W9-AEJ-918

Sixteenth Annual Winterthur Conference, 1970

PRINTS IN AND OF AMERICA TO 1850

WINTERTHUR CONFERENCE REPORT 1970
JONATHAN L. FAIRBANKS, CHAIRMAN

Prints in and of America to 1850

Edited by John D. Morse

WINTERTHUR

Published for
The Henry Francis du Pont Winterthur Museum
Winterthur, Delaware

The University Press of Virginia
Charlottesville

John Dewey Library
Johnson State College
Johnson, Vermont

769.943
W736p
74-4952

Copyright 1970 by The Henry Francis du Pont
Winterthur Museum, Inc.
First published 1970
The University Press of Virginia
Standard Book Number: 8139-0323-8
Library of Congress Catalog Card Number: 76-135506
Printed in the United States of America

CONTENTS

ILLUSTRATIONS

<u>American Beginnings: Prints in Sixteenth-Century Mexico</u>*

*Illustrations are woodcut book frontispieces printed
in Mexico unless otherwise noted.

<u>Seventeenth-Century American Prints</u>

Prints and Scientific Illustration in America

Jacob Perkins, William Congreve, and Counterfeit
Printing in 1820

American Lithographic Technology before the Civil War

The Grand Triumphal Quick-Step; or, Sheet Music Covers in America

Prints and the American Art-Union

Printmaking Demonstrations

FOREWORD

THE Winterthur Conference Committee selected the 1970 Conference theme "Prints in and of America to 1850" in the fall of 1968. At the same time it appointed Jonathan L. Fairbanks, associate curator in charge of conservation, chairman of the program committee to plan the content of the meeting. Mr. Fairbanks for several years had pursued not only a professional interest in the history of American prints but a personal and technical interest in printmaking.

For the most part, the general format developed over the years for the Winterthur Conference was followed: a three-day program of papers and discussions held in the Lecture Hall, an exhibit illustrating the Conference theme utilizing materials largely drawn from the Winterthur collections, demonstrations and discussions of related craft techniques and conservation practices held in the Research Building, and an invited group of specialists in the field. An important innovation was the preparation of a list of resources for print research which appears as an Appendix to this Report. The success of the Conference is largely due to the enthusiasm, resourcefulness, and diligence with which the program committee and its indefatigable chairman planned these several features.

Although statistics do not express the character or spirit of a gathering such as this, it is interesting to note that among 218 persons attending the Conference, there were 37 invited resource specialists, 51 members of the Winterthur Museum staff, 6 faculty members of the University of Delaware, 45 Winterthur graduates, 15 Winterthur fellows in residence, 47 wives of participants, and 9 special guests. Persons came from as far away as British Columbia, Canada, and from professions as varied as publishing, music teaching, and printmaking.

The annual Winterthur Conference on Museum Operation and Connoisseurship was first held in 1954. The initial purpose of the Conference was to contribute to the course of study of the fellows enrolled in the Winterthur Program in Early American Culture. A second, equally important

objective gradually developed as the policy of inviting graduates
of the Program provided an occasion for the exchange of information and ideas between graduates (numbering about 100
in 1970), fellows, and the Museum staff. More recently, a
limited number of resource specialists has been invited from
other museums, universities, and historical agencies across
the country: art historians, collectors, antiquarians, editors,
and authors have joined the Winterthur community of fellows,
graduates, staff, and university colleagues in a study of
some aspect of the arts in early America and their preservation.

                              E. McClung Fleming

INTRODUCTION

THE Sixteenth Annual Winterthur Conference, which was held
March 19-21, 1970, on the subject "Prints in and of America
to 1850" served a variety of useful ends. It identified an
area of the American arts--graphic art before the Civil War--
which has received little systematic attention in recent years.
At a time when practically no professional meetings were
being held on the subject, it provided an opportunity for
interested scholars to confer. It brought together, from a
surprising number of different professions, print experts and
buffs who were not acquainted but who discovered a common
interest in developing a neglected field and who resolved to
hold follow-up meetings in the near future. Finally, through
its papers, exhibit, and demonstrations, the Conference made
a substantial contribution to the limited scholarly literature
on the subject.

Because the main function of prints is communication--by
both picture and word--their messages are immediate and
explicit. Most print-aware persons looking at the past
through the medium of prints have discovered that historically
remote happenings seem alive and current. For this reason,
prints break down artificial barriers between the past and
present. And yet not all past events and personalities can be
well understood by comparison with recent experiences or
through the colored glasses of contemporary life. It is
presumptious to try to fit the great variety of life in early
America within the few shallow lines etched on recent memory.
Relating everything today with everything yesterday is an
all-too popular pastime. Admittedly, the historical process
is a tight-rope walk balanced between the past and the present,
with old events taking on new meanings in the light of
current happenings.

The growing desire among many people to make better use
of pictorial source material in examining the American past
has made print curators busy public servants exhibiting
prints, and leaving them little time for research and publication. Books by Stauffer, Peters, Brigham, Wainwright,
and Hamilton, among many others, are invaluable references,

but more research remains to be done before a definitive book on prints made or used in America can be published; hopefully, this Report supplies some of the basic information and points out new directions for such a book.

To assess fairly the role of the printmaker in early American life, one needs to recognize that many fundamental changes have taken place in the dozen or more generations that have passed since the first prints were produced in Colonial America. Were we to meet a printmaker of early America at first hand, would we find him thinking of himself as a graphic artist and creative designer as we look on the printmaker today? Or would we find that he considered himself an artisan and, perhaps, a merchant of things?

Today the printmaker or graphic artist usually designs his own plate and therefore creates an original work of art. The basic task of the early printmaker was more commercial--to reproduce as accurately as possible the work of another--the work usually being a painting or a drawing.

Modern photomechanical reproduction has almost eliminated the need for hand copying on stone or copperplate. Most graphic artists today concentrate their attention on innovative designs for limited editions. Today the rarity of an early print may make us forget that the original intent of the print-maker was to mass-produce an image. Each improvement in graphic technology was toward cheaper, more numerous, and more accurate reproductions of the original image. With the advent of specialized technology in the nineteenth century, the graphics industry required so many different talents that it is not possible thereafter to speak of the "printmaker" as a single species. And today it is generally true that most noncommercial printmakers consider themselves independent artists.

Art is always undergoing redefinition, and our feeling about a print or any object is transformed once it gains the sanctuary of a private collection, a museum, or is included in a written work. It is one of the more interesting tasks of curators and scholars to call attention to these associated values and to study the meaning of objects that have been overlooked or misinterpreted. In these areas, as well as others, the 1970

Winterthur Conference was productive beyond expectation and
resulted in an exceptionally enthusiastic exchange of information and ideas. Some participants suggested that this vast
subject be explored further through annual meetings, with
appropriate institutional sponsorship in the host cities.

As conference chairman, I am most grateful to the speakers,
whose originality of insight and sense of discovery gave the
Conference a unique quality, which I think every reader of
this Report will recognize.

I wish to thank also those who demonstrated printmaking
techniques and methods of paper conservation which made
possible a common understanding of techniques and nomen-
clature. Sally Frost Knerr, professor of art, School of
Gibbes Art Gallery, Charleston, South Carolina, and Jerome
Kaplan, head of printmaking, Philadelphia College of Art,
demonstrated lithography. Intaglio printing was demonstrated
by Jay Cantor, visiting critic, College of Architecture, Art,
and Planning, Cornell University; Martin E. Weil, architect,
Price and Dickey, Media, Pennsylvania; and Stephanie
Munsing, Winterthur fellow. Dr. Elizabeth Harris, assistant
curator, Division of Graphic Arts, National Museum of
History and Technology, Smithsonian Institution, and Darrell
Hyder, production manager, Barre Publishers, showed printmaking by letterpress. Mr. Hyder also distributed his booklet,
The Printing Processes: A Brief Introduction to Their Charac-
teristics, as a souvenir of the Imprint Society, Barre,
Massachusetts. Anne E. Clapp, conservator of paper at the
Winterthur Museum, prepared an exhibit and explained and
demonstrated print-and-paper conservation, philosophy, and
methods. The exhibition of Winterthur prints was selected
and hung by Nancy E. Richards, assistant curator, and
R. Peter Mooz, teaching associate.

For this Report, we thank John D. Morse, head of the
National Extension Office, his editorial assistant, Louisa F.
Turley, and his secretary, Carolyn J. McVeigh.

Jonathan L. Fairbanks

OPENING REMARKS

Donald H. Karshan

AN OPENING statement at such a scholarly rendezvous should consist of some form of meaningful overview. By overview, I mean a look from afar at this pursuit of knowledge of the early American print and its relevance to contemporary life.

There have been several major artistic activities in this nation since World War II that may be changing our way of looking at and appreciating these modest prints, maps, and broadsides. We know that New York has replaced Paris and Berlin as the artistic center of the world. Witness, for example, the abstract expressionists of the 1950s; the neo-dada, pop, and color field artists of the 1960s; and perhaps even the conceptual artists of the early 1970s. As the Americans avidly collected the impressionists in the 1890s, the Germans of today are acquiring American pop art and its circle more voraciously than any other collectors. We find our particular brand of aesthetics fanning out intercontinentally. This new-found leadership in creating and influencing art has encouraged us, in turn, to reexamine what has already been done here, going back to our most naive beginnings in the seventeenth century. Because of the innovative element in present-day painting and sculpture styles, we are urged to search for the roots of these styles in our artistic past. This is a deep longing, I suspect, for a profound cultural identity and continuity. This longing goes further in explaining the current rash of exhibitions of and publications on all phases of American imagery than do the vicissitudes of the art market per se.

In our search for a corollary, we realize that our visual experiences of the last dozen years or so have better equipped us to view the early American print. Do not the flags and targets of Jasper Johns help us to see more clearly those

emblematic, matter-of-fact images in our eighteenth-century
prints? Do not the journalistically oriented statements of
Robert Rauschenberg, James Rosenquist, and Andy Warhol also
bring us closer to the commentary of many of these early
engravings? And how about the deadpan portraits of pop
artist Robert Indiana and proto-pop artist Larry Rivers? Is
there not also a strange and familiar ring to the fact that
many of our important artists of the 1960s were sign painters
and itinerant commercial artists? And how will conceptual
art, which often uses language as its sole vehicle, enhance
our response to those assertive broadsides?

The early American print, being so rare, is, in a sense,
very much out of the turbulent art market. Undisturbed then,
we can examine these graphically concise images and attempt
to extract from them those meanings that go beyond their
ability to verify and illuminate events and personalities.

American graphic art today, so widespread as to be a
virtual printmaking renaissance, is becoming more and more
preoccupied with informational material and the relationship
between the viewer's "need to know" and the nonprecious
and open-ended attributes of the multiple. Graphic images
reflecting the urgencies of colonial life and of continental
expansion are paralleled today in images of the priorities of
ecology, domestic dissent, and space exploration. The
earliest maps of our land--convoluted utterances of survival
and strategem--are echoed today by the maps and charts of
our earthwork and spacework artists. There is no better time,
then, to reexamine and show to the American people these
printed documents of our far past. They may now be understood as significant prototypes of the communications of our
own disturbed and challenging era.

Sixteenth Annual Winterthur Conference, 1970

PRINTS IN AND OF AMERICA TO 1850

AMERICAN BEGINNINGS
PRINTS IN SIXTEENTH-CENTURY MEXICO

Richard E. Ahlborn

FROM the viewpoint of the cultural historian, the development
of printing, and the purposes to which it was put in the later
1400s, may be described as the principal event marking the
shift from the medieval to the modern mechanics of civilization. The development and use of this mechanism appear
to parallel and, at times, to predict major adjustments in the
structures of social institutions, and of individual freedom.

Each of us recognizes certain mechanical differences
between the medieval scriptorium and the early Renaissance
print shop. Perhaps the chief difference is between movable
type and hand-formed letters. The great advantage held over
manuscripts by pages composed of movable type is that of
rapid duplication and, thereby, wider, cheaper distribution.
Moreover, the invention of reusable, replaceable, and inter-
changeable elements of type face, borders, and illustrative
engravings contained cultural implications beyond the
mechanics of printing.

The same font could spell out a prayer, then be broken
down and reset to print a profane poem; the letters of the
law could be literally realigned into a revolutionary tract.
And the same stylish border could serve all four statements.
Predominant, however, is the technological fact that a few
movable elements now allowed total flexibility of message
content, a situation not overlooked by religious and civil
officials.

Church and state officials perceived the potentialities of
printing within their own systems of control. Licenses,
permits, taxes, and even force of arms were used by
officialdom to maintain surveillance over the new technology.
Despite such safeguards for "the public good," as well as

efforts within the craft to keep its secrets, the knowledge
and application of movable-type printing spread west and
south from Germany in the generation prior to the Spanish-
financed discovery of the Americas.

Spain, through her privileged membership in the Holy
Roman Empire, was in close contact with Germany and Italy.
Associations with papal and Hapsburg lineages awarded Spain
a unique opportunity to dominate European civilization by
1500, in both cultural ascendancy and territorial extension.
The development of printing was well suited to traverse
these coordinates, even if under massive official protection.

The launching platen of printing from Europe to the
Americas was Seville. Printing was first established in Spain
at Valencia on the Mediterranean coast in 1474. Within
three years, Seville, the cultural center of the peninsula
since the thirteenth century, began to produce books with the
use of movable type and decorative woodcuts. Not surprisingly, the first printers of Seville were Spanish-born. However, it was three Germans known as the Tres Alemanes
Companeros who produced a work in 1493 that first mentions
nuevo mundo, the New World.[1] Other printers from the
German empire, including parts of Switzerland, Poland, and
Flanders, brought their skills and tools to Seville before 1500.

This Germanic impact is demonstrated by the continuing
popularity of Gothic face over Roman among both the Spanish
public and the government consumers. Although the Roman
face was promptly introduced from Venice to Seville by
Spanish-born printers, Gothic faces, probably brought from
Spanish-held Naples, were used by famous German printers
such as the Crombergers.[2]

Jacome Cromberger (Nuremberg) and his descendants were
the Sevillian printers most prominent for their influence in
the New World. Through three generations, the
Crombergers impelled the technology and the actual equipment of printing across a century, and two continents. The
elder Cromberger also had contacts other than printing in
the New World. Before his death in 1528, Jacome had established land claims, commercial interests, and even relatives
in the Caribbean area. Along with financier Jacob Fugger,

Cromberger speculated by outfitting ships for voyages piloted by the English adventurer Sebastian Cabot.[3] Apparently, Jacome Cromberger was as much entrepreneur as imprinter, but it fell to his heirs to transmit printing technology to the Americas.

Two important prints that influenced Mexican production were portadas, or frontispieces, in books from the Cromberger presses. That of the 1519 Suma de geographia, written by Fernandez de Encisco, a lawyer and speculator living in Santo Domingo,[4] presents a schematic globe set in early Renaissance borders (fig. 1). The second crucial work from Seville appeared in 1530, when Juan Cromberger, son of Jacome, brought out Father Montesino's Vita Christi. A copy in the original parchment bindings is located in the National Library of Mexico; its frontispiece is pure Mannerist whimsey into which a Germanic Nativity scene intrudes (fig. 2). The Vita contains Gothic characters used in Seville before 1500 appearing later in early Mexican imprints such as the 1544 Doctrina breve, muy provechosa . . . written by the father of Mexican printing, Bishop Juan de Zumarraga, O. F. M. The colophon of this manual for priests in the New World reads "at the place of Juan Cromberger, by command of the bishop and at his cost."

Zumarraga, the remarkable Franciscan and first bishop of Mexico, labored to spread his humanist philosophy with the aid of printed face and image. The Franciscan missionaries watched over many of the earliest events in Mexican printing, which were, accordingly, of a pragmatic, religious nature. From archives in Seville, we know that Zumarraga requested papermakers and printers for Mexico in 1533.[5] In that year, he and Viceroy Mendoza visited Juan Cromberger and encouraged him to explore business prospects for printing in Mexico. To this end, a factor named Esteban Martin was sent to Mexico. The 1539 records of the cabildo, or Town Council, of Tenochtitlan (Mexico City) stated that the emprimydor Esteban Martin had lived there for five years and could become a citizen. With the lack of paper, strict censorship, and other restrictions, it was probably the urging of the bishop, more than anything reported by his

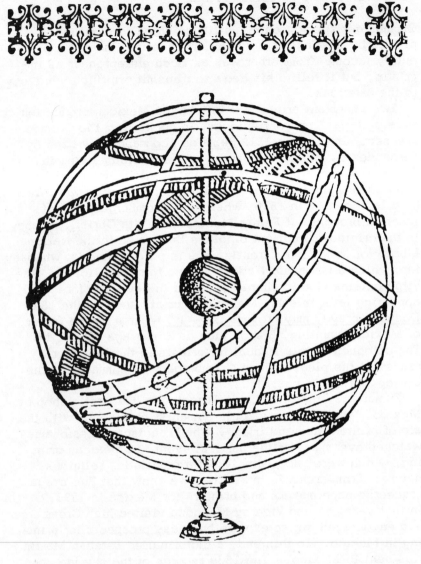

Fig. 1. Frontispiece from Fernandez de Encisco, *Suma de geographia* (Seville, Spain: Jacome Cromberger, 1519). Woodcut. Height of page: 10 5/8"

Fig. 2. Frontispiece from Father Montesino,
<u>Vita Christi</u> (Seville, Spain: Jacome Cromberger,
1530). Woodcut

factor, which moved Cromberger to establish the first
American print shop.

In accord with a contract drawn up by Juan Cromberger,
his Italian-born nephew, Juan Pablos, arrived in Mexico with
fonts and a press in 1539. The contract specified that Pablos,
"a composer of cast letters," was to direct the entire operation, including a Negro slave and a pressman, for 20 percent
of the gross profit, with 80 percent returned to Cromberger,
the "Royal fifth" in reverse. The first work bearing the
colophon of Pablos was the 1546 Doctrina christiana mas
cierta y verdadera . . . , also written and paid for by Bishop
Zumarraga. Within the year, however, Pablos found it necessary to seek financial support from Viceroy Mendoza. For
the next fifteen years, American printing managed to survive
conditions in Mexico and even produced images of strong
visual impact.

The frontispiece of Pablos's Doctrina typifies the earliest
American woodcuts: a separate, central design framed with
stock elements in the style of the period (fig. 3). Perhaps
the earliest known American print is the 1544 frontispiece
for Doctrina breve, muy provechosa, which has as the central
motif the Spanish coat of arms with the Order of the Golden
Fleece, a compartment with strapwork baskets of fruit, and
caryatids on a plinth (fig. 4).

A decade later came the triumph of the career of Pablos.
Three of his products appeared in 1554, each bearing an important print. The Recognitio Summularum by Father Veracruz,
the first American philosophical work for students, uses a
cut of Saint Augustine, a representation suitable to later
popular taste. Next, the Constitutions of the Archbishopric
and Province of Tenochtitlan displays a strapwork crest with
other European designs supported on a Mexican cactus. The
third design introduced by Pablos in 1554 is known as the
Whitchurch compartment (fig. 5). Edward Whitchurch was an
English printer of humanist works, such as the Paraphrase of
Erasmus (London, 1548-49) in which the compartment first
appeared, and which was known to Latin scholar Princess
Mary. Through her Spanish tutor and her marriage to Philip
of Spain or, for that matter, even through the great book fair

Fig. 3. Frontispiece from Bishop Zumarraga, <u>Doctrina</u>
<u>christiana mas cierta y verdadera</u> (Mexico: Juan
Pablos, 1546). Woodcut

Fig. 4. Frontispiece from <u>Doctrina breve, muy</u>
<u>provechosa</u> (Mexico: Juan Pablos, 1544). Woodcut·
Height of page: 9 5/8"

¶DIALOGO DE DOCTRINA
Chriſtiana, en la lengua dˀ Mechuacã, Hecho
y copilado de muchos libros de ſana doctrina, por el muy Reuerendo padre Fray Maturino Gylberti dela orden del ſeraphico Pa
dre ſant Frãciſco. Trata delo que ha de ſaber
creer, hazer, deſſear, y aborrecer, el Chriſtia-
no, Va preguntando el diſcipulo al Maeſtro.

¶YYETI SIRANDA YQVI A-
ringahaca Dialogo aringani, ychuhca hĩ-
bo chupengahaqui Chriſtianoengani,
yngui vca tata chẽ caſireq̃ Fray
Maturino Gilberti ſant Frãciſco tata. Teparimento am
baqueti. Ma hurengua
reri curamarihati
tepari huren-
dahperini. Ca hurendahperi mayo-
cucupanſtabatihurendaeq̃embani.
Bño de. 1559.

Fig. 5. Frontispiece woodcut used by Edward
Whitchurch in England in 1546 and used by 1554
in Mexico by Juan Pablos

at Frankfort, the Whitchurch compartment presumably reached
Spain and then Mexico shortly after 1550. At this time,
Pablos was cutting new blocks to introduce the first Roman
face to Mexico. The compartment continued to be used by
Pablos and later Mexican printers until 1638.[6] Despite such
innovations, Pablos went on using Mannerist border cuts, as
we see in his 1558 work, Arte en la lengua de Mechuacan,
by Father Gilberti. The next year, however, witnessed the
return of Pablos in Gilberti's Vocabulario to a figurative compartment fitted out with religious symbolism of sin and
sacrifice (fig. 6).

At the death of Pablos in 1561, the development of Mexican
prints for the next decade had already passed into other hands.
In 1558, the exclusive privileges granted Pablos had been
annulled in favor of a type caster from Seville, Antonio de
Espinosa. His use of initial letters, two colors or tints, and
more open designs marked European influences that became
significant achievements in the art of the American print.
Three fine examples again serve as frontispieces; the first,
in a deluxe edition in the New World of the Missale Romanum
in 1561, has a border composed of prophets, Catholic prelates,
and above, God the father (fig. 7). Second, there is a
magnificent Renaissance treatment of the stigmata crest with
botanical symbols in a 1567 edition of Instituta ordinis
beati Francisci (fig. 8). The saint is represented in the
frontispiece of another work, Vocabulario en lengua Mexicana
y Castellano (1571) by Father Molina. Finally, a woodcut
of Germanic character shows a Crucifixion with Mary and
John the Evangelist, and is repeated in two works from 1569
by Espinosa, then reused twenty years later by his one-time
collaborator, Pedro Ocharte.

By the 1560s, Mexican printing began to expand its personnel. In 1562, a Normandy-born printer, Pierre Chart, arrived
in Mexico as Pedro Ocharte; he married the daughter of Juan
Pablos and leased the printing establishment from his widow.
Beginning his career by working with Antonio de Espinosa,
Ocharte dominated Mexican printing through the seventies
and eighties. Later in the century, sons of Ocharte's two
marriages, Melchor and Luis, nurtured the transplanted
technology and art into the seventeenth century.

Fig. 6. Frontispiece from Father Gilberti, <u>Vocabulario en lengua de Mechuacan</u> (Mexico: Juan Pablos, 1559). Woodcut

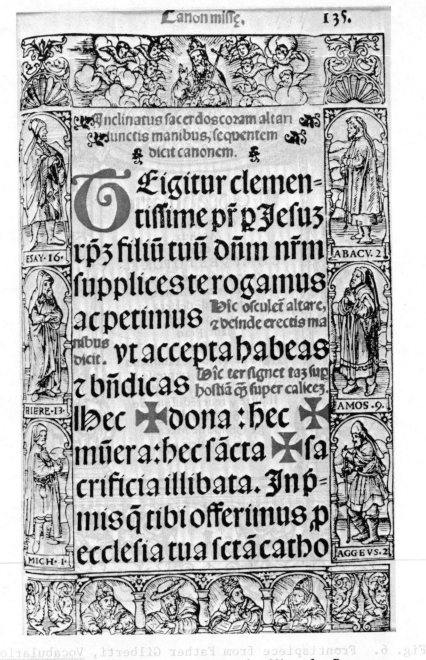

Fig. 7. Frontispiece from the Missale Romanum
(Mexico: Antonio de Espinosa, 1561). Woodcut

Fig. 8. Frontispiece from the _Instituta ordinis beati Francisci_ (Mexico: Antonio de Espinosa, 1567). Woodcut

The accomplishments of Ocharte were considerable, and not easy to come by. The frontispiece to the Doctrina christiana breve . . . of Father Annunciacion, published by Ocharte in 1565, portrays a complex theme, probably symbolic of aid granted by the Virgin Mary as the "Rosario" to Pope Pius IV, whom she directed to join forces with Philip II of Spain in order to defeat Soliman the Turk at Malta (fig. 9). In 1568, Ocharte used a woodcut of St. Francis receiving the stigmata (clearly derived from a fifteenth-century oil of northern European origin) to introduce what is probably the first pedagogical work printed in America, Cartilla para ensenar a leer, an alphabet book (fig. 10). However, in 1570, Ocharte was called before the Holy Office of the Inquisition after putting out an early medical text with a classic early Renaissance compartment from Spain (fig. 11). He was accused of spreading Lutheran ideas such as the questioning of papal authority and veneration of and intercession by the saints. Ocharte confessed under torture, suffered punishment, and returned to printing. In 1576 appeared the magnificent third edition of the antiphonary Graduale Dominicale. Its frontispiece prudently presents a landscape with two saints, Peter and Paul, set in a frame of strapwork (fig. 12). This print, as well as the small initial-letter cuts within the score, may be the work of Juan Ortiz, an "engraver of images" known to be an employee of Ocharte.[7]

By the opening years of the seventeenth century, lesser events documented and confirmed the character of Mexican printing. European printers continued to provide up-to-date printing styles and technology within the confines of official requirements. Ocharte shifted his affiliation with Espinosa to one with a young printer from Turin, Antonio Ricardo, who proceeded on to Peru where he established the first press in Lima in the 1580s; meanwhile Pedro Balli of Salamanca produced such required texts as the 1595 Regla de los Frayles Menores. The print shop under the widow of Ocharte moved out to the convent and college of Santiago Tlaltelolco. There, in 1597, work, board, room, and clothing for 170 pesos per year were provided as penance to Cornelius Adrian Cesar. Born in Holland, apprenticed to the Christophe Plantin press,

Fig. 9. Frontispiece from Father Annunciation, _Doctrina christiana breve en lengua Espanola e Mexicana_ (Mexico: Pedro Ocharte, 1565). Woodcut

¶ Cartilla para enseñar a leer, nueuamente enmenda-
da, y quitadas todas las abreuiaturas que antes tenia.

A a b c d d e f g h i k l m n
o p q r ʒ ſ s t v u r y ʒ ꝯ ꝯ 9

Fig. 10. Frontispiece from <u>Cartilla para ensenar a</u>
<u>leer</u> (Mexico: Pedro Ocharte, 1568). Woodcut. Height
of page: 11 3/8"

Fig. 11. Frontispiece from Francisco Bravo, _Opera Medicinalia_ (Mexico: Pedro Ocharte, 1570). Woodcut

Fig. 12. Frontispiece from <u>Graduale Dominicale</u>, 3d
ed. (Mexico: Pedro Ocharte, 1576). Woodcut
attributed to Juan Ortiz

and employed in Leyden, Cesar was brought to New Spain by
Zuniga Acevedo, Count of Monterrey and Viceroy of New
Spain. An admitted Lutheran, Cesar was sentenced to three
years in jail and the wearing of penitential clothing. The
famous Martin[ez] family of Spanish printers, first extended
to Mexico by Esteban, agent of Cromberger, was continued
after 1600 by Henrico. The 1606 Tratado primero del mundo
en general del Reportorio de los tiempos, y Historia natural
desde Nueva Espana, by Henrico Martinez, uses a device
similar to the schematic globe employed by Cromberger eighty-
five years before. In a sense, the Old World had become the
New.

The sixteenth-century Mexican print evidences few stylistic and thematic changes, and then only in accord with
textual material of which it was technologically an integral
part. Mannerist elements began to drop from usage shortly
after mid-century; on the other hand, Renaissance motifs
continued to be challenged by late Gothic and strap designs
into the third quarter, perhaps due to the persistent influence
of northern European printers and their works in Mexico. At
the same time, thematic changes reflected current styles:
purely decorative and figurative elements shifted from
Mannerist to High Renaissance treatment. The use of crests
in strapwork, however, nearly disappeared during the last
third of the century, and then escutcheons appeared in a
more up-dated Italian Renaissance style. We noted the use
of the compartment, or architectural frame of plinth, pillars,
and pediment, in the earliest Mexican frontispieces, at a
time when Spain continued her liking of crests. Religious
subjects, including arms of the orders, continued into the
seventeenth century.

I would suggest that the period of 1565-75 represents a
watershed for Mexican prints. Not only did strapwork and
figurative design lessen in frequency, but the Gothic face
was seriously challenged by the Roman. I believe that these
stylistic shifts corresponded in part with the arrival of
French-born Pedro Ocharte, who initiated a new direction
for Mexican printmaking. The movement was away from
personal, highly emotive, Counter Reformation images to

more impersonal, rationalistic, even abstract designs; in effect, saints were replaced by symbols.

It seems clear that Mexican religious prints had settled into a predictable pattern by 1600. Although a second center of printing was established at Puebla by mid-century, the themes of Mexican imprints and the means used to illustrate them remained unchanged. Missals, antiphonaries, religious tracts, and regulations for the orders, with the later additions of novena prayers and histories of locally popular saints, have remained in production for three centuries. These imprints were stylistically oriented to traditional Spanish taste; woodcuts continued to serve Mexican illustrators until after 1800, when zinc and copper plates began to predominate. The subtle shading achieved in mezzotint portraits did not have the same basic appeal, or impact, for the Spaniard as the late medieval religious woodcut of Germanic origin. The cheap religious prints, popular to this day in Spanish-speaking America, were not widely available until the nineteenth century.[8]

Imprints of secular content, such as guild regulations, laws and statutes, and official proclamations, as well as texts and treatises on natural science, often gave up grandiose frontispieces in favor of multiple lines of Roman face in contrasting sizes printed in two colors. Not only were cuts, type, and paper scarce, but a local oil used to liquify colors caused staining.[9] Borders of repeated elements and a few crests and emblems of symbolic importance to the aristocracy replaced most figurative illustrations on secular imprints after 1600.

The decorative and didactic prints of sixteenth-century Mexico not only reflect their European origins but serve as indicators of national and ethnic values. Nevertheless, Mexican prints stand in sharp contrast to those of English-speaking North America. Without a considerable commercial class, Mexico had no reason to produce images of the merchant and his town or to feed a growing nationalistic appetite. Maps proved more useful than cityscapes to civil and military authorities in Mexico. Portraits of the truly prominent officials, whether secular or religious, were done in oils.

In Mexico, the art of printmaking remained an integral part of the printer's craft. Few blocks had their images separately struck and sold. The masses were simply too poorly educated to provide a market, and all aspects of printing were nominally under strict regulations. Thus while stylistic invention and radical content were restricted in Mexican printing, its visual impact and technical level was not challenged in North America for more than a century.

Notes

1. Carlos R. Linga, "Los primeros tipografos en la
Nueva Espana y sus precursores europeos," IV Centenario
de la imprenta en Mexico (Mexico, 1939), pp. 500-01;
Conrad Haebler, Tipografia Iberica del siglo XV (Leipzig,
1902), p. 47.
2. Linga, pp. 493, 512; Emilio Valton, Impresos
Mexicanos del siglo XVI (Mexico, 1933), pp. 24-29;
Vicente de P. Andrade, Ensayo Bibliografico del siglo XVII,
2d ed. (Mexico, 1899), no. 10, p. 14.
3. Linga, p. 522.
4. H. Harrisse, Biblioteca Americana vetustissima
(New York, 1866), no. 97, pp. 168-69.
5. Valton, pp. 6-13, 37.
6. Valton, p. 57, as used by Juan Ruiz; Lucy Eugenie
Osborne, "The Whitchurch Compartment in London and
Mexico," The Library, ser. 4, VIII (Dec. 1927), 303.
7. Valton, p. 37.
8. See Oscar Lewis, La Vida, A Puerto Rican Family in
the Culture of Poverty (San Juan and New York, 1966); The
Children of Sanchez (New York, 1966) for uses of these
prints in Puerto Rico and Mexico.
9. Valton, p. 123. The local oil was distilled from
chia, a lime-leafed sage.

Other Works Consulted

Icazbalceta, Joaquin Garcia. Bibliografia Mexicana del
    siglo XVI. Mexico, 1886
Medina, Jose Toribio. La Imprenta en Mexico. 8 vols.
    Santiago de Chile, 1912
Sulaica Garate, Roman. Los Franciscanos y la imprenta en
    Mexico en el siglo XVI. Mexico, 1939
Documentos para la historia de la Tipografia Mexicana.
    Biblioteca del Congreso de la Union. Mexico, 1936

SEVENTEENTH-CENTURY AMERICAN PRINTS

Richard B. Holman

PRINTS made in English-speaking America in the seventeenth century were so few, so primitive, and so generally unimpressive that we would overlook them but for one point; they were the beginning of American print making, just as the seventeenth century was the beginning of this nation. So I do not apologize for inviting your attention to a scattering of inept engravings. Incunabula are always important.

A surprising thing about early American printmaking is that it began so late. In view of the fact that serious and successful settlement of the country began before 1610, it is hard to believe that the earliest datable print did not appear until 1670. And yet 1670, exactly three centuries ago, sixty-three years after Jamestown and fifty years after Plymouth, is the accepted date.

Why did not John White of the Roanoke Colony attempt a few engravings? He made masterful water colors. Thankful as we are for de Bry of Frankfort, it would have been pleasant if White himself had tried his hand on a block of American pine or a bit of bartered copper. Why did versatile men like Champlain and Lescarbot, who came in 1603, never multiply one of their maps or fix some of the scenes reflected in their words? Apparently they did not. Nor did any of the voyagers, explorers, or first settlers.

Another odd feature of seventeenth-century American prints is that they all seem to have been made in the Massachusetts Bay Colony. It is improbable that none were made elsewhere. A printing press was not necessary; rubbed proofs of wood blocks can be made with equipment no more complicated than a kitchen spoon. Surely someone must have

been living in one of the other colonies before 1700 who knew
of wood-block printing and who felt a desire to multiply some
design and scatter it to other people and places. Yet, so far
as is known, the earliest print made in English-speaking
America was a woodcut portrait of the Reverend Richard
Mather made about 1670 by John Foster. The date is not
established beyond challenge. However, both date and attribution have been accepted for so long by so many, and seem
so probable, that it is commonly supposed that they are
established fact.

The Woodcut Process

Early American prints were woodcuts, just as the first
European and Asian prints were. Why this should be is
obvious. Wood was available and easy to cut or carve, and
a woodcut could be easily printed. Copper and iron were
valuable, scarce, and harder to work.

Woodcuts are, of course, printed from a block or blocks
of wood on which a design has been cut. Traditionally the
blocks have tended to be "type-high" to make it possible to
lock them in a chase with type and so print text and illustration in one operation. Over the years the most satisfactory
woods have been fruit woods and boxwood. Box is especially
suited to work on the end-grain. For work on the plank side,
such as we are concerned with in early America, apple and
pear would have been best. Whether our pioneers were aware
of this is not known, because none of their blocks has survived.
All we can say is that the results of their work do not suggest
fruit wood. In any case, for larger sizes their likeliest choice
would have been white pine. Eastern white pine was plentiful
and available in any size, and it could have been worked
easily.

In all probability the first woodcuts were made with a
knife, though this would be hard to prove. A gouge would
have been simpler to use, but a knife probably easier to find.
E. H. Richter, Curator of the Print Department at the Museum
of Fine Arts, Boston, in 1904 organized a trail-blazing
exhibition of early engraving in America. He described

John Foster's work on his Richard Mather portrait and on his
map of New England as "Knife work on relief block." And
that is the way they look--two cuts to each line, one on each
side of every black line. However, it must be stated that
when Foster died in 1681 his estate contained "turning tooles
Carueing tools playns &c."[1] Either the lathe tools or the
carving tools may have been gouges well adapted to cutting
wood blocks, and there is no way of knowing whether or
how much he may have used them.

Woodcuts are very much like letterpress. The parts that
stand up print; the parts cut away do not. The woodcut engraver has an awkward job; he must think of his black lines
as something to be left after removing all else. In addition,
of course, he has the difficulty common to all engravers, that
of reversing everything, including letters and words, so that
the print will read properly. If he gets some unexpected results from time to time, even after he becomes experienced,
it need surprise no one. Our earliest engraver, John Foster,
was neither experienced nor trained. But he was intelligent
and of an experimental turn of mind, which was even better.

The First Print

Foster was born in Dorchester in the Massachusetts Bay
Colony in 1648. His father was a man of substance, the town
brewer and a captain in the militia. The son went to college,
Harvard necessarily, and graduated in 1667. He ranked third
in his class of seven, socially, not academically, for
Harvard graduates were so ranked until 1773. Instead of
entering the clergy as might have been expected, he taught
school in his native village. But in 1675 he left teaching
to become a printer in Boston. He was encouraged in this
move by his friends, Increase Mather and John Eliot, both
well-known clergymen, the latter the famous "apostle to
the Indians." How Foster, a member of the intelligentsia,
came to take up one of the mechanic trades is yet to be
explained. It was an unusual step in the seventeenth century.

In 1908 a volume containing twenty early New England
pamphlets, mostly sermons, printed in Boston or Cambridge,

was added to the Harvard College Library. Originally some of
the pamphlets belonged to the Reverend William Adams of
Dedham, Massachusetts. His son, the Reverend Eliphalet
Adams of New London, Connecticut, had them bound, as he
noted on a flyleaf, "in 1701-2." Bound in with one of the
pamphlets, The Life and Death of that Reverend Man of God,
Mr. Richard Mather . . . (Cambridge, 1670), was a woodcut
portrait without printed title or signature (fig. 1). The date
of the pamphlet has become associated with the print. It
was long supposed that the print was the frontispiece to the
pamphlet and was therefore America's first book illustration,
but this has not been conclusively proved. Neither do we
know why the portrait was engraved on two separate blocks
dividing the shoulders and the torso.

On the Harvard print is a handwritten inscription,
"Richardus Mather. Johannis Foster Sculpsit" (fig. 2). The
handwriting is that of William Adams, whose Harvard class
was 1671, only four years after Foster's. It may be assumed
that the two men were acquainted. So, although we have the
best possible testimony that Foster engraved the blocks, we
do not know incontrovertibly that he did so in 1670.[2] The
discovery of the print, placed as if it were an illustration,
has not proved that the date of the pamphlet is the date of
the print. In the first place no known duplicate pamphlet
provides corroboration. Other copies do not contain the print.

The Harvard impression is unique in other respects. Although there are four other known impressions from blocks,
the Harvard impression differs from all four.[3] It is on different paper. At least three of the others, and probably all
four, are on paper with an eighteenth-century Pro Patria
paper mark.[4] One has not been examined. The blocks of
the Harvard print match, making the line of the shoulders
continuous and natural; in the others there is a distinct step
as in the one at the Massachusetts Historical Society (fig. 3).
It lacks the others' scratched lines of the sleeves and jacket-
opening. It appears to have been printed on a press; the
other four show evidence of being "spooned" proofs. The
four have printed titles, though the type is differently

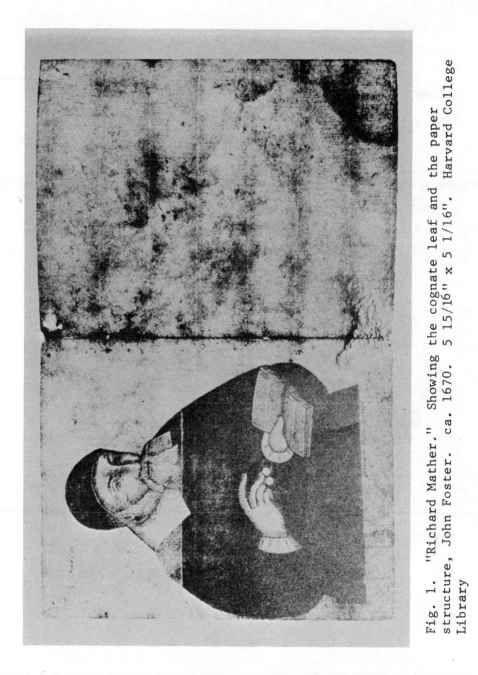

Fig. 1. "Richard Mather." Showing the cognate leaf and the paper structure, John Foster. ca. 1670. 5 15/16" x 5 1/16". Harvard College Library

Fig. 2. "Richard Mather." Woodcut in the first state,
John Foster. ca. 1670. 5 15/16" x 5 1/16". Harvard
College Library

Mr. Richard Mather.

Fig. 3. "Richard Mather," in the later state,
showing the step in the line of the shoulder
caused by unequal expansion of the wood blocks,
John Foster. 6 1/8" x 5 1/8". Massachusetts
Historical Society

positioned in each case. In sum, there is something here
which needs explanation.

The step in the line of the shoulders apparently results
from printing with damp blocks, although why they were damp
is still an unsolved problem. Wood, of course, expands
very much when wet and very much more across the grain
than with it. Here we have horizontal grain in the upper
block and vertical grain in the lower. This seems clear and
simple and gives us the feeling of getting somewhere. It is
a pleasant change.[5]

But back we go to the fog. There is in the Peabody Museum
of Salem, Massachusetts, a piece of badly mutilated paper
which once was part of the map of New England known as the
Wine Hills map (fig. 4). Whether Foster engraved the Wine
Hills as well as the White Hills map is a question we will
mention later. But there is at least no doubt that the Wine
Hills map was printed in 1677. The Harvard impression of
the Richard Mather portrait and the mutilated map in Salem
seem to be on the same paper. There is no discoverable
paper mark in either. The paper of the map fragment shows
a count of sixty grid lines to 50 mm. From one chain line to
the seventh (six intervals) the measurement is 145 mm. The
paper on which the Mather portrait is printed shows the same
counts. This is at least a curious coincidence. The thickness of the two pieces of paper shows a little difference--
about 0.0042 of an inch for the Harvard print, about 0.005
for the Salem map--but in handmade paper such a matter is
of no moment.

The implications of the similarity of paper, one sheet used
in 1677 and the other supposedly used in 1670, are very un-
settling, although, of course, not conclusive. When one
remembers that Foster had no press of his own until 1675,
and the Harvard impression of the Mather was apparently
made on a press, the puzzle begins to shape up nicely, as
a seventeenth-century problem should. Presumably Foster
had access to a press in Cambridge. Or perhaps one of the
Cambridge printers could have printed Foster's block. But
what about the 1677 paper? One can only hope for more
light, and for some careful study of paper used by the
Cambridge and Foster presses.

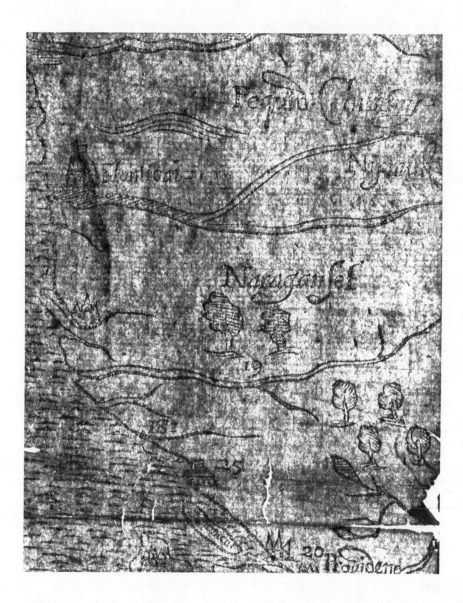

Fig. 4. "Wine Hills Map." Enlarged detail of the fragment in the Peabody Museum of Salem, showing paper structure. Probably John Foster. 1677

If the Richard Mather portrait were not our first print it
would still have claim to distinction as a work of primitive
art, no matter when it was made. Gillett Griffin of Princeton
summed it up very well in an article in Printing and Graphic
Arts in 1959:

> The Mather woodcut portrait remains unique for its
> time and place. No precedent for it has survived.
> How many were printed of any edition, why and for
> whom, are unanswered questions. The later print-
> ings may have been done for the Mather family
> exclusively. It seems reasonable to suppose
> Foster was moved to make it out of his own re-
> spect and fondness for Mather. Although crude,
> it has undeniable fascination, directness and
> sincerity. The simple bold contrast of black and
> white, together with the expressive delineation
> of the head, made a vivid American icon. As a
> work of primitive art it can hold its own. It is
> a sound cornerstone of American printmaking.[6]

To this can be added an anticlimax. We are taught to
worship at the shrines of Thomas Bewick, the Englishman,
and Dr. John Anderson of New York for pioneering the art
of white-line wood engraving in the 1790s. Yet Anderson
was not the first American to use the white line. In the
seventeenth century, when John Foster represented the appearance of Mr. Mather's white beard, he either instinctively
or accidentally adopted the white-line technique. Let us not
claim too much for Foster, but let us not overlook this fact.

The Lost Indian Items

On September 4, 1671, John Eliot wrote to the Commissioners of the United Colonies asking that John Foster be
paid " 3 4 or 5" pounds for "cutting in wood the Scheame
of our Indian A. B. C. & our Indian Dialogs."[7] The Commis-
ioners paid £4, which was no trifling sum in 1671. After
Foster died in 1681 the building that housed his printing

business was valued at £15, and this was after the cruel
inflation brought on by King Philip's War. A payment of £4
suggests an engraving job of importance, but we cannot say
for certain; no copy has been found.

A work entitled Indian Dialogs, printed in 1671, does
exist. There are two copies, one in the New York Public
Library and one in the Bodleian. But these are in the Indian
language. At any rate, there are no bits of woodcut work at
all in the little volumes in New York and in Oxford.

If the Indian ABC and the Indian Dialogs were actually
printed, and Eliot's words imply this, they must have been
printed in Cambridge, where the presses were in 1671, and
where Marmaduke Johnson was the official printer for Indian
work. It was Johnson's business which Foster bought after
Johnson had moved it to Boston late in 1674, and suddenly
died. I think we may reasonably assume that Foster had
more than casual acquaintance with the printing trade before
he entered it.

Still, the only direct word we have on the matter is in a
letter from Samuel Green, the Harvard College printer, to
John Winthrop, Jr., of Connecticut, dated July 1675. Green
complains that Foster has been permitted to enter the printing trade. Foster, he writes, is "a young man who had no
skill at printing but what he had taken notice of by the by."[8]
The facts are probably colored here by competitive feeling.

There is circumstantial evidence, too, but it does not go
wholly to Green's credit. Foster issued an almanac for 1675.
It must have been published toward the end of 1674, six
months or so before he became a printer. It was printed by
Green. The title page is a pretty rough bit of work. One is
tempted to observe that circumstances were perhaps right
for a neophyte to enter the printing business successfully.
Perhaps Foster looked at this title page and decided that a
bright Harvard man could certainly do better. This almanac
was important for another reason. It contained two unimpressive woodcuts by Foster which seem to be our first
scientific illustrations.

Annals of the Town of Dorchester by James Blake, under
the year 1681, notes "this year died Mr. John Foster, son

of Capt. Hopestill Foster; School-master of Dorchester, and
he that made the then Seal of Arms of ye Colony, namely an
Indian with a Bow & Arrow &c." Surprisingly enough he is
not called a printer, nor is the method mentioned by which
he made the seal or arms. Still, we must assume from this
that his making of the seal was important, more important
than some of his other accomplishments. Just what did he
make?

He did not design the seal. The largely naked Indian
with his bow and arrow and a ribbon of words issuing from
his mouth, "Come Over and Help Us," had come from
England with the first settlers. The original seals were of
silver, for impressing wax, and were made in London by
Richard Trott in 1629, nineteen years before Foster's birth.[9]
No one seems to have bothered to name the man who thought
up the Indian and his words. Was this sort of thing done by
the College of Heralds?

In 1672 John Usher of Boston, an enterprising merchant,
importer, and bookseller, published a volume with the title,
The General Laws and Liberties of the Massachusetts Colony:
Revised and Reprinted. By Order of the General Court
Holden at Boston, May 15th, 1672. It was printed at
Cambridge by Samuel Green. On the leaf opposite the title
was a woodcut of the seal of the Colony. There is no
question that Foster made such a cut, nor that he had such
a cut which he used very often after he went into business
as a printer in 1675.[10] But the two cuts differ. Did he make
both? The Usher cut was used for years by Green. The
other cut was used for years by Foster. Samuel A. Green,
historian and Foster scholar, gave Foster credit for making
both, pointing out that no other woodcut engraver was available. Matt B. Jones, historian and student of the Colony
seals, thought Foster made only the one used in his own
shop, the Usher cut being presumably imported. To me,
simply looking at the woodcuts, it seems unlikely that both
were made by the same hand, and fairly likely that Foster
made the one used in 1672 by Usher and afterwards by Green.
However, this required a reasonable explanation of why
Green's cut looks like Foster's work and Foster's cut looks

like some other man's work when there was probably no other
man. Also Jones raised a good point when he wrote: "if we
attribute this cut [the 1672 cut used by Green] to Foster, we
must explain why he did a better job for Usher in 1672 than
he did for himself in 1675."[11] This is a fair statement; the
1672 workmanship is superior.

Nevertheless I am tempted to believe that Foster is in
some way involved with the 1672 cut. In 1960 in an article
on the Foster map, I singled out the tree symbols for
particular mention:

> The tree symbols, indicating forested areas, are
> worth noting. As far as my present knowledge
> goes they are unique in design. They somewhat
> resemble the trees of the map in William Wood's
> New England's Prospect of 1634, also a woodcut
> map, but the resemblance is not complete. Foster's
> typical tree symbol has two lines outlining the
> trunk meeting in a point in a cloud-shaped mass
> of foliage marked by lines of shading [cf. fig. 4].[12]

This is a good description of the three trees seen between
and beside the legs of the Indian in the 1672 cut, and the
resemblance is noteworthy. But as far as I am concerned
up to the present moment we have no good answer to Matt
Jones's question about Foster's doing a better job for Usher
than for himself. There is a third woodcut seal, very crude
indeed, which we will come to a little later.

James Thomas Flexner in his First Flowers of Our Wilderness pays his respects to a woodcut with which John Foster
"embellished so many of his books . . . that it seems
practically his trade mark" (fig. 5). Flexner shows no
hesitancy in attributing the woodcut to Foster on stylistic
grounds alone:

> Two winged cherubs, fat, bouncy and naked, are
> blowing trumpets while between them a skeleton
> climbs comfortably out of his coffin. The design
> is held together by flowered borders similar to

Fig. 5. The book ornament probably cut by Foster
as first used in 1672 in the Laws and Liberties of
the Massachusetts Bay Colony. Used over and over
by Foster after 1675 when he became a professional
printer. 5 1/8" x 4 7/16". Boston Athenaeum

those that run down the sides of tombstones.
This mingling of fat flanks with bare bones, of
putti with a death's head, reflects amusingly the
marriage of convenience between the Middle Ages
and the Renaissance which was Puritan culture.[13]

And Foster, being a Puritan, would, of course, engrave
something like this!

My own opinion is that the book ornament may well have
been cut by Foster, although to my eye it resembles his
other work not at all. It was used after 1675 in several
items from the Foster press as well as before 1675 in at
least one non-Foster imprint, The Laws and Liberties of 1672.
To me it seems likely that if Foster cut the Colony seal in
Usher's volume he may almost be assumed to have cut the
decoration as well, and vice versa. But I cannot explain
why the ornament ended up in his hands rather than Green's.

The dissimilarity of the book ornament to Foster's other
work may simply reflect his sources. It looks very much like
a piece of simple copying. The little central medallion may
have come from a tombstone design, but the ornate strapwork
border is surely from some engraved title page or the
cartouche of some Ortelius or Mercator map. Outright copying was common in sophisticated Europe of the time. Why
not here, too?

The Hubbard Map

Most ambitious of Foster's engravings was the map of
New England (fig. 6) which Randolph Adams says antedates
by five years the earliest datable engraved map in Latin
America.[14] It has provoked more discussion than any
American print before Revere's copy of Pelham's "Boston
Massacre." Its problems have even been referred to as a
controversy.

From June 1675 to the autumn of 1676 New England
experienced an epidemic of Indian fights known ever since
as King Philip's War. The Indians almost won it. Before
the end of 1677, eight accounts of the war had been

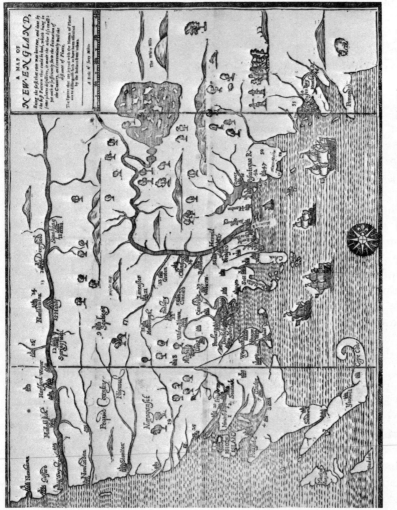

Fig. 6. "A Map of New England" ("White Hills Map"). Woodcut, John Foster. 1677. 11 11/16" x 15 5/8". John Carter Brown Library, Brown University

published in London, one of them in verse. The best of them was in the picturesque prose of the Reverend William Hubbard, teacher of the First Parish in Ipswich, Massachusetts. Foster printed a Boston edition of it in the spring of 1677; Thomas Parkhurst published a London edition a surprisingly short time later.

Hubbard's narrative of King Philip's War is distinguished among books in that it contained the first map ever engraved and published in America. This deservedly famous production (first American map and first book illustration in one) bears no name of cartographer, engraver, or printer. But in the words of an eminent and cautious scholar, Lawrence C. Wroth, it has been "generally conceded to be the work of John Foster."[15] It is the best known of Foster's engravings and the least rare. Randolph G. Adams, in his valuable study of Hubbard's Narrative, gave the locations of sixty-two maps in 1939 still in copies of the book.

The map shows New England from Nantucket to Pemaquid Point and from New Haven almost to the White Mountains. Its orientation is odd in that it looks west instead of north. This is not uncommon among early maps of the Atlantic coast. People were still mentally in Europe; their maps tended to look across the ocean. The Foster map is a fairly primitive example of the wood engraver's art. It suggests the woodcut maps of 150 years earlier rather than the typical European copperplate map of the seventeenth century. Despite one published objection to my statement of some years ago, I shall repeat it. To any one with a taste for American beginnings it is a fascinating map of unsurpassed beauty.

The title of the map was set in type and mortised into the block. It is long and informative: "A Map of New-England, Being the first that was ever here cut, and done by the best pattern that could be had, which being in some places defective, it made the other less exact, yet doth it sufficiently shew the Scituation of the Countrey, and Conveniently well the Distance of Places." Three statements seem to be implicit in this little flood of words: first, the engraver was perfectly aware that he was producing the first printed

American map; second, it was based on another map; and
third, he knew that it was not too accurate but good enough
in the circumstances.

We now know, thanks to Miss Jeannette Black of the
John Carter Brown Library, what the other map was, though it
has not been found and may never be. Miss Black has found,
in the public records of Massachusetts, that a man named
James Taylor had been paid to make a copy of an earlier map
by William Reed, who in turn had been paid to make up a
map showing the northern and southern boundary claims of
Massachusetts, based on the somewhat impractical limits
granted in 1629. The Taylor copy was taken to London and
used to make a map for the use of the Lords of Trade and
Plantations which is now in the John Carter Brown Library.
This is a seriously simplified statement, but a reasonably
accurate one.

The Secretary of the Colony was Edward Rawson, who
lived in Newbury. In traveling between the capital and his
home he literally passed the door of William Hubbard. The
records show that there were enough copies of the Reed map
so that one could have been on file in Rawson's office. "The
best pattern that could be had" must have been supplied in
one way or another to Hubbard by Rawson. Whether Hubbard
traced, copied, or simply handed the map to Foster is not
known. There seems to be no question, however, that
Foster cut the wood block. And so we call it the Foster map.

The Foster map is printed from a block incised on the
plank or side grain of the wood, probably with a knife. It
measures roughly 12 by 15 inches. Needless to say, it is
very unlikely that a genuine example exists without the
creases resulting from being folded into the book.

It seems probable that Hubbard or Foster made a tracing
which Foster fastened face down on the block. Transparency
could have come from oil or varnish applied after the paper
had dried on the block.[16]

The map has a number of decorative details: five sailing
vessels, a compass rose, a bear, a fox, two Indian hunters,
a rabbit (or porcupine), a forest of little trees, and house-
shaped symbols to mark the settlements. But there is no

representation of an Indian fight. The house symbols all lean
rather drunkenly to the left.

Scattered over the map are reference numbers, some
attached to named or unnamed towns, some not. According to
three lines of print below the title, "The figures that are
joyned with the Names of Places are to distinguish such as
have been assaulted by the Indians from others." But this
is not entirely accurate. Some figures stand alone, some
with nameless towns, and other towns which are known to
have been attacked seem to have lost their figures. Many
of the legends naming the settlements are crudely cut and
oddly spelled; some suffer very much from misdirected cuts
with the knife. The form of some of the letters suggests
the handwriting of the time; others strongly resemble printed
characters. It appears that Foster worked from a manuscript,
but corrected and amended it by using type mortised into the
block.

The key numbers are very largely chronological in
sequence, starting with King Philip's stronghold, Mount
Hope, as No. 1, then with the earliest scenes of trouble in
order, all the way to the last encounters in Maine in the
spring of 1677, numbered up to 55. It is plain that some of
the cutting was not completed until immediately before
printing. Some numbers are missing. It has been shown from
Hubbard's own Advertisement to the Reader that the author
made continual changes and additions in the text. It appears
that Foster worked in somewhat the same way as far as the
map was concerned.

There are two variant forms of the same map, both intended
to illustrate Hubbard's book, both printed in 1677, both
printed from wood blocks and very similar in style, size, and
general appearance. Luckily for those who wish to distinguish between them there is one curious difference. On one
we find a group of mountains north of Lake Winnepesaukee
named "The Wine Hills," on the other the same group named
"The White Hills." It is customary to refer to the Wine
Hills or the White Hills map.

The significance of the variants has for a long time
attracted attention and created a tremendous tangle of

ideas among scholars in the nineteenth century. All attempts
to say why there were two variant maps and all attempts to
say who cut the "other" one, whichever that other one was,
simply failed. Some booksellers of the time added nothing
to our understanding by removing maps from expensive
London editions of Hubbard and tipping them into valuable
Boston editions which lacked the map. One famous bookseller went so far as to advertise that he had published
facsimiles of both forms of the map on old paper, the one
"to be with difficulty distinguished from the original" and the
other "a perfect facsimile."[17] He was not stretching the
truth very far.

Finally Randolph Adams entered the field. His theory was
that the point might be cleared up if an experienced man looked
at all the books. So he set out to examine, or have examined,
a significant number of copies of Hubbard's Narrative in both
editions. On the basis of fifty of each he was able to state
that the White Hills belonged wholly to the Boston edition,
the Wine Hills wholly to the London edition. Apparent exceptions turned out to be facsimiles or maps more or less
recently inserted. Most things said and many things written
before Adams made his report are suspect, misleading, or
totally wrong.

The questions, then, are who made the Wine Hills, or
London, block? Was it made by Foster or by an Englishman?
Was it made in Boston, and if so, was it made before the
White Hills or after? Which, in other words, was the
earliest engraved American map? But, of course, neither
block may be the earlier, except in point of printing and
publishing. The blocks may have been cut concurrently
with every intention of sending one to England. There is
no proof; simply hints and inductions. At least we can say
with assurance that the White Hills map, undoubtedly engraved by John Foster, was the first map to be engraved,
printed, and published in English-speaking America.

Three years ago David Woodward, presently of the New-
berry Library in Chicago, contributed an article on the two
maps to Imago Mundi in which he made some sound contributions, as he should, and found some serious faults with

some of my conclusions of 1960.[18] It would serve no purpose to say more at the moment, except to point out that the
more informed discussion, the more progress.

There are other, minor, Foster blocks. Presumably there
are also undiscovered major works as well. We live in hope
of discovery. Before leaving him it would be fitting to say
something more of the man.

Before he died of tuberculosis at thirty-three, Foster had
engraved the first print in English-speaking America, engraved the first map, and written a paper on "Comets, their
Motion, Distance and Magnitude" which seems to be among
our very first astronomical publications (fig. 7).[19] He had
done something more than dabble in medical science and
mathematics. He may, too, have been our first native-born
painter of portraits. His view of Boston and Charlestown
from East Boston, engraved in Amsterdam and seemingly lost
forever, may have been our first acceptable landscape. In
an age when such mingling had little precedent he combined
a practice of some of the mechanic arts with the accepted
intellectualism of the day. The inventory of his estate lists
his "Gittarue Viall wether glasses," a frustrating jumble
which at least suggests an interest in music and meteorology.

There is exaggeration but much truth, too, in the words of
John Allen Lewis quoted in Sibley's Harvard Graduates:

> After a while I came to look on Foster as one of the
> great men of that great age,--a scholar, a thinker,
> a printer, engraver, chemist,--a man worthy of the
> love, friendship, and admiration of the Mathers.
> Had Foster lived to the age that Franklin reached,
> Franklin might have been called a "second Foster."[20]

For all this, there is still very little known about Foster,
and what we do know has been uncovered by many people.
We have no reason to believe that all the significant facts
have yet been found. We almost know what we are talking
about but not quite.

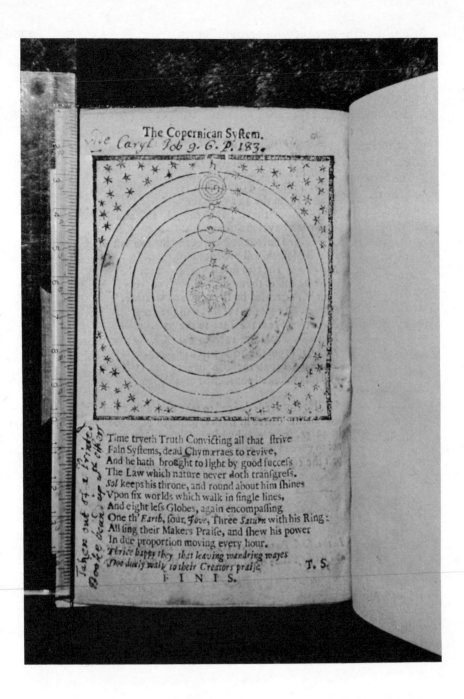

Fig. 7. "The Copernican System." An astronomical chart, John Foster. 1681. 3 1/16" x 2 15/16". Massachusetts Historical Society

The Harp Player

We can speak with assurance of only three American engravers in the seventeenth century. After Foster came the
anonymous producer of a rough-and-ready but appealing woodcut portrait thought to represent King David playing the harp
(fig. 8). The third was the man, almost certainly John Coney
the silversmith, who engraved copperplates from which
Massachusetts paper currency was printed in 1690. In
addition there was at least one engraver whose existence
can be inferred. Perhaps "alleged" would be the more suitable word.

Let us look at King David. Since we are ignorant of the
engraver's name we can follow the European practice and
call him the Master of the Harp Player. The print he made
was an illustration, at least in the sense that it was printed
in the <u>Cambridge Ephemeris. An Almanack of Coelestial</u>
<u>Motions, Configurations &c. For the year of the Christian</u>
<u>Aera, 1684</u>, N. Russell, Astrotyr. (Cambridge: Printed by
Samuel Green, 1684). The copy in the Massachusetts
Historical Society seems to be unique. The print is reproduced in Sinclair Hamilton's "American Book Illustrations
Prior to the Nineteenth Century" (Princeton, reprint, 1968).
The paper of the frontispiece and that of the body of the book
seem to be identical; apparently the cut did not get bound in
adventitiously as the Richard Mather did.

The woodcut of King David is not a finished or polished
piece of work. Nor does it elucidate anything in the
almanac. I do not believe that it serves any didactic or
religious purpose. It is intended, I think, as a work of
pure decoration, and yet there is an emotional quality to it.
The artist seems quite simply and directly to be celebrating
his enthusiasm for a great man of the Old Testament. Without concerning ourselves at all with the Puritan ethos, we
can accept the fact that in early New England, King David
was regarded with much the same approval shown by his
descendants and coreligionists. This woodcut seems to be
a purely lyrical outburst, an unusual thing at any time; in
seventeenth-century Boston and Cambridge--an event of
considerable rarity.

Fig. 8. "The Harp Player" ("King David").
Possibly by Richard Pierce, made during the
1680s. 5 1/16" x 3". Massachusetts
Historical Society

The Master of the Harp Player is nameless, but his style
of work is individualistic. If another example of his work
were to appear, it might be fairly easy to make the attribution.
Perhaps this example is the woodcut seal of the Massachusetts Bay Colony used by Richard Pierce of Boston in printing
a few official documents in the 1680s, in the time of Governor
Andros (fig. 9). Its origin is unknown, but it has such a
home-grown look that it seems unlikely to have been professionally cut in England. Perhaps Pierce cut it, but there
is nothing to prove it. At this point, and very tentatively
indeed, I suggest a possibility. There is some sort of
similarity, a similarity of crudity, of use of blacks, of
naivete and inexperience between the King David and the
Richard Pierce seal.

The First Copperplate Engraving

The so-called Colony Bills of 1690 are reputed to be the
first examples of intaglio engraving as well as the first
paper money in what we think of as the United States. John
Coney engraved the copperplates from which they were
printed under the supervision of an interested committee of
five.[21] Although the bills were not particularly distinguished pieces of engraving, they probably looked acceptable
to people who came into possession of them at that time.
John Coney, then, was our first engraver on metal.

A feature which may or may not have helped the notes was
a last appearance of our aboriginal friend, the Indian of the
Colony seal. On the 1690 bills he appears in even more
disheveled condition than before (fig. 10). He still stands
between some trees--two mangy conifers--and he has re-
gained his ribbon of words, "Come over and help us." But
somehow in his last appearance during the 1600s the words
came out backwards, and most people must read them in a
mirror.

Another matter of no small importance begins with the
Colony notes of 1690. As David McNeely Stauffer points
out in his indispensible American Engravers upon Copper
and Steel: "This Massachusetts paper money was

Fig. 9. Woodcut seal of the Massachusetts Bay
Colony used by Richard Pierce of Boston in the
1680s

Fig. 10. A slightly enlarged
view of the seal on a 1690
colony bill, engraved by John
Coney

counterfeited almost as soon as issued; and this fact is
sufficient evidence that the Colonial authorities did not
employ all the engraving talent then available in New
England."[22] So we can say of our second engraver on copper
that he seems to have been a modest and retiring individual
and no seeker of personal publicity.

The next piece of the engraver's art to appear was also a
copperplate, but no one counterfeited it as far as we know.
A copy of an English original, it was a portrait of Increase
Mather, engraved by Thomas Emmes of Boston. Its year of
publication was 1701, so it belongs to the next century.

NOTES

1. Samuel Abbott Green, John Foster, the Earliest American Engraver and First Boston Printer (Boston, 1909), p. 52.
2. Gillett Griffin, "John Foster's Woodcut of Richard Mather," Printing and Graphic Arts, VII, no. 1 (1959), 1-8; Sinclair Hamilton, "Portrait of a Puritan, John Foster's Woodcut of Richard Mather," The Princeton University Library Chronicle, XVIII, no. 2 (Winter 1967), 43-48.
3. Four other Foster prints of Mather are located at The American Antiquarian Society, The Massachusetts Historical Society, Princeton University, and the University of Virginia.
4. Griffin, p. 6.
5. Richard B. Holman, "Some Remarks on Mr. Richard Mather," Printing and Graphic Arts, VII, no. 2 (1959), 57-63.
6. Griffin, p. 7.
7. Green, p. 6.
8. George E. Littlefield, The Early Massachusetts Press, II (Boston, 1907), 10.
9. Matt B. Jones, "The Early Massachusetts-Bay Colony Seals," Proceedings of the American Antiquarian Society, XLIV (April 1934), 13-44.
10. Ibid., p. 12.
11. Ibid., p. 11.
12. Richard B. Holman, "John Foster's Woodcut Map of New England," Printing and Graphic Arts, VIII, no. 3 (1960), 55.
13. James Thomas Flexner, American Painting: First Flowers of Our Wilderness (Boston, 1947), p. 26.
14. Randolph G. Adams, "Hubbard's Narrative," Papers of the Bibliographical Society of America, XXXIII, 26.
15. Lawrence C. Wroth and Marion W. Adams, Woodcuts and Engravings, 1670-1800 (Providence, 1946), p. 16.
16. Holman, "Map," p. 67.
17. Henry Stevens, Bibliotheca Geographica y Historica (London, 1872), items no. 1959 and 1960.

John Dewey Library
Johnson State College
Johnson, Vermont

18. David Woodward, "The Foster Map Controversy: a
Further Examination of the Evidence," Imago Mundi, XVI
(Amsterdam, 1967).

19. Foster's woodcut for an astronomical chart was used
in the almanac of 1675 now at the American Antiquarian
Society in Worcester, and that of 1681 at the Massachusetts
Historical Society in Boston.

20. John Langdon Sibley, Biographical Sketches of
Graduates of Harvard University in Cambridge, Massachusetts (Cambridge, 1881), II, 222.

21. Andrew McFarland Davis, Currency and Banking in
the Province of Massachusetts-Bay (New York, 1900).

22. (New York, 1907), I, p. xxii.

PRINTS IN COLONIAL AMERICA
SUPPLY AND DEMAND IN THE MID-EIGHTEENTH CENTURY

Joan Dolmetsch

IN DECEMBER 1743, Robert Pringle advertised in the South
Carolina Gazette: "Just imported in the Ship Samuel, Capt.
Warden from London sundry Goods, particularly a very choice
Collection of Printed Books, Pictures, Maps and Pickles to be
sold very reasonable." In the formative days of restorations,
citing such a simple reference seemed documentation enough
to answer visitors' inquiries concerning the appropriateness
of most print usages. But having literally come of age
together, neither restorations nor visitors are any longer
completely satisfied by such facile bits of information as
that prints were part of the cargoes transported to these shores.
The necessity for further documentation, to name names, so
to speak, has become essential in an attempt to make such
projects more meaningful not only to the public at large but
also to associates in the profession.

Based on this need for more information, the 1966 decision
of Colonial Williamsburg to open additional exhibition
buildings offered an excellent opportunity to undertake a
study not of Colonial American prints (a subject already
well explored) but rather a study of prints known to
have been in Colonial America. What is presented here is
far from a finished project, nor is an end foreseen. These
findings are based on readings of early colonial newspapers,
letters, and inventories and the correlation of this information
with pertinent English print documentation in an effort to
present as complete an account of mid-eighteenth-century
usages as possible.[1] However, as long as historical
documents are discovered, read, and assimilated, more
information is certain to be discovered.

Daniel Fisher, traveling through the Northern Neck of
Virginia in 1755, noted in his journal that he stopped at a
Rappahannock ordinary which had:

> as elegant an appearance as any I have seen in the
> country, Mr. Finnays or Wetherberns in Williamsburg
> not excepted. The chairs, Tables, &c. of the Room
> I was conducted into was all of Mahogony, and so
> stuft with fine large glaized Copper Plate Prints:
> That I almost fancied myself in Jeffriess' or some
> other elegant Print Shop.[2]

"Elegant" shops such as this Virginia traveler was remembering
were numerous in London during this mid-eighteenth-century
period. They abounded in prints selling for a few shillings
plain, another penny or two colored. These were ready to be
admired and discussed in England; to be packed as part of the
personal belongings of those leaving for the colonies; to be
ordered by settlers upon their arrival here from their friends
or London agents; or to be added to cargo by the ship captains
who knew of the ready market for these printed sheets.

But no matter who the purveyor or purchaser of such prints
might have been, one fact was quickly established: the
colonists' desire for the latest and best engravings available.
Considering this, it is little wonder that the works bearing
William Hogarth's name were a constant in mid-eighteenth-
century advertisements of shipments reaching all the colonies.
And indeed, they continued to be among the best-selling
prints long after Hogarth's death.

Notices appearing in the <u>Boston Gazette</u> between the years
1757 and 1760 informed the public that Nathaniel Warner had
a regular supply of Mr. Hogarth's works, including among
others "The Harlot's Progress," "Paul Before Felix," and
"The Rake's Progress." In a letter to a brother studying in
England, Thomas Jones of Williamsburg requested that more
Hogarth prints be purchased for him, and specified that he
already had in his possession "A Midnight Modern Conver-
sation," " The Rake's Progress," "The Harlot's Progress,"
and "The Roast Beef of Old England."[3]

But if one were to have recorded the best-selling of all Hogarth sets in the colonies at this period, surely "The Idle and Industrious Prentice" would have carried home the honors (figs. 1, 2). It was advertised almost continually after its publication in 1747 and was still available for sale in shops such as Stephen Whiting's in Boston in 1771, six years after Hogarth's death. The popularity of this set is not really difficult to understand when one considers the colonists' penchant for the Roman virtues. Anything depicting the triumph of good over evil sold exceedingly well.

Not far behind such Hogarth sets in appeal were those engravings (often based on paintings) of Biblical stories, sometimes called "scripture pieces." The 1770 inventory of the personal estate of His Excellency Lord Botetourt taken in the Governor's Palace, Williamsburg, lists thirty-four such pieces. Sarah Green of York County, Virginia, had pictures of "Solomon's Temple" and "Rachel and Leah." Alexander Spotswood of Orange County, Virginia, had a scripture piece of "The History of Women Taken in Adultery."

From the colonists' pictorial obsession with Biblical interpretation and Roman virtues, it was only a short step to their zeal for Roman antiquities. Joseph Royale of Williamsburg lists in his 1766 inventory "6 prints--Ruins of Rome and 2 in its original splendor." At almost the same time Matthew Clarkson in the Pennsylvania Gazette was featuring complete sets of "Roman antiquities."

These prints in themselves are an interesting study, for often they were designed and published for quick sale to people who had visited Rome and wanted a memento of their journey. Such customers did not demand complete accuracy in these prints, preferring instead many varied ruins in a single one-page picture, no matter what the actual distance from one ruin to another might be.

Two of the more popular engravers of such works during this period were Johann Sebastian Muller, who worked in England from the paintings of Pannini, and Giambattista Piranesi, who worked in Rome from his own designs. One of Piranesi's Roman designs is the "Colonna Antonina" (fig. 3). Illustrated are the Palazzo Ghigi, the Piazza Colonna,

Fig. 1. "The IDLE 'PRENTICE Executed at Tyburn." Black and white line engraving, Pl. 11 of set, William Hogarth. 10 3/4" x 16 1/8". Colonial Williamsburg

Fig. 2. "The INDUSTRIOUS 'PRENTICE Lord-Mayor of London." Black and
white line engraving, Pl. 12 of set, William Hogarth. London, 1747.
10 7/8" x 16 1/8". Colonial Williamsburg

Colonna Antonina.

Fig. 3. "Colonna Antonina." Black and white line
engraving, Giambattista Piranesi. Rome, ca. 1755.
22 1/2" x 16 1/4". Colonial Williamsburg

and the Strada Del Corso, an area of about six blocks compressed into one engraving.

The appropriate companion pieces to these antiquities were, of course, portraits of the Caesars. These were sometimes used in small numbers, such as the four listed in a 1749 rural New England inventory of William Dudley, or in larger groupings such as the twelve registered in the Williamsburg inventory of John Burdett. The portrait of "C. IVLIVS CAESAR" is just one example of those published and circulated well into the eighteenth century, in both England and the colonies (fig. 4).

But not all the prints coming into the colonies were of such a somber or moralistic nature, or of such Hogarthian wit and satire. As early as 1690 the inventory of David Fox of Lancaster, Virginia, listed "25 pictures of Sences [sic]," which were located in his hall. The hall and stairs were favorite display locations for prints, as is confirmed by the record of a York County, Virginia, resident who had fifty-two in his hall, plus many in other rooms. In 1758 John Welco advertised in Boston "A Number of Metzitinto prints, large and small pictures suitable for a Stair-case." Such sets of engravings as the "Sences" were an integral part of the decorative furnishings both here and abroad. Among others were "Elements," "Seasons," and "Arts and Sciences." Engraving and publishing such prints in England in great numbers, artists made a common practice of "borrowing" (a polite term) ideas from one another, rarely changing more than costumes and publication information.

One publisher well known for such ornamentive items was Robert Sayer. The business between Sayer and the Virginia Colony is well documented in the daybook of Joseph Royale, Williamsburg printer. Between the years 1764 and 1766 Royale ordered from Sayer "sundry prints" totaling £98:5:5. Alexander Purdie, another Williamsburg printer, purchased sixteen Sayer prints in gilt frames, and Hugh Walker, also of the city, obtained in 1764 one dozen Sayer prints in gilt frames.

These prints, popular in their original form, were also a source for another type of artistic endeavor. Peter Pelham

Fig. 4. "C. IVLIVS CAESAR." Black and white line
engraving, Aegidius Sadeler, from a painting by Titian.
13 7/8" x 9 1/2". Colonial Williamsburg

in a 1738 Boston Gazette announced: "Young Gentlemen and Ladies, may be taught Dancing, Writing, Reading, Painting on Glass and all sorts of Needle Work." If a correct young lady became bored with needlework, she could properly turn to artistic pursuits as a viable alternative. Thus painting on glass became one of several exceedingly popular pastimes.

Whether the glass paintings were done by a professional in a shop or by a young lady in her home, a mezzotint print was often selected as the subject. The already present shading of this engraving technique made it an ideal medium for such purposes. Matthew Clarkson in a 1755 Pennsylvania Gazette advertised "a great variety of metzotinto pictures for paintings on glass," as did Nathaniel Warner of Boston. The 1761 Virginia inventory of Benneh Neals listed "1 sett 12 months painted on glass in frames."

The transfer "November," is one of a set designed and engraved about 1750 by Thomas Burford which has an interesting history (fig. 5). Purchased in London when the Colonial Williamsburg staff was furnishing the Peyton Randolph House, two arrived in this country broken. Normally such an accident represents a complete loss, for once such a transfer is damaged little can be done to restore it. However, in this instance an exact replacement for one of the broken ones was located in New York, suggesting the possible popularity of this particular set for use as transfers.

Sea pieces were another type of fancy print noted in many advertisements and inventories. The Pennsylvania Gazette of May 1, 1755, carried a listing of a particularly unusual item. Alexander Hamilton announced that he had available "Vandeval's Green Sea Pieces." That there was some experimentation of color printing by 1755 is an established fact. But to my knowledge this is the earliest suggestion of such colored prints reaching the colonies, and the only one so far located. In order to determine the precise nature of such prints, marine museum personnel both here and abroad were consulted. Information received from the National Maritime Museum, Greenwich, England, indicated that the engraver Elisha Kirkall did a series of colored prints derived from paintings of marine pieces by Van de Velde and other

Fig. 5. "November." Hand-colored glass transfer, T.
Burford. One of a set of twelve. London, 1747. 14"
x 9 1/8". Colonial Williamsburg

notable artists.[4] At about this time John McKendry, curator
of prints at the Metropolitan Museum of Art, obtained for the
museum collection a green engraving by Kirkall. However,
it was done after a Vandiest canvas (fig. 6). The unique
muted grey-green ink used in the printing of this sea piece
is an interesting indication of the colonists' taste for unusual
items.

Hamilton's May 1755 advertisement in the Pennsylvania
Gazette, aside from mentioning this unusual sea piece,
provides a formidable list of prints for sale:

> . . . variety of pictures viz sciences painted on
> glass, scenes, months, seasons, cartoons, hunting
> pieces, Roman Antiquities, parts of the day by
> Hogarth, roast beef of Old England, distressed
> poet and enraged Musician, humours of a fair,
> March to Finchely, midnight conversation, India
> settlements, Vandeval's green sea pieces, industry
> and idleness, judgment of Hercules, Paul before
> Felix, in the Dutch taste, sleepy congregation,
> the lottery and several other humerous pieces by
> Hogarth . . . .

A recurring question in Williamsburg concerns the use of
botanical plates removed from bound volumes and hung or
used in some manner as decorative objects. The John Custis
Letter Book of 1717-1741 contains the following letter written
in 1734 from his Williamsburg home to a Mr. Cary:

> I am very much pleased with the flour [sic] pieces
> you sent me: but the man has not done me justice
> in not sending the thirteenth print with the sub-
> scribers names which I find he has sent to other
> Gentlemen, Coll Lee for one. I hope you will
> order him to send it me still, I believe I have
> got him severall Customers.[5]

The 1764 inventory of Williamsburg merchant William Prentis
includes "12 Fruit P - - - - [illeg.; prints or pictures] valued

Fig. 6. "Moonlit Harbor Scene." Mezzotint engraving
in color, Elisha Kirkall, from a painting by A.
Vandiest. Metropolitan Museum of Art, Elisha
Whittelsey Fund

at £8." Although it would be unwise to name any one set of
prints as the subject of these references, certain facts cannot
be overlooked. In 1730 Robert Furber published the first
edition of <u>Twelve Months of Flowers</u>. The plates were engraved
by H. Fletcher after paintings by Pieter Casteels. The work
detailed month by month flower seeds and bulbs which might be
ordered from Furber for planting in one's garden. The thirteenth
plate which accompanied this work contained the names of subscribers who had financially aided Furber in this project. This
was followed in 1732 by <u>Twelve Months in Fruit</u>. Certainly it
would be difficult to find a set of flower or fruit pieces more
closely paralleling the descriptions in the letter and in the
inventory than those issued by Furber.

Another reference showing that botanical prints served for
other than scientific ventures is this curious advertisement
which appeared in the <u>Pennsylvania Gazette</u> on September 9,
1756:

> This Day is published a Catalogue of a curious
> collection of Prints: consisting of several hundred
> representations of Trees, Shrubs, Plants, Herbs,
> Fruits, Flowers &c. and neatly coloured after
> nature. Being well adapted for furniture, and
> ornamenting of apartments, closets &c., like-
> wise fit for japanning, or to serve for patterns
> for drawing embroidery &c. divided into lots;
> which will be sold very cheap for ready money
> the lowest price being marked in the catalogue.
> The sale to begin on Monday the 13th day of
> September at the Public Register Office of
> Intelligence, within two doors of the Indian
> King in Market street, Philadelphia where
> catalogues may be had gratis.

Unfortunately, it is not easy to pinpoint with any degree of
accuracy a reference such as this. At this period a great
many design books were reaching the colonies, but as a
general rule they contained designs of a vast variety, rather
than being limited to strictly botanical representations.

However, volumes of Ehret and Linnaeus were being published
in Europe, and it is possible that these may have been used
as sources of design in the manner indicated in the Gazette
notice.

Landscape or scenic engravings comprised one of the
largest single groups of prints in both import and export trade
of this period. The natural curiosity of people provided an
impetus for artists both here and abroad to depict views of
buildings and grounds, cities and villages, which could not
personally be visited. Thomas Monck in 1744 provided the
colonists of South Carolina:

> sundry curious Prints colour'd & plain viz
> Churches, noblemen's and gentlemen's seats,
> belinheim bridge, Landskapes of Porto Bello,
> Carthegens, and Havanna . . . plans of
> Prague and of St. Sebastian . . . rotundas of
> Rome . . . sets of views of Guernsey, Jersey . . . .

In 1755 the people of Pennsylvania could purchase from
Matthew Clarkson "a neat sett of views of Kensington gardens
and Hampton-Court," while in Boston, Rivington and Miller
offered "splendid Views of some of the most remarkable
Places in North-America and of the most magnificent Palaces
and Gardens in England " (fig. 7). The purchasers of views
were people such as G. Mercer of Stafford County, Virginia,
who owned among other things: "Kip's Views of Noblemen's
Seats, 8 Views of Scotland and 100 Views of Brabant and
Flanders."

If for any reason a person was unable to afford the price
of one of these prints to hang in his own home, a traveling
show was provided by such people as Thomas Williamson,
who advertised as follows in the February 21, 1750, Maryland
Gazette:

> Notice is hereby Given That there is lately arrived
> at Annapolis, and to be seen at the House of
> Mr. Thomas Williamson sundry curious and de-
> lightful PROSPECTS of most of the PUBLIC BUILDINGS,

Fig. 7. "A View of the Palace from the South side of
the Lake and the Temples of Bellona and Æolus, & the
House of Confucius in the Royal Gardens at Kew."
Hand-colored line engraving, William Woollett. London,
ca. 1760. 14 1/2" x 21 3/4". Colonial Williamsburg

PALACES, HOSPITALS &c. in Europe: Views of
SHIPPING, Inside Prospects of sundry CHURCHES,
RIVERS, LAKES and FOUNTAINS. It is the same
which has been advertised in the Pennsylvania
Papers for the six Months past, and has given
Universal Satisfaction to all who have seen it.

As we shall continue in Town by [sic] a few
Days (intending for Virginia), those Gentlemen
who have a mind to satisfy their Curiosity by
sending to the House above said, shall be
waited on at their own Houses.

The interest of the colonists about happenings in England
was evenly matched by the Englishman's curiosity concerning
the New World. As early as 1585 John White had recorded
scenes of the land, water, and inhabitants of the Virginia and
Carolina areas in watercolor. The seventeenth century saw
an increase in such drawings, and by the eighteenth century
a number of views of colonial settlements and towns were
available in England. Most often the sketches were made on
these shores and then returned to England for engraving and
publication. An early one by Peter Schenk of "Niue Amsterdam-
Noord Americaes" was widely circulated in Europe as a single
plate and then later was used as a part of the decorative
design on maps. The "South East View of New York" was
"Drawn on the Spot" by Captain Thomas Howdell of the Royal
Artillery and engraved in England in 1763 by P. Canot (fig. 8).

Sometime shortly before 1739 Bishop Roberts sketched a
watercolor view of Charleston which was returned to England
for engraving and publication by W. H. Toms. Other town
views quickly followed such as the one advertised in the
Pennsylvania Gazette of March 25, 1755, by Nicholas Scull
of "East Prospect of the City of Philadelphia." This was
drawn by George Heap under Scull's direction and then
engraved by G. Vandergucht in England. It appeared in many
states including a much reduced version which appeared in the
London Magazine, October 1761. The continued popularity
of this print is reflected in citations such as that in John
Pleasant's inventory recorded in Cumberland, Virginia, in 1765.

Fig. 8. "A South East View of the City of New York, in NORTH AMERICA." Hand-colored line engraving, Captain Thomas Howdell. London, ca. 1763. 12 1/2" x 20". Colonial Williamsburg

Equally as important to town views in the chronicling of
the New World was the interpretation of its natural history.
Probably the most important figure in this field was Mark
Catesby. After traveling and recording in drawings the natural
life of the southern colonial areas, Catesby returned to England
to study the art of engraving and to make his findings available
to the general public. The slow process of this publication
began in 1729 and continued over a period of years. The plates
were then offered in bound volumes or as single sheets in
London shops and in colonial shops such as that of H. Gaines
of New York, who offered them for sale in 1755 (fig. 9).

One type of print seems to have appeared in every source
of documentation, that of portrait engravings, more popularly
referred to in the eighteenth century as "heads." Whether
personal to a family or of a general nature, inventories both
rural and town seemed to contain one or more such engravings.
General advertisements tended to carry long listings of such
items. The Waldron Phoenix Belknap, Jr., study of the
relationship of these prints to American colonial painting is
well known.

An entire study could be written about portrait prints
available in the colonies, but this study will list only a
few: in 1719 a resident of York County, Virginia, had small
pictures of King William and Queen Mary; also in York, in
1739, was a "neat picture of King Charles the 2nd"; others
include "The Judges of England," the "King of Prussia,"
"King Ferdinand," "Admiral Boscawen," "Mr. Gerrick [sic]
Actor," "Mr. Beard, Singer," and "The Hon. William
Pitt, Esq."

Pitt, because of his pro-colonial political maneuvers, was
perhaps one of the most popular of all portrait figures, but one
of the most difficult to characterize because of his changes in
government positions. One such engraving by Richard Houston,
after a portrait by Hoare, underwent so many alterations that
Houston eventually reworked the whole print (see fig. 14, p. 153).
An impression of this was listed in an inventory of a rural North
Carolina resident in 1769.

However, the epitome in portraiture not only of Pitt but of
all heads, and one which seems an appropriative resume of

Fig. 9. "Muscicapa nigriscens. The blackcap Flycatcher." Hand-colored etching, Mark Catesby. London, 1731-43. 13 3/4" x 10 1/4". Colonial Williamsburg

the prints of this mid-eighteenth-century period, is "Worthy
of Liberty, Mr. Pitt," painted and engraved about 1768 in
London, by Charles Willson Peale (fig. 10). This was quickly
available for sale in the colonies. Peale somehow instilled
in one grandiose portrait of Pitt as a "noble Roman" all of the
ideas and sentiments so popular in mid-eighteenth-century
colonial America; ideas and sentiments destined, however, to
undergo radical changes in the following years.

Fig. 10. "Worthy of Liberty, Mr. Pitt scorns to
invade the Liberties of other People." Black and
white mezzotint engraving, Charles Willson Peale.
London, ca. 1768. 23 1/2" x 15 1/4". Colonial
Williamsburg

NOTES

1. Research facilities for studies such as this exist at
the Research Department and the Department of Collections
of Colonial Williamsburg and at The Institute of Early American
History and Culture, Williamsburg, Virginia.

2. Extract from ancestral journal quoted in Louis Pecquet
du Bellet, Some Prominent Virginia Familes (Lynchburg, Va.,
1907), II, 791.

3. Manuscript Division, Jones Papers, Library of
Congress.

4. The spelling of the Van de Velde name varies greatly
in early documents concerning the various artists in the
family.

5. John Custis Letter Book, 1717-1741, Manuscript
Division, Library of Congress.

THE GRAPHIC ARTS IN COLONIAL NEW ENGLAND

Sinclair H. Hitchings

NOT long ago, Isaac Bashevis Singer said that he was spending all his time writing for children because "they don't give a hoot about the critics, they have no use for psychology, they detest sociology . . . they still believe in God, the family, angels, devils, witches, goblins, logic, clarity, punctuation, and other such obsolete stuff."

I have a feeling that the imagery of early New England might interest Mr. Singer. In successive New England editions of The Prodigal Daughter--the first one that survives is a Boston edition of about 1737-41--the devil appears "in his true form, naked, with horns, tail and a cloven hoof."[1] He is sinuous, he coaxes yet he stalks, he is seen in stark silhouette, the alien prince of darkness. He also appears in one illustration dressed as a gentleman. Clad in his finery and carrying a cane, he casts a shadow. This was a mistake. The cut survived and was used again, but with the shadow removed. If you meet a man who casts no shadow, beware!

Successive generations of study of the early history of British North America have brought us, in our own times, to a vantage point which we ought to use when we talk about a particular activity such as the graphic arts in colonial society. We always need more information, true, but what we now possess has become almost embarrassing in its abundance. No one library brings it together in one place; many of the facts about the visual arts are not yet clearly understood in the broader context of life in the colonies. The sheer quantity of photographic reproduction in our magazines and books, however, has brought us to a more comprehensive sense of the imagery of that world. We can think of seventeenth- and early-eighteenth-century printers' ornaments in comparison to

the ornamental vocabulary of New England furniture makers of
the time. We can see, together, the crude colonial cuts of
eclipses and the handsome London-made telescopes which our
American astronomers bought and used. We know the death's-
heads on early gravestones and the crude images of skeletal
time with his scythe on mourning broadsides. We know the
symbols of authority--the lion and unicorn as seen in royal
arms on official broadsides, or in sculpture in the presumably
eighteenth-century carving now at the Massachusetts Historical
Society, or in the round in the form of separate figures mounted
on Boston's Town House, today's Old State House. We know
the pine-tree shilling, the pine tree printed from simple cuts
on colonial paper currency, the carved pine cone placed atop
the dome of Bulfinch's Massachusetts State House in the early
years of American independence. When Nathaniel Hurd cut
dies for the Province of Massachusetts Bay in 1755 to be used
in embossing legal documents, three of his designs were: for
four pence, a schooner; three pence, a pine tree; two pence,
a codfish, symbolism that naturally brings to mind the sacred
cod carved in wood and hung in the State House in Boston.
Less well known is the chart of Canso Harbor, Nova Scotia,
by Cyprian Southack, which was engraved by Francis Dewing
in Boston in 1720, showing a very early representation of New
England fishermen hauling cod into an open boat. A putto in
the cartouche of this chart has a large codfish tucked firmly
under his chubby, childish arm. There are surprisingly many
of these homemade symbols in New England--of land, sea,
people, and livelihood. The seal of the Plymouth Company, a
die cut by Thomas Johnston in 1753, displays a codfish and an
anchor. Two other processions of colonial images have implications worthy of book-length studies in words and pictures:
the portraits of New England divines, in paintings, line engravings, mezzotints, metal cuts, woodcuts, and the re-
current image of the Indian. I have, incidentally, found
exactly one piece of evidence that anyone in colonial New
England ever attempted to draw or paint a New England Indian.
To them, "an Indian was an Indian," to adapt the title of an
instructive publication by Bradford F. Swan.[2] Virtually every
representation of an Indian in the art of colonial New England

came out of an already-established tradition in which major
landmarks are the De Bry engravings after John White's watercolors of Carolina Indians and Simon's mezzotints after
Verelst's paintings of the four "Indian Kings" from the Mohawk
and Hudson River Iroquois tribes who were taken to London in
1709. I should advance this as a theory, not as fact, for the
colonial representations of Indians are not so few, ranging
from John Foster's Indian on a woodcut Massachusetts seal
to Shem Drowne's metal weathervane that swung above the Province House in Boston. When Paul Revere in 1772 engraved a
picture of King Philip, he modeled features, dress, and pose
on one of Simon's mezzotints of sixty years earlier, took details from another of the mezzotints, and used a 1766 print
after Benjamin West as the model for a group of Indians in the
background. This became the approved likeness, despite its
untruth. Sixty and more years after Revere's engraving, King
Philip was served up to Americans in at least one lithograph
based on Revere's print.[3] Art much prefers to follow art
rather than nature.

The concept of drawing is at the heart of the meaning of
graphic; so in talking about the graphic arts in Colonial New
England, I include drawings as well as prints. In terms of
history, it is helpful to do this, for in the much smaller world
of the seventeenth century, and to a very considerable extent
in the eighteenth century, manuscripts sufficed for many needs.
Presumably John Winthrop made his sketch map of Boston and
environs, of about 1637 or 1638, for his personal use and that
of a few close associates.[4] Later in the century, the Colonial
Office in London, as well as individuals and other agencies,
found it useful to have copies made of certain manuscript maps
and charts; from what evidence we have, one, two, or three
copies could usually meet the demand. We know far too little
about the information possessed by English and colonial sea
captains in the seventeenth century, but we do have various
indications that most of what they knew, they carried in their
heads.

Manuscript maps and charts nevertheless testify to their
need for information on paper, as they testify to the prevailing
concern with the boundaries of land ownership throughout New

England. The graphic arts in Rhode Island and Connecticut
share an ancestor in the manuscript map of 1642 by Nathaniel
Woodward and Solomon Saffery entitled "A description of the
extent of the bounds of Massachusetts Bay Patent."[5] Manuscript surveys of parts of what is now the coast of Maine were
made even earlier.

The graphic art, both drawings and prints, produced in New
England in the seventeenth century was the result of what
people in the colonies needed, what they had time for, and
that for which they were willing to spend money. Another way of
defining their motives would be to point out that their drawings
and prints served the purposes of piety, as in the woodcut of
Richard Mather; utility, as in manuscript charts and printed
paper currency; and authority, as in the royal arms and colony
arms which were used again and again on broadside proclamations. Happily, even in the seventeenth century in New
England one or two prints seem to have been done just for the
sport of it, like the woodcut figure of 1684 of King David playing a harp.[6]

To the south, New Amsterdam had a transatlantic perspective that opened on the age of Rembrandt. The earliest New
York view, engraved and printed in Holland, is of 1626-28;
there are two beautiful watercolor views of the 1640s; and the
separate engraved views and insets on maps issued in Holland
in the seventeenth century are a gold mine of information.[7]

New England, in contrast, did not need these frills. Old
England, as far as the graphic arts are concerned, was not
very sophisticated and did not begin to be more so until the
period of importation of Dutch painters and engravers during
the Restoration. It was to Amsterdam, not London, in the late
1670s, that John Foster's no-longer-surviving view of Boston
was sent to be engraved.

In theocratic New England, teachers of religion sought the
printed word, not the printed picture. An exception, perhaps,
was the Apostle Eliot, who joined forces with John Foster--
Eliot as author, presumably, Foster as illustrator--in the production of an ABC, printed from woodcuts, for the Indians. In
the first publishing heyday of the American Tract Society in
the 1820s, evangelistic publishers understood the necessity of

reaching some people with words, others with pictures. In
the 1670s, the Reverend Mr. Eliot was ahead of his time. [8]

If another reason is needed for the paucity of graphic art
in seventeenth-century New England, there was also what
Carl Bridenbaugh accurately calls "a rigidly self-imposed
censorship of the press."[9] This carried on an English tradition. The press in Cambridge, the only printing office in the
colonies before the second Cambridge printing business was
set up by Marmaduke Johnson in 1665, was firmly under the
thumb of the church. Stephen Daye and, later, Samuel Green
and Marmaduke Johnson were worthy men, but do not look in
their products for the spice of the unpredictable. It took a
press in Boston across the river, and the ingenious, inquiring
mind of John Foster, to bring a little salt and pepper into
Massachusetts printing. Among these meager bits of season-
ing were the first almanac cuts, including a native New England
rendering of the anatomical man, or man of signs, that naked
figure possessing both male and female characteristics in
which parts of the body are identified with signs of the zodiac.
This figure is an old, old expression of man's longings for
fortune, luck, a good moon; and Foster's cut and its successors
in New England are only a step away from magic in their primitive symbolism. They are an element of the imagery of the
times well worth a philosophical inquiry comparable to that of
George Lyman Kittredge in The Old Farmer and His Almanac.

Studying the graphic arts in New England in the first generations of English settlement, I have often remembered what
Walter Whitehill has said about the study of Spanish Roman-
esque architecture in the twelfth and thirteenth centuries: the
facts are so far apart that you have to spend a great deal of
time thinking about each one. I would identify the first period
of the graphic arts in colonial New England as "before John
Foster," or before the first Boston press of 1675; these are two
different ways of saying the same thing.

After this period, which we might mark out as 1620 to 1670-
75, there were decades of slow development in the graphic
arts in which a scattering of cuts and engravings were made for
various purposes. This period extended from the 1670s to
about 1715, and in it you can glimpse a fact that becomes

increasingly apparent later; wherever the printing press goes,
the graphic arts almost certainly go. One of the earliest
pieces of graphic art in New England is the arms of Connecticut
of 1673. At that time, of course, there was no place to print
important Connecticut laws and resolves except at Cambridge
in the Massachusetts Bay Colony. The cut, which is quite a
polished piece of work, probably was made in England; in New
England, Samuel Green used it in printing the title page of <u>The
Book of the General Laws for the People within the Jurisdiction
of Connecticut</u> (1673). When the first Connecticut press was
established in New London in 1709, cuts of the colony seal
and the royal arms became a part of printer's stock as a matter
of course. The need for currency was pressing in Connecticut
at this time, calling for graphic art of another kind and the
help of a silversmith who could produce copperplate engraving
and printing. For this purpose, Connecticut hired a Massachusetts silversmith, Jeremiah Dummer, who engraved the
Connecticut currency of 1709.

About 1715 or a little before, a surge of growth, civic ambi-
tion, and new ideas began in Boston. The architectural
symbols included the brick Town House built after the fire of
1711; Long Wharf, built at the same time; and Boston Light, the
first lighthouse in the colonies, completed in 1716. Boston
attracted British craftsmen during these years of expansion as
never before. Francis Dewing, the first professional printmaker to settle in the city, and also the first in the colonies,
came in 1717 and stayed about five years. He went back to
England, after the experiment, and continued his career as an
engraver there. Meanwhile another professional, William
Burgis (figs. 1, 2), was in Boston, spending most of the 1720s
there, and at the end of that decade a one-two team of painter
and mezzotint engraver, John Smibert and Peter Pelham, arrived
to carve out a permanent place for the artist in Boston life, a
full century after the founding of the community.

There was one more important infusion of graphic skills into
Boston in this period. James Franklin, a native Bostonian, went
to England to learn printing and brought back the equipment to
set up his own shop. Today we remember Franklin largely for
the work done in his printing office by his younger brother

Fig. 1. "A South East View of yᵉ Great Town of Boston in New England in America."
William Burgis, 1743. 23 1/2" x 52". Winterthur Museum

Fig. 2. A detail of the Burgis view of Boston (1743 issue), showing the center section of this four-foot-long print. Winterthur Museum

Benjamin, starting in 1717, the first year the new press was in
operation. James Franklin was a clever man who learned not
only letterpress printing in England but also the technique of
printing linens, calicoes, and silks, a skill which he advertised in the Boston Gazette. He adorned a number of his publications with relief cuts which he engraved on wood or type
metal. After discovering Franklin's previously unknown work
as a book illustrator, Lawrence Wroth in 1946 put his head
together with Clarence Brigham, and they found eleven cuts in
publications of 1717, 1718, and 1719 that may have been made by
Franklin.[10] As with the work of so many of the graphic artists
of colonial America, these cuts have never been reproduced all
in a single publication. Bringing pictures together in this way
is a part of the learning process in which we have a long way
to go.

A new era of activity in the graphic arts opened with the beginnings of the French and Indian Wars in the 1740s. The men
who carried on Boston's efforts in the graphic arts were
Pelham and Thomas Johnston (figs. 3, 4, 5, 6), who apparently
had learned engraving from Burgis before 1728.[11] Patriotism
was a potent stimulus to printmaking. Both engravers took
images that existed in manuscript or in oil portraits and multiplied them for a ready audience. Pelham's big, ambitious
"Plan of the City and Fortress of Louisbourg" of 1746 reproduced a design by Richard Gridley. Two patriotic portraits in
mezzotint, of Sir William Pepperrell and Governor William
Shirley, followed. Pelham engraved them in 1747, basing them
on portraits by Smibert. Later pictorial landmarks of the wars
are a pair of large and intricately detailed prints, part map,
part view, part diagram, engraved by Johnston: Samuel
Blodget's "The Battle of Lake George," issued as an engraving
in 1755, and Timothy Clement's "Plan of Hudsons Riv[r.] from
Albany to Fort Edward (& y[e] Road from thence to Lake George
as Survey'd)," engraved and printed in April 1756.[12] Better
known is Johnston's engraving of "Quebec, the Capital of
New-France," 1759 (fig. 4.) Like other views published in
Boston before the Revolution of 1775, and like a number of
eighteenth-century English views, this print has a curiously
archaic flavor, going back in its exaggerated silhouettes of
church towers to the tradition shared by fifteenth-century

Fig. 3. "Sir William Pepperrell." Mezzotint engraving, Peter Pelham, after painting by John Smibert. Boston, 1747. 17 1/2" x 11 5/8". Winterthur Museum

Fig. 4. Bookplate for William Smith.
Engraved by Thomas Johnston about 1750.
Winterthur Museum

Fig. 5. Trade card of Lewis Deblois. Engraved by Thomas Johnston, 1757. Winterthur Museum

Fig. 6. "Quebec, The Capital of New-France." Engraving, Thomas Johnston. Published by Stephen Whiting, 1759. 6 3/4" x 8 7/8". Winterthur Museum

German woodcut views and sixteenth-century views engraved
on copper.[13]

As early as the fall of 1743, James Turner was working in
Boston. We know nothing about his career before this time,
but the range of his skills, as he advertised them in the <u>Boston
Evening Post</u>, suggests thoroughgoing experience in England.
Even to attempt to make a living at engraving, in this era, men
had to exploit every possible application of their skills. Turner
described himself as "Silversmith & Engraver." He said that he:

> Engraves all sorts of Copper Plates for the Rolling
> Press, all sorts of Stamps in Brass or Pewter for the
> common Printing Press, Coats of Arms, Crests,
> Cyphers, &c., on Gold, Silver, Steel, Copper,
> Brass, or Pewter. He likewise makes Watch Faces,
> makes and cuts Seals in Gold, Silver, or Steel:
> or makes Steel Faces for Seals, and sets them
> handsomely in Gold or Silver. He cuts all sorts
> of Steel Stamps, Brass Rolls and Stamps for
> Sadlers and Bookbinders, and does all sorts of
> work in Gold and Silver.[14]

John Greenwood, a pupil of Thomas Johnston, tried his hand
at both painting and mezzotint engraving in these mid-century
years, as did Peter Pelham's stepson, John Singleton Copley.
Nathaniel Hurd made the first of his surviving prints, which
come down to us as a surprisingly large group of roughly
seventy engravings on copper, more than fifty of them bookplates. Hurd engraved everything from caricatures to trade
cards, from a compass rose to portraits, from a masonic certificate to currency. He engraved seals and dies, including the
seals of Brown and Dartmouth. His versatility and his apparently lucrative bookplate business reflect a substantial
market for the sometimes useful but mostly decorative imprints--
"luxury products," perhaps--of his copperplates (fig. 7.) Only
Paul Revere rivaled him in reaching this prosperous urban
market through a wide variety of engravings, beginning in the
early 1760s, a dozen years or more after Hurd's first efforts.

This summing up can be quickly completed by the mention

H-ds-n's SPEECH from the Pillory.

WHAT mean thefe Crouds, this Noife and Roar!
  Did ye ne'er fee a *Rogue* before?
Are *Villains* then a Sight fo rare,
To make you prefs and gape and ftare?
Come forward all who look fo fine,
With Gain as illy got as mine:
Step up——you'l foon reverfe the Show;
The *Croud* above, and *few* below.

Well—for my Roguery here I ftand,
A Spectacle to all the Land:
High elevated on this Stage,
The *greateft Villain* of the Age.
My Crimes have been both great and many,
Equal'd by very few, if any:
And for the Mifchiefs I have done
I put this *wooden Neckcloth* on.

There *HOW* his brawny Back is ftripping,
Quite callous grown with often whipping.
In vain you wear your *Whip-Cord* out,
You'l ne'er reclaim that *Rogue fo ftout*.
To make him honeft, take my Word,
You muft apply a *bigger Cord*.

Now all ye who behold this Sight,
That ye may get fome profit by't,
Keep always in your Mind, I pray,
Thefe few Words that I have to fay.
Follow my Steps and you may be
In Time, perhaps, advanc'd like me;
Or, like my fellow Lab'rer *HOW*,
You'l get at leaft a *Poft* below.

Sold by N. HURD, near the Exchange, and at the *Heart* and *Crown* in Cornhill, *Bofton.*

Fig. 7. "H-ds-n's Speech from the Pillory."
Engraved and published by Nathaniel Hurd, 1762.
10" x 8". Winterthur Museum

of a native Bostonian, Richard Jennys, Jr., who made mezzotints in Boston in the late 1760s which Hurd published, and
Samuel Okey, a London engraver who came over to Newport
several years before the Revolutionary War and made mezzotint portraits (fig. 8.) A quick survey of this kind, however,
does not really give an idea of the diversity and number of
people who had a hand in the graphic arts in colonial New
England. So much research has been carried on within very
sharply defined areas of subject matter that a conscious effort
is needed to reach a broad view of the need for various kinds
of graphic art, of the graphic skills available or developed in
response to demand, and of the practitioners themselves.

First of all, there were the professional surveyors, map
makers, and chart makers. William Reed of Boston may have
ranked as a professional, or he may simply have been the most
competent person available, when the Massachusetts General
Court employed him in the summer of 1665 "together with some
other gentlemen of the Court, to draw up an exact mapp of his
majesties colonie of the Massachusetts." A man who earned
his living in this business was Philip Wells, who in the late
1680s was employed by Governor Andros to put information
about Boston Harbor into coherent form in a manuscript chart.
Earlier, Wells had been Governor Dongan's surveyor in New
York and had surveyed grants and holdings of land for a number
of individuals. He had been assigned by the governor in 1684
to make a survey of Staten Island and was appointed in the
same year as one of the commissioners to run the boundary line
between the provinces of New York and Connecticut. Wells
was the creator, at about this time, of "A sand draught of
New-York Harbour," showing shoals, flats, and bars, with
a few soundings.[15]

In the 155 years of the colonial period in New England
(1620-1775), there were more men who made drawings in the
course of government service than can be listed here. Probably the most productive, as well as one of the most cantank-
erous, was J. F. W. Des Barres, whose "American Neptune,"
beautifully engraved and printed in London and showing in detail the coasts of the British North American colonies as he
charted them in the 1760s and '70s, has been called the most
lavish set of charts ever produced.

Fig. 8. "Mr. Samuel Adams." Engraving, Samuel
Okey after the portrait by J. Mitchell. Published
by Charles Reak, Newport, April, 1775. 13 3/4" x
9 3/4". Winterthur Museum

Among the men in government service were British Army and
Navy officers whose skills oftentimes included drawing. No
chapter of the iconography of eighteenth-century America com-
pares in detail with the maps, charts, plans, and views taken
by British officers during the Revolutionary War. The picture
they give can be supplemented by the information put down in
graphic form by French officers and by Americans both in and
out of uniform. The graphic record of the American Revolution
has never been brought together in one publication; we do not
even have, in the pages of a book, all the views and plans of
New York or Boston during the British occupations. We do have
a prod, however--the prospect of bicentennial celebrations
beginning in 1975.

An officer who came to America long before the Revolution
and who devoted himself, more than most, to labors with pen,
pencil, and paper, was Colonel Wolfgang William Romer. A
military engineer, Romer had learned his skills in the service
of the Prince of Orange and had come to England with Prince
William in 1688. He was given an American assignment as
chief surveyor to Lord Bellomont in New York in 1697, made
surveying trips inland and along the New England coast, designed fortifications for New England seaports (notably Boston,
where Castle William, commanding port of Boston Harbor, was
built from his designs), and ended his American duty in 1706.
The evidence I have seen suggests that he possessed a sophisticated knowledge of plan making and draftsmanship, and that
he also had on his staff at least one expert draftsman to put
plans in final form. (Philip Wells, incidentally, may have had
a draftsman on his staff, too, for his chart of Boston Harbor
not only reads "By Phillip Wells" but also has the signature
of "M. Carroll.")

In the British Museum are more than a dozen sketch maps
and plans dated 1699, showing Saco River, Saco Fort, Casco
Bay, the old fort and the proposed fort at Pemaquid, forts and
islands at the mouth of the Piscataqua, and Castle Island in
Boston Harbor with proposed new fortifications. Another
series of about ten drawings is dated 1705; these cover some
of the same places, along with Salem and Marblehead, and
outline newly completed fortifications. Three drawings,

apparently done in 1705, show Fort William and Mary on the
Piscataqua. One is a flat plan of the fort and includes profiles
of four areas; the second is "The Profil belonging to the
Icqnographycal Draft of the Fort William & Mary on Piscataqua
River in America"; the third is a long view of the fort, with
important buildings and landmarks identified. This must rank
among the important early American views, more than fifteen
years earlier than any surviving view of Boston. It may be the
handiwork of Romer himself. One of the plans of 1699 is "By
J. Dudley," and many of the drawings of 1705, not including
the group of three just mentioned, are signed "J. Redknap."

Captain Cyprian Southack, the first New England coast-
guardman, labored for decades to bring into print various separate charts and a coastal survey finally published as The New
England Coasting Pilot about 1728. Later there were full-time
surveyors, men who had greater skill and better equipment,
such as James Cook, later of Pacific fame, who surveyed the
coast of Newfoundland and Labrador between 1762 and 1767,
and Des Barres, gathering information for the "Atlantic Neptune."

Men in government, such as John Winthrop in the 1630s, had
always needed detailed maps and charts; the time eventually
came, in colonial America, when information of this kind was
much more abundant and there was leisure for a colonial admin-
istrator or army or navy officer ashore to make drawings which
would show his friends, or a larger English audience, what
the New World looked like. Thomas Pownall's drawings, which
we know from engravings issued in England in the 1760s, are
the observations of a cultivated and versatile man. This is
also true of three of the finest eighteenth-century drawings of
America which are known, the very spirited and informative
pen-and-wash prospects of Boston in 1764 made by a British
naval officer, Captain Richard Byron.[16]

The most accomplished of the sea captains, Cyprian Southack
included, taught themselves to draw and were able to make their
own manuscript charts. Recording soundings and coastline in
an accurate "draught" was a skill which might be extended and
enhanced, leading to naval, military, and civil architecture.
Captain John Bonner, who died in 1726, four years after the
publication of his detailed map of Boston, was remembered by

his contemporaries as "a Gentleman very Skillful and Ingenious in many Arts and Sciences; especially in Navigation,
Drawing, Moulding of Ships, &c."[17] Peter Harrison came to
architecture by way of navigation and chart making. His
manuscripts and drawings were destroyed by a mob in New
Haven in 1775, but a few of the drawings which were elsewhere at the time survive today. The earliest, a plan of
Louisbourg and vicinity of 1745, made during his youthful
career as a sea captain, is in the Public Record Office, London.
It shows the coastline and a few soundings. Drawings of Fort
George, which Harrison designed to defend Newport Harbor
(the fort was begun but never finished), date from 1755-56 and
are in the Public Record Office and the Huntington Library.
"A Plan of the Town and Harbour of Newport on Rhode Island,"
1755, a handsome piece of chart making, is also in the Public
Record Office. His architectural career is preserved for us in
the buildings themselves, including Newport's Redwood
Library, Touro Synagogue, and Market House, King's Chapel
in Boston, and Christ Church in Cambridge. None of his
drawings for buildings is known to survive.[18]

Although government officials, sea captains, official
surveyors, and British Army and Navy officers on duty in the
colonies sometimes made and used their own manuscript maps,
charts, and plans, they frequently did not go further to seek
the engraving and printing of their designs for a wider audience.
In the colonies, however, a class of men grew up who devised
means of printmaking as a practical matter of make-do. These
were the printers who needed cuts for various purposes and
often had to produce them, themselves, or do without. Some
of their needs, of course, were met from the beginning by cuts
imported from England as standard printers' stock--headpieces,
tailpieces, and initial letters. What they lacked, they sometimes could contrive. John Foster was the first of these
printer-printmakers; Richard Pierce, who may have learned
both printing and printmaking from Foster, seems to have been
the second. In the manuscript Jeffries Papers (Vol. I, p. 122)
at the Massachusetts Historical Society, Stephen Riley years
ago came on a receipt of December 2, 1687, by Pierce acknow-
ledging payment for various items connected with printing.

Among the work mentioned are the following items:

        To ye Cutting of ye Seale of ye Prdt & Council   --0--15--00
        To ye Cutting of ye Kings Arms   --0--15--00

Sir Edmund Andros was governor of Massachusetts at the time.
Pierce's receipt seems to establish that Andros did not bring
over cuts of the seal and the "Kings Arms" when he came from
England. It also appears likely that Pierce made the cuts
himself.
    There are others whom we know to be in this succession of
printer-printmakers. James Franklin ranks with John Foster as
one of the most resourceful. A little before Franklin's Boston
printing career began, cuts were being made in the Boston
printing office of Thomas Fleet, whose first Boston imprints
date from 1713.[19] Isaiah Thomas, chronicling the history of
printing in America before 1825, noted that:

    the principal performances of Fleet, until he began the
    publication of a newspaper, consisted of pamphlets for
    booksellers, small books for children, and ballads. He
    made a profit on these, which was sufficient to support
    his family reputably. He owned several negroes, one
    of which worked at the printing business, both at the
    press and at setting types; he was an ingenious man,
    and cut, on wooden blocks, all the pictures which
    decorated the ballads and small books of his master.
    Fleet had also two negro boys born in his house;
    sons, I believe, to the man just mentioned, whom
    he brought up to work at press and case; one named
    Pompey and the other Cesar.[20]

    Isaiah Thomas himself has left us testimony that he made
some cuts while he was an apprentice in the printing office
of Zechariah Fowle in Boston in the early 1760s. There are
some crude cuts engraved by Thomas in Fowle's 1767 printing
of The New Book of Knowledge, as well as cuts signed IT in
the 1766 printing by Fowle of History of the Holy Jesus, just
as there are earlier cuts in one of Thomas Fleet's imprints
which are signed PF, probably Pompey Fleet.

Almost as old a line of succession as the printer-printmakers
in colonial New England were the silversmith-printmakers. The
ancestor of these men, and of all native New England printmakers, was Joseph Jencks, who cut the die for New England's
first currency, the pine-tree shilling, in 1652. John Coney engraved the plates for the Massachusetts paper currency of 1702,
and probably for the earliest issue of paper money in the
colonies, the Massachusetts bills of 1690. Among his other
work was the Harvard College seal which he engraved in 1693.
Unfortunately it has not survived.

Reliance on the silversmiths for the engraving of plates for
paper currency was a natural consequence of their role in mint-
ing metal coinage. Much more than the letterpress printers,
they knew the intricacies of intaglio engraving; hiring them was
the best security that could be had (and it was far from fool-
proof, at that) against counterfeiters. There was also the
question of precise control over the quantity of bills printed.
The silversmiths to some extent acted as bankers and occupied
a place of special responsibility in the community. Even so,
they undoubtedly were closely supervised. The only real account we have of the process was written not by a Boston
silversmith but by a Philadelphia printer. Benjamin Franklin
describes in his autobiography how machinery was improvised
and security guaranteed by the presence of legislators when
New Jersey needed an issue of paper currency in 1728.

The first two-color printing in the British colonies in North
America seems to have been the handiwork of one of these
silversmith-printmakers. For the Massachusetts paper currency
of 1708, two copperplates were used: one for the cipher printed
in reddish-brown as background, the other for the statement of
authorization and value, printed in black.[21] We do not know
who made these plates. A good possibility is Jeremiah Dummer,
who the next year, 1709, engraved the plates for the first
Connecticut currency. The list of these silversmith-printmakers
continues to grow; when the Massachusetts Historical Society
reproduced, in one of its picture books, a selection of the
Society's prints and drawings, the bookplate of Paul Rivoire
(1702-54), founder of the Revere family in America, was

shown, with Stephen Riley's comment that the plate presumably was engraved by Rivoire himself.

Nathaniel Morse, also a silversmith, engraved currency and a crude copy of an English copperplate portrait, and later on, Nathaniel Hurd and Paul Revere were the most prolific of the printmakers of colonial New England. Nathaniel's brother Benjamin made prints and painted coats of arms, in addition to his work as a silversmith. To this succession should be added the name of Abel Buell, silversmith, counterfeiter, jeweler, lapidary, type founder, engraver, mintmaster, armorer, inventor, "ingenious mechanic," investor, and veteran of repeated financial disasters. Buell's almost endlessly versatile and restless career was launched in his home state of Connecticut in the 1760s.

Of all the men mentioned so far, not one, with the possible exceptions of several surveyors and chart makers, was a professional graphic artist, making his way in the world by the earnings of his pen, pencil and graver. Francis Dewing, William Burgis, and Peter Pelham were the first men to come to live in New England who had made their living in old England as printmakers. Dewing, as far as we can tell, brought the first professionally made copperplate press to the colonies in 1717. The announcement which he published on his arrival in Boston suggests that he possessed a wide range of skills in engraving and printing, and probably was fully equipped. Earlier printing from copperplates seems to have been very much a matter of improvisation. With further study, it would be possible to piece together a sequence of evidence which would show us the beginnings and spread of professional copperplate printing in various colonial centers. Franklin's adventures in devising a copperplate press in New Jersey in 1728 affirm the rarity of such presses in the colonies at that date, and as late as 1750, it is doubtful if in all the colonies there were more than four or five.

Although Dewing, Burgis, and Pelham were professionals, they could not sustain themselves in New England by the earnings of their graphic art. Pelham, the only one of the three who stayed, made prosperous marriages and supplemented the family income by teaching school. His engravings brought in something; so did his few portraits in oils.

About James Turner, who arrived in Boston in 1743 and continued work as an engraver in Boston and Philadelphia until
his death in 1759, we are less sure. No doubt he was both
silversmith and engraver, as he said in his Boston advertisement of 1745; today, no pieces of his silver are known, while
a substantial and varied group of his engravings survive, including a portrait, a trade card, maps, a chart, magazine
cuts, and engraved music. His skill as a copperplate printer
must have been a source of income, too, for a number of his
imprints call attention to his role not only as engraver but as
printer. In the imprint of John Greenwood's "Jersey Nanny,"
Greenwood is identified as having painted the picture and then
engraved it; it was then "Printed by J Turner, for J Buck, &
Sold by him at the Spectacles, in Queen Street Boston."[22]

The small quantity of their surviving work makes it extremely
doubtful that Richard Jennys, Jr., working in the 1760s, and
Samuel Okey, at work just before the Revolution, kept body and
soul together through their efforts as engravers. Joseph
Callender, beginning his career just before the Revolution,
did earn a living as an engraver, in part because of a job
as a diesinker for the Massachusetts Mint. Christian Remick,
whose skills were in drawing and watercolor, seems to have
had firsthand knowledge of the inadequate market for graphic
art which all but the most professional, and most versatile, of
these men encountered. He came to Boston in the late 1760s,
produced a number of watercolors that survive, and worked for
Paul Revere, coloring impressions of Revere's "Landing of the
Troops" and "Boston Massacre." But it was not enough, and
he died in the poor house in 1773.[23]

In all the colonial period, there is no artist, with the exception of John Greenwood, in whose life printmaking and painting
were to exist together as important commitments. Peter Pelham
is a near exception, though his portraits in oils seem to have
been few. John Singleton Copley tried his hand only very
briefly at printmaking. Greenwood, who found printmaking a
different but not necessarily inferior medium, is the person
who came closest to being a painter-engraver. He had learned
engraving from Thomas Johnston, and perhaps it was Johnston,
too, who gave him his first instruction in painting. His print

of Yale College in 1749, printed by Johnston, is in strong,
sharp outline. It is in an old tradition of topographical and
architectural engraving, but it has an individuality which
gives it a special place among colonial New England prints.
Even more in a class by itself is Greenwood's "Jersey Nanny,"
a salute to the memorable presence of this huge, picturesque
woman on the streets of Boston. As Edgar Richardson points
out, this is the first American genre picture. These interesting beginnings were subordinate, at the time they were made,
to Greenwood's role as a painter of portraits. Later, in
Holland and England, he became a professional engraver of
importance turning out mezzotints which met the London standards of the day. His career, to this point, is almost like
Pelham's in reverse. Ultimately, he became a successful
London art dealer.

A tally of those who had a particular interest in the graphic
arts in colonial New England includes the scriveners and the
writing masters whose work at least had borders on the world
of draftsmanship and printmaking. Boston had no one like
Lewis Evans of Philadelphia, accountant, scribe, and map
maker. In Abel Buell of Connecticut, many different interests
in the graphic arts can be seen together, including the practice
of calligraphy, the engraving of maps, and the cutting of
punches for type molds.

There were the counterfeiters, such as Thomas Odell, who
imitated Massachusetts £4 notes and tried to pass them in
Philadelphia in 1705. He did not pull it off, and later spent a
year in jail.[24] There were men pursuing projects of public
benefit in spite of their limited skills, men like old Captain
John Bonner who was bound to give the world a map of the
thriving town of Boston and did so with the help of Boston's
first professional copperplate-engraver-in-residence, Francis
Dewing. And there were the publishers, men we need to know
much more about. The most important, in colonial New England,
seem to have been William Price at the King's Head and Looking
Glass in Cornhill, Boston, for fifty years beginning about 1720;
Stephen Whiting at the Rose and Crown in Union Street for
roughly thirty years after 1740; and J. Buck at the Spectacles
in Queen-Street in the 1740s and 1750s. Charles Reak of

Newport was doing some ambitious publishing of Samuel
Okey's prints in Newport in 1773, 1774, and 1775. It was
natural enough for the more professional of the engravers to
do their own publishing at times, and Pelham, Turner, and
Hurd were among those who sometimes added the role of publisher to their skills as engravers and printers.

The map makers and chart makers, the government surveyors,
the cultivated men in government service, such as Pownall and
Byron, who counted the ability to draw as a useful and pleasur-
able accomplishment; the printer-printmakers, silversmith-
printmakers, and professional graphic artists; the scriveners
or writing masters whose skills drew on the graphic arts; the
counterfeiters; the print publishers and printsellers such as
Price, Whiting, and Buck--all these men, seen together, give
a much broader idea of the place of the graphic arts in colonial
New England.

The audience for the graphic arts, and in particular the
picture-collectors of the times, are still another essential part
of the story. It cannot be told here, for the sifting and organiz-
ing of material that is needed would yield a full-length study
in itself. Information about the ownership of pictures continues
to accumulate. At all events, the audience was there, supporting the business of printselling in Boston after 1720, and among
its members were men who eagerly welcomed new graphic efforts,
who collected prints produced abroad and at home, and who sent
the native New England products across the Atlantic to family
and friends, as well as to associates in the worlds of government and learning.

For generations, information about the graphic arts in the
American colonies has accrued in the form of many brief notes
and findings and articles in the proceedings and published
collections of learned societies, as well as in bibliographies,
in booksellers' and printsellers' catalogues, in exhibition
catalogues, in catalogues of public collections, and in surveys
like David Stauffer's American Engravers upon Copper and
Steel. We could profit greatly from a bibliography that
gathered all these bits and pieces together. Winterthur's
Prints Pertaining to America presented a listing of publications
which is a very welcome step in that direction.

As a field for study, the graphic arts in colonial New England, but more broadly the graphic arts in British North America, with related chapters of activity in Canada and the Caribbean, is wide open. In the history of colonial New England alone, at least four printmakers--William Burgis, Thomas Johnston, James Turner, and Nathaniel Hurd--deserve full-dress treatment in fully illustrated books. We have one enduring monument of that kind, Brigham's perennially useful Paul Revere's Engravings. On the same bookshelf belong Lawrence Wroth's Abel Buell and Carl Bridenbaugh's Peter Harrison. Nathaniel Hurd received something close to book-length treatment in Hollis French's book of 1939, Jacob Hurd and His Sons Nathaniel & Benjamin, Silversmiths, 1702-1781, but much more is now known about Nathaniel's printmaking. The prints themselves continue to surface. A fact about Hurd which has begun to sink in is his stature as one of the most versatile of the New Englanders who made prints, and one of the most prolific. Only for Revere, among all these men, do we have record of a larger production.

Our failure to put available facts together can be emphasized by a look at some of the things we know about the originals of printmaking in colonial New England, the actual copperplates, woodblocks, and engraved designs in relief on type metal. Surprisingly many eighteenth-century coppers, engraved in New England, are still in existence today. Why no one has taken a look at this subject, I do not know, but I offer it as one more opportunity for a detailed study. Most recently, the American Antiquarian Society received from a Canadian descendent of Mather Byles two early copperplates, both in excellent condition. One is the portrait of Increase Mather engraved in London by John Sturt in 1689, with the inscription on the plate later altered to read "Aetatis Suae 85. 1724." This bit of expert tampering undoubtedly was carried out in Boston in the 1720s by William Burgis, Francis Dewing, or one of the silversmiths. The other plate is the original copper of Peter Pelham's mezzo-tint portrait of Mather Byles, engraved in Boston about 1740. As far as I know, this is the earliest surviving original of a print made in New England. The preservation of the plate of Paul Revere's "Boston Massacre" is well known. It is in the

Massachusetts Archives, along with part of the plate of his
"Landing of the Troops." The original copper of his engraved
certificate of service at the North Battery is at the Massachusetts Historical Society. Restrikes of colonial currency and
colonial bookplates testify to the survival of a number of
eighteenth-century copperplates in private hands. Years ago
a woman in Concord, New Hampshire, loaned a friend in Boston
a copperplate which had on one side a section of a chart and
on the other side four engravings for New Hampshire paper
currency of the 1740s. Her friend showed the plate to George
Goodspeed, and an unsuccessful attempt was made to purchase
it. The plate went back to Concord and has not been heard of
since. Also in private hands is the plate on which Nathaniel
Hurd engraved an invitation to a party given by two graduating
Harvard men in 1767. A restrike from the plate was sent to the
American Antiquarian Society years ago with a note about the
engraving and the two young men, Thomas Bernard and Edward
Oxnard, who gave the party. I hope these incidents may whet
someone's appetite. A checklist of surviving coppers engraved
in colonial New England, and an essay on them, could be extremely enlightening.

Of course, original blocks and plates with designs engraved
or cut in them have been carefully preserved at many times in
many places because of their potentialities for multiplying
copies of an image. Some of Durer's woodblocks survive, and
so does at least one of Rembrandt's coppers. There was nothing
new about the care sometimes taken by eighteenth-century New
Englanders in preserving blocks or plates to be used again, and
it proves their respect for these originals of prints. About 1743
James Turner engraved, probably on type metal, a stylized and
somewhat primitive view of Boston which was used as a head-
piece in each issue of the American Magazine and Historical
Chronicle. More than thirty years later, this cut had migrated
from Boston to Portsmouth, New Hampshire, and was still in
excellent condition. Apparently it had been carefully preserved in the Boston and Portsmouth printing offices of Daniel
Fowle, one of the printers of the magazine. In 1756, after a
bitter dispute with the Massachusetts General Court over
censorship, Fowle left Boston, taking his equipment to

Portsmouth to found the first press there. Among his later
Portsmouth imprints is a broadside of 1775, <u>Declaration by the</u>
<u>Representatives of the United Colonies of North-America, now</u>
<u>met in General Congress at Philadelphia, Setting forth the</u>
<u>Causes and Necessity of Their Taking Up Arms</u>. Turner's cut
is used in the upper right-hand corner. A title, in type, is
placed below it: "A View of that great and flourishing City of
Boston, when in its purity, and out of the Hands of the
Philistines."[25]

William Price, one of the most enterprising of the men concerned with the graphic arts in eighteenth-century Boston,
carried the preservation and updating of engraved copperplates
to great lengths, much to the benefit of historians. His printselling career seems to have begun during the years Francis
Dewing was engraving in Boston. He and John Bonner together
published the Bonner Map of 1722, and Price retained the plate.
He also acquired the plate on which Dewing had engraved, for
Captain Cyprian Southack in 1717, "A New Chart of the English
Empire in North America." He was the publisher of the big
Burgis view of Boston, of about 1725; this was engraved in
London by Harris and was so big it had to be made in three
sections, each printed from a separate copperplate and then
pieced together to produce a single picture. The plates were
sent to Boston, and these, too, Price could count among his
assets.

He nursed along the plate of the Bonner map for more than
forty years, reissuing it, with extensive alterations, in 1733,
1739, 1743, 1760, and 1769. There may also have been issues,
although no copies of them survive, in 1729 and 1754. With
the help of Thomas Johnston as engraver, many changes and
additions were made. Price found in the white spaces of the
original design--the sizable areas not covered by the uneven
shoreline and topography of the Boston peninsula--room to in-
sert advertisements of the goods he sold in his store, as well
as altered dedications and new information. His name appears
in the 1733 issue in four different places. The original collaboration of Bonner and Dewing received a heavy overlay of
Price and Johnston. Presumably all this work produced market-
able prints, from which Price made money. For the historian,

successive issues of the map provide a running record of the
size, configuration, and major buildings of Boston for almost
half a century.

The 1743 issue of the Bonner map contains what may be the
first attempt at a printed picture of Faneuil Hall, completed the
year before. Also in 1743, Price published a reissue of the big
Burgis view. This contained a number of additions, including
an incongruous sandwiching-in of what also purports to be a
picture of Faneuil Hall. Whatever its defects, it includes a
clear delineation of Shem Drowne's grasshopper weathervane.

On the 1733 issue of the Bonner map, a border of scratched
lines obscures the earlier imprint containing the names of
Bonner and Dewing, while Price's name keeps cropping up
among the spate of words which have been added to the plate.
Also added is the name of T. Johnston, barely readable under
the cartouche containing the dedication. There is at least a
strong possibility that Johnston also made the engraved additions to the big Burgis view and worked over the 1717 plate of
"A New Chart of the English Empire in North America." With
extensive changes and additions, the plate of the "New Chart"
found its way back to the press after a good many years of
idleness, and prints from it, as revised, were published by
Price in 1746. The preservation, revision, and reissuing of
the Southack chart, the Bonner map, and the Burgis South East
View cast some light on the very small world of the graphic
arts in the eighteenth-century Boston.

It would be reasonably safe to say that more prints were
made in New England between 1750 and 1775 than in all the
years of English settlement before that time. Those were the
years of prolific output by Nathaniel Hurd and, starting soon
after 1760, by Paul Revere. As our stock of information continues to grow, we should be able to form an idea of the
quantity of prints which have not survived to our own times.
Trade cards are especially perishable; labels are even more
so. At one point in his study of Paul Revere's engravings,
Clarence Brigham has this to say: "In Revere's Day Book
there are many charges for advertising cards and bill-heads
for merchants, or for the sale of prints. But since no
specimens of such cards have survived, there is no way of

describing them or proving that they were engraved." That
may be a practical conclusion for an author dealing with a
wealth of material and laboring, after many years, to bring
his study to a conclusion, but I think we can be safe in
thinking that these prints were, indeed, engraved. The list
of such entries which Brigham put into print is one more re-
minder of how much we have yet to learn.[26]

NOTES

1. The quotation from Singer is from an article on presentation of the National Book Awards, New York Times, Thursday, March 5, 1970. For The Prodigal Daughter, see d'Alte A. Welch, "A Bibliography of American Children's Books Printed Prior to 1821," Proceedings of the American Antiquarian Society, vol. 77 (1968), 106, 115-17.

2. An Indian's an Indian, or, The Several Sources of Paul Revere's Engraved Portrait of King Philip (Providence, 1959).

   In London, Indians who came for adventure or diplomacy frequently were persuaded to sit for their portraits. There they were curiosities, exotic, romantic. To most of the white settlers of New England they were the enemy. A different outlook is reflected in the sympathetic and convincing portrait of Ninigret (died ca. 1690), a sachem of the Narragansetts. The picture is at the Rhode Island School of Design, Providence. Oliver LaFarge wrote that it "is probably a copy of an earlier one which may well have been the earliest direct portrait made of an American Indian other than Pocahontas" (A Pictorial History of the American Indian, [New York, 1956], p. 81). See also Alden T. Vaughan, New England Frontier: Puritans and Indians, 1620-1675 (Boston, 1965), pp. xvii, 207.

3. LaFarge, p. 80.

4. The map is in the British Museum (ADD. 5415, G. iii).

5. Howard M. Chapin refers to the original in the Massachusetts Archives (p. 1, book marked "Collonial 1629-1720" and numbered 2 and 3 [1866]) in his Contributions to Rhode Island Bibliography No. V: Check List of Maps of Rhode Island (Providence, 1918).

6. See Sinclair Hamilton, Early American Book Illustrators and Wood Engravers, 1670-1870 (Princeton, 1968), cat. no. 5, p. 4; reproduced as fig. 4. Also, the cover of this book.

7. I. N. Phelps Stokes, The Iconography of Manhattan Island, 1498-1909 (New York, 1915; reprinted New York, 1967).

8. Many of us, however, probably overestimate the pictorial character of this early landmark of the graphic arts in America. We tend to visualize it as having brief text on each page, or perhaps a single letter of the Indian alphabet, illustrated by a small woodcut scene. In that form it would be akin

to an illustrated New England primer. George E. Littlefield has
a more plausible theory. He felt that the ABC "was more in the
nature of a writing book, similar to the familiar writing book of
our boyhood days, in the headlines of each page of which were
printed in script, from engraved blocks, first slanting and carved
lines, then the letters of the alphabet, and later words and
sentences. The children had already been taught their letters
and syllables from the hornbooks and common primers which
Mr. Eliot had imported, but the copies in these writing books
were to be in the Indian language, and from them the Indian
children were to be taught to write and read the Indian language,
and to them Eliot gave the name of 'Indian A B C' " (The Early
Massachusetts Press, 1638-1711 [Boston, 1907], II, 4-6).

9. Cities in the Wilderness: The First Century of Urban
Life in America, 1625-1742, 2d ed. (New York, 1955), p. 128.

10. Wroth and Marion W. Adams, American Woodcuts and
Engravings, 1670-1800, introduction by Clarence S. Brigham
(Providence, 1946), p. 7.

11. Johnston did a thoroughly competent job of engraving
William Burgis's map of Boston, published in 1728.

12. Even larger than either of these is Johnston's "Plan of
Kennebeck & Sagadahock Rivers," 1754, which sets forth the
claims of the Plymouth Company to lands along the Kennebec
River. Excellent pictorial source books for these and many
other early American prints are Massachusetts Historical
Society, Prints, Maps and Drawings, 1677-1822 (Boston, 1957);
The Associates of the John Carter Brown Library, The French and
Indian War: An Album (Providence, 1960); the recent extraordinary trio of exhibition catalogues, The Associates of the
John Carter Brown Library, A Collection's Progress (Providence,
1968), American Antiquarian Society, A Society's Chief Joys
(Worcester, 1969), and Massachusetts Historical Society,
Collecting for Clio (Boston, 1969); and the even more gener-
ously illustrated exhibition catalogue which reproduces many
of the prints of the Middendorf Collection, American Printmaking: The First 150 Years (Washington, 1969). All are in
print in paperback, and several have been issued in hard-
cover editions.

13. Though primitive by comparison, Johnston's "Quebec"
of 1759 echoes the style of the city-views on copper which
were published in the six volumes of Civitatis Orbis Terrarum,
1572-1618.

14. Quoted by David McNeely Stauffer in his American Engravers upon Copper and Steel, pt. 1 (New York, 1907), p. 278.

15. The reference to William Reed is in Records of the
Governor and Company of the Massachusetts Bay (Boston,
1854), IV (2): 182. Information on Philip Wells and his works
is from Stokes. Probably the first accurate chart of Boston
Harbor, including a number of soundings, is the one prepared
by Wells. The original is in the Rare Book Department, Boston
Public Library.

16. Byron's drawings are owned by the Bostonian Society
and are on permanent exhibition in the Old State House, Boston.

17. Boston News-Letter, Jan. 27-Feb. 3, 1726. Bonner's
obituary occupies one paragraph.

18. Carl Bridenbaugh, Peter Harrison, First American
Architect (Chapel Hill, N.C., 1949).

19. The man of signs cut which was used in a number of
almanacs printed by Fleet from 1716 through 1723 seems to be
one of these homemade cuts. Among the almanacs in which
it can be seen, in the exceptional collection of the American
Antiquarian Society, is Thomas Robie's for 1716 (Boston, 1716).

20. Isaiah Thomas, The History of Printing in America
(Albany, 1874), I, 98-99.

21. In letterpress printing, the first use of two colors came
a little later. William Keith's Letter to His Majesty's Justices
of the Peace for the County of Chester, printed by William
Bradford in Philadelphia in 1718, is the earliest American book
known to contain rubrication, (Frederick R. Goff, "Rubrication
in American Books of the Eighteenth Century," Proceedings of
the American Antiquarian Society, vol. 79, pt. 1 [1969], 31).

22. The print is reproduced in Museum of Fine Arts,
Centennial Acquisitions (Boston, 1970), p. 109.

23. A notation of Remick's death was discovered by
Stephen Riley in a manuscript volume of Records of the Over-
seers of the Poor of Boston. See The Massachusetts
Historical Society, 1791-1959 (Boston, 1959), where the notation is reproduced on p. 43.

24. Bridenbaugh, <u>Cities in the Wilderness</u>, p. 22.

25. A copy of the broadside is owned by the American Antiquarian Society. There are many evidences of long survival and reuse of cuts. About 1745, for instance, Thomas Fleet used a crude cut depicting a U-shaped curve of shore and houses enclosing water and ships. As printed by him on a broadside entitled <u>New England Bravery</u>, the cut was supposed to represent the taking of Louisbourg by New England forces under General Pepperrell. Three decades later it reappeared illustrating a broadside titled <u>Two Favorite Songs, Made on the Evacuation of the Town of Boston, by the British Troops, on the 17th of March, 1776</u>. See Hamilton, cat. no. 81, p. 27. Worthington C. Ford reproduces the cut and lists both appearances of it (Ford 833 and 2040) in his <u>Broadsides, Ballads, &c., Printed in Massachusetts, 1639-1800</u> (Boston, 1922).

26. Clarence S. Brigham, <u>Paul Revere's Engravings</u>, 2d ed. (New York, 1969), pp. 174-75.

Printmaking by the letterpress or relief process.
Darrell Hyder and Elizabeth Harris place the frisket
down over the paper to hold it in place. The
Washington hand press (ca. 1840-60), a gift to
Winterthur from Mr. and Mrs. Walter M. Whitehill,
and Mr. and Mrs. Wendell D. Garrett, was made by
R. Hoe & Co., New York and London.

THOMAS HOLLIS AND THE ARTS OF DISSENT

Frank H. Sommer III

THE relationship between two English dissenters of the
eighteenth century--Thomas Hollis III and Thomas Hollis V--
and their dissenting friends in Massachusetts--found an interesting expression in paintings, prints, and coins. I hope
that the few examples included here will give the reader a
sense of that interplay which took place in political,
"dissenting" art and ideas between England and America in
the eighteenth and early nineteenth centuries.[1]

The Commonwealthman in England and America

In his brilliant book The Origins of American Politics,
Bernard Bailyn has pointed out that eighteenth-century
Americans were British, and that it is impossible to understand politics in our country in that century unless one also
understands the British politics of the era.
    The England of George II was dominated by the conserva-
tive Whigs led by Sir Robert Walpole. Among the Whigs was
a radical branch opposed to Walpole who were what Professor
Caroline Robbins has called "The Commonwealthmen," that
is to say, the radical Whigs. They were the followers of
the politicians and political theorists who had led the Civil
War against Charles I and the Revolution of 1688 against
James II. Their heroes were John Milton and Oliver
Cromwell, Algernon Sidney, John Hampden, Henry Neville,
Edmund Ludlow, Marchamont Nedham, Andrew Marvell, and
John Locke. They believed that England (with Switzerland
and Holland) was a land of liberty--was, in fact, the land
of liberty--in principle. Liberty, in principle, they
believed was secured by the British constitution which

guaranteed a constitutionally restrained monarch as the
head of state, an aristocracy represented by the House of
Lords, and a democracy represented by Commons. The
Commonwealthmen believed, however, that in practice the
constitution was violated under George II by Robert Walpole,
the "Robinarch," who, as prime minister, usurped the powers
of the king and, according to them, made himself the de
facto head of state. Whether ruled by king or minister,
Great Britain under George II was politically stable because
it was controlled from the top by rulers who had a firm grip
on place and favor.

In principle, Colonial Americans accepted British consti-
tutional theory, but in practice American society was less
stable than the British because of comparative lack of
control from the top, the absence of an aristocracy, and
the dominance of the people. The English radical Whigs
looked on the American colonies with ever-increasing favor
as the land for the practical development of the British
constitution, the land in which to nurture the principles of
the Civil War and the Revolution of 1688, the land of
British civil and ecclesiastical liberty.

Members of the Hollis family were among the most active
and generous English radicals who helped to develop the
dream of British liberty in America. The founder of the
Hollis fortune was a Yorkshire whitesmith (d. ca. 1662-63)
who was the first of the known Thomases of his family. It
was his eldest son, Thomas II, who expanded the family
business beyond the English provinces. He was apprenticed
in the manufacturing town of Sheffield and then went on to
London where he established a branch of the cutlery
business. That the second Thomas was much interested in
the religion of the Dissenters is indicated by the fact that
in London he leased Pinner's Hall for their worship. His
interest in charity is indicated by his establishment of the
Hollis Hospital in Sheffield. Thomas II set a pattern of
interest in practical charity and dissenting religion which
was inherited by the next Thomas.

The successor of Thomas II was a third Thomas (1659-
1731), who increased the family fortunes and developed his

father's religious and charitable interests. It was Thomas III who was the first member of his family to take an active interest in the college of Dissenters at Cambridge, Massachusetts. Although he gave books to the younger college in New Haven, his American donations were concentrated on Harvard. His interest had been captured by the college's brilliant scholar and president, Increase Mather. This interest was developed by Mather's successors--and other alumni such as Benjamin Coleman.

The Harvard--and the New England--of Increase Mather's day was undergoing a revolution. Perry Miller has shown that the 1720s represented a watershed in the development of the New England way. Samuel Willard's great Summa of 1727, unlike that of Aquinas, was an encyclopedic compilation of theology which was fast losing its hold on most owners of the "New England Mind." Jonathan Edwards and Samuel Hopkins were resistance fighters for the orthodox or the old "Saints." But the majority of the professional thinkers of New England in the late seventeenth and the first fifty or sixty years of the eighteenth century were breaking away from the way of the early "Saints," widening the standards of admission to church membership, cultivating science and historical research, breaking with orthodox theological determinism, and even accepting some of the graces of Anglicanism, such as "church" and "chapel" buildings (instead of meeting houses)--those formerly detested symbols of the Established Church which the Quaker George Fox had described as "steeple houses." Increase's son Cotton, together with most of his clerical contemporaries portrayed in surviving portraits, wore clerical bands, gowns, and cinctures which to the modern eye are indistinguishable from those of the Anglican clergy. They even--in contrast to their "Saintly" predecessors--covered their own hair with elaborately curled and powdered wigs.

It is symptomatic of the new spirit that the descendants of the men who had scourged Quakers and driven the Baptists into Rhode Island accepted the gifts to the college of Thomas Hollis III, a man whose sympathies were Baptist. In the tactful words of Edward Wigglesworth, the first Hollis

Professor of Divinity, Hollis was one who "though he was
not strictly of our way, nor in judgment with us in the point
of infant baptism, yet his heart and hand was the same to us
as if we had been one in opinion and practice with him."

The gifts were many and most generous. Between
1718-19 and his stock-taking in 1727, Thomas III's gifts
("exclusive of gifts not vendible") amounted to roughly
£4,900. This total was invested at 6 percent and yielded
£294 a year. This sum was used to pay the salary of the
"Hollis-professor of Divinity," the "Hollisian Professor
of Philosophy and Mathematics," the "treasurer or
Accomptant of the College," scholarships for "ten Poor
Students in Divinity," and, finally, to "supply Deficiencies"
(presumably a "slush" fund).

The "gifts not vendible" were kept in Harvard Hall, the
second building of its name, until destroyed by fire in
1764. At that time the major buildings of the College were
Harvard Hall, Stoughton College, and Massachusetts Hall.
A unique print in the Massachusetts Historical Society by
William Burgis shows the buildings in 1726 (fig. 1). Harvard
Hall is to the left, Stoughton is in the middle, and Massachusetts on the right. In Harvard Hall was an "Apparatus
Chamber" in which scientific equipment was preserved. In
1722 Hollis gave a 24-foot refracting telescope. After
graduating from Harvard in 1721, young Isaac Greenwood
studied science with Newton's friend, the noted John
Theophilus Desaguliers in London. Greenwood met Hollis
there and is thought to have interested him in further en-
riching Harvard's "apparatus." In 1726-27 Harvard received
as a gift from Hollis "a complete Apparatus for the Mathematics, bought of Hawksbee." The unvirtuous Greenwood
was elected the college's first Hollisian Professor of
Philosophy and Mathematics at the age of twenty-five in
1727. Although he lectured and published assiduously for
ten years, his career at Harvard perished in 1738 when his
devotion to Bacchus brought about an abrupt termination of
his professorship.

The library of the college was located on the second
floor of Harvard Hall. It contained the many books Hollis

Fig. 1. "A Prospect of the Colledges in Cambridge in
New England." Engraving, William Burgis. Boston, 1726.
19" x 24 5/8". Massachusetts Historical Society

had given and the fonts of Hebrew and Greek types he sent.
Like many benefactors before and since he also had sent his
portrait, "as large as the life." This was in "a gilt frame,
which, with charges, cost £28." It was accompanied by
"his statutes and orders relating to his benefactions, hand-
somely framed, with a glass before it, which cost £8." The
original painting was done by Joseph Highmore in 1722 when
the sitter was seventy-one. The portrait is lost, but Peter
Pelham, the stepfather of John Singleton Copley, did a
mezzotint after it in 1751 (fig. 2). Hollis is dressed in a
full-bottomed wig and (surprisingly) a flowered dressing
gown. He sits facing right in a tall armchair holding some
of his papers on a draped table. He stares directly at the
spectator, but with a gentle smile very much like that of
his great-nephew Thomas V. From a letter written after the
fire by President Holyoke, it would seem that the portrait
was accompanied by an escutcheon painted with the Hollis
arms. How the family became armigerous is not recorded.

Other gifts were given by the brothers of Thomas III
and by his nephew, Thomas IV (who sent Harvard its first
recorded microscope); but it was the third Thomas and his
great-nephew, Thomas V (the son of Thomas IV), who were
the family's most generous donors to Harvard. Thomas
Hollis V is the major actor in our story.

Jonathan Mayhew and Thomas Hollis V

The Harvard developed by the Mathers; Greenwood; Thomas
Hollis III; Edward Wigglesworth (ca. 1693-1765), the first
"Hollis Professor of Divinity"; and John Winthrop (1714-79),
the second Hollis Professor of Natural Philosophy and
Mathematics, was a very different place from the citadel of
the saints. Professor Winthrop's ancestor of the same name,
the first governor of Massachusetts Bay, and Professor
Wiggleworth's father, Michael, the author of the Day of
Doom, would not have felt at home. Theology had been
greatly liberalized. Not only was a conversion experience
no longer a necessary qualification for church membership;
when George Whitefield (1714-70) attempted his "revivals,"

Thomas Hollis late of London Merch.t a most generous Benefactor to Harvard College, in N.E having founded two Professorships and ten Scholarships in the said College, given a fine Apparatus for Experimental Philosophy, & increased the Library with a large Number of valuable Books &c.

Ob.1731. Æ.71.

Jo. Highmore pinx.t 1722.   P.Pelham ab Orig.ti fecit et vend.t 1751.

Fig. 2. "Thomas Hollis." Mezzotint, Peter Pelham, after a painting by Joseph Highmore. Boston, 1751. 11 5/16" x 9 3/4". Houghton Library, Harvard University

he was strongly opposed by the college and by the ministers of Boston. Locke ruled philosophy and Newton, science. Harvard and the ministers worked out a modus vivendi with the Anglicans, the Quakers, and, as with the Hollises, the Baptists. Life in the Massachusetts of the 1740s was largely quiet. Reason ruled the faculty of the college and the pulpits of the Commonwealth. Charles Chauncey (1705-87) was perhaps the leading minister of Boston's ten churches in the 1740s and certainly the leader of the theological liberals of his generation. He was a devoted opponent of "Enthusiasm," of the establishment of Anglican bishops in New England, and of Edward's black and white picture of total depravity and irresistible grace.

Into the bright, new world of New England of the 1740s came a brave young man. Jonathan Mayhew (1720-66) was a poor boy from Martha's Vineyard. His father, Experience, was a missionary to the Indians on the island. After graduating from Harvard in 1744, Jonathan was called to Boston's West Church in 1747.[2] Rumors of young Mayhew's radicalism had preceded him, but, in spite of hostility from most of Boston's other ministers, he found a friend and patron in the liberal Chauncey.

Jonathan Mayhew became a leading figure in the formation of the ideology of the American Revolution. To the neglect of the Puritans, historians of American history in general and of the Revolution in particular have emphasized the importance of the role of its secular leaders. Modern scholarship frequently forgets that the War of Independence was fought for religious as well as political freedom. Mayhew strove for both. His pulpit and his sermons were his weapons.

Mayhew was not an original thinker; he was a successful propagandist. Opposed to the religious enthusiasm of Whitefield and Edwards, he fought for free will and against the divine tyrant in theology; in church polity and in civil politics he was opposed equally to the tyranny of the state and its rulers.

His career began conventionally, and successfully, with a series of lectures on Christianity and morality for the

young. Their publication was, rather surprisingly, followed
by the apparently unsolicited award of the degree of Doctor
of Divinity from the University of Aberdeen in 1750. Some
of the pulpit fire which filled his church on Sundays and
also filled his Thursday lectures blazed from the printed
page and touched his Scottish readers. The rest of his work,
whether directly from the pulpit or on the printed page,
also met with great success.

The gifted preacher won a devoted audience. The con-
gregation of the West Church contained a few men of wealth,
such as Harrison Gray. There were few poor. The typical
members were small merchants and shopkeepers. "More than
any other in Boston, it was the church of enterprising,
ambitious, usually self-made men . . . who were impatient
of restraining traditions in any area of human activity."[3]
A tradition recorded by Esther Forbes in her biography of
Paul Revere is that the future patriot came to listen to the
popular preacher and was punished by his father for associ-
ating with radicals.[4] As we shall see, there is considerable
reason to think that Revere was well within the orbit of
Mayhew's influence, if not as a boy, then at least in his
more mature years.

Although Mayhew preached many times and published a
great deal, his contemporaries generally commented that the
most influential of his sermons was A Discourse concerning
Unlimited Submission and Non-resistance to the Higher
Powers . . . The Substance of which was delivered in a
Sermon preached in the West Meeting-House in Boston The
Lord's Day after the 30th of January, 1749-50 (Boston, 1750).
His topic was "whether disobedience and resistance may not
be justifiable in some cases." The occasion was the annual
Anglican celebration on the anniversary of the execution of
Charles I, an event which had taken place January 30, 1649.
A volume of eighteenth-century English sermons on what
amounted to the Feast of Saint Charles I shows the lengths
to which Anglican priests went to promote the execution as
the martyrdom of their Defensor fidei.[5] The custom came to
New England, and was a thorn in the side of men like Mayhew
who regarded the action of the Commonwealth in trying and

executing King Charles on grounds of treason as wholly
justified.

It is difficult for us in 1970 to realize how violently
radical a break with the past the "regicides" had made. The
execution of Louis XVI roused shudders among the American
Federalists in the late eighteenth century. The issue as
it concerned their own kings was even closer to the bone
among Boston conservatives in 1750. It is significant that
John Adams regarded the sermon as one of the most important
statements on liberty published by an American before the
Revolution.

The sermon was reprinted in London by the Reverend
Richard Baron, a dissenting minister passionately concerned
with the issues of religious and civil freedom and later
intimately connected with Thomas Hollis. Mayhew's pamphlet
was included in a two-volume anthology of radical material
collected and edited by Baron, called The Pillars of Priest-
craft Shaken (London, 1752). In the dedication of his
anthology, Baron stated the purpose of his work: "The
design of this Collection being to emancipate the minds of
men, and to free them from those chains in which they have
been long held to the great disgrace both of reason and
christianity." In the dedication of the second volume he
said that it was the priests of the Anglican Church "that
bred all the discord betwixt King Charles I and his parliament." It was they who:

> hurried on that prince to those illegal practices,
> which afterwards justly brought him to the block:
> for it is evident that he deserved it, and that
> the people were under a necessity either of cutting
> him off or of being slaves themselves without re-
> demption. . . . It is the duty of all men to
> oppose and break their power by all possible means.

In his introductory remarks on Mayhew's sermon, Baron
excused the author for preaching politics. But it was true
that young Mayhew's discourse was aimed more directly at
civil liberty than ecclesiastical. The pastor of the West

Church argued that loyal obedience should be given only to
good and just rulers. When the ruler harms society, we are
bound to throw off our allegiance to him and to resist. The
divine right of kings is "fabulous and chimerical." No
government is to be submitted to at the expense of the
common good and safety of society.

Charles I was a tyrant ruling in an absolutely lawless
and despotic manner. Resistance to him was made in defense
of the rights of the people. Mayhew went on to argue that
even God is bound by the laws of truth, wisdom, and equity;
but Charles set himself above those laws as much as above
the written laws of the realm. Those who put Charles to
death were not guilty of rebellion. The priests made him a
martyr as a reproach to those who are not of the Established
Church: "And he was a martyr in his death, not because he
bravely suffered death in the cause of truth and righteous-
ness, but because he died an enemy to liberty and the rights
of conscience; i.e., not because he died an enemy to sin,
but dissenters." Because our ancestors put Charles to
death, "we are represented in the blackest colours, not
only as schizmaticks, but also as traitors and rebels."

Mayhew at the end of his sermon pointed out to his
audience that it should be contented and dutiful to George II
since he ruled by law and his people enjoyed "under his
administration all the liberty that is proper and expedient
for us." But the heart of his final message was a threat
that anticipated things to come:

Although the observation of this anniversary seems
to have been (at least) superstitious in its original;
and although it is often abused to very bad purposes
by the established clergy, as they serve themselves
of it, to perpetuate strife, a party spirit, and divisions in the Christian church; yet it is to be hoped
that one good end will be answered by it, quite
contrary to their intention: it is to be hoped, that
it will prove a standing memento that Britons will
not be slaves; and a warning to all corrupt coun-
sellors and ministers, not to go too far in advising
to arbitrary despotic measures.

In spite of the sugar-coating of loyalty to a just government
that ruled by law, the threat of rebellion to unjust government was remarkably bold and open. New England's devotion
to civil disobedience was openly proclaimed by Mayhew--
the intellectual ancestor of John and Samuel Adams, Henry
David Thoreau, and William Lloyd Garrison.

Mayhew's contemporaries applauded--or detested--his
message; his spiritual descendants developed and applied
it; but in England it had an immediate effect on Richard
Baron and, if not immediate, had by 1754 on Thomas Hollis V
an impact that had important consequences for Harvard, New
England, the United States, and the cause of liberty both
civil and ecclesiastical.

The fifth Thomas Hollis was physically a big man, highly
intelligent, extremely kind, of great esthetic taste, a
creator (or in contemporary terms an "inventor") of visual
designs, a neurotic, an extreme eccentric, and above all a
passionate servant of British liberty in particular and--to a
lesser extent--liberty in general. It is no coincidence that
he signed one anonymous newspaper article "The Roast Beef
of Old England." There can be no doubt that, somewhat like
Hilaire Belloc, he was a "professional" Englishman (though
with better reason than that French writer). In several of
the books inscribed by him, he wrote a capsule description
of himself: "Thomas Hollis of Lincoln's Inn, an Englishman,
a lover of Liberty, his Country, and its excellent Constitution as most nobly restored at the Happy Revolution."

Hollis was a rich man who seems to have taken little
interest in the business from which his fortune flowed. Instead he devoted himself to collecting works of art, writing,
editing, publishing, bestowing charity, and learning. He
was a member of the Royal Society, the Royal Society of
Antiquaries, the Free Society of Artists, and the Society for
the Encouragement of Arts, Manufacturers, and Commerce.
His circle of friends both at home and abroad was wide. In
England among his well-known friends and acquaintances
were Samuel Johnson, Laurence Sterne, Oliver Goldsmith,
Robert and James Adam, Sir William Chambers, William Pitt,
James Stuart, and Nicholas Revett. In Italy, he had many

friends, most of whom are forgotten today, but he also knew
and corresponded with men well known to the student of
eighteenth-century Italy, such as Consul Smith, Winckelmann,
Piranesi, the younger von Stosch, and the art and music critic
Count Algarotti. In Massachusetts his circle included
Edmund Quincy, Edward Holyoke, and above all--though they
only corresponded and never met--his great friend Jonathan
Mayhew.

Hollis spent a large part of his time and fortune acting
as a self-appointed missionary in the cause of British liberty.
His day-to-day diary for the years 1759 to 1770 (now in the
Houghton Library) reveals that a great deal of his activity
was carried on anonymously. He sent his propaganda to
English institutions, such as the British Museum, Christ's
College, Cambridge (sacred to him because of its association with his hero Milton), and Trinity College (also revered
because of its connection with Newton, another hero), and
to many English friends and acquaintances. But the diary
makes clear that most of his gifts went to other countries
where he felt that they would be most useful in propagating
his cause. He sent portrait busts of the British "Worthies,"
such as Locke and Newton, to Leiden University in the form
of a set of thirteen waxes. To Switzerland he sent much of
the literature written by the major propagandists of the
Commonwealth and the Revolution of 1688, and he even edited
and printed a Latin grammar of English so that the foreign
reader could learn to read the books. Other gifts went to
Italy, France, and Sweden. But it was to the British
colonies, and especially Massachusetts, that he sent most
gifts. A large library, scientific instruments (or at least
the money to buy them), a portrait of Thomas III, and prints
were among the gifts.

It is on the prints that I want to concentrate in this
paper. Neither time nor space permits a full account of the
Hollis "Liberty prints," as he called them, but a few
selected examples will show how his mind worked and the
impact of his methods and ideas on the American patriot and
above all on the American printmaker.

The Cameo and the First Britannia

In 1754 Hollis returned from several years of touring the
Continent. He had enjoyed his travels, but never was to
leave England again. On his return he became acquainted
with the Reverend Richard Baron, the editor of Mayhew's
sermon, A Discourse concerning Unlimited Submission. We
know that Hollis was greatly moved by the sermon, for in
the same year he employed an artist named Lorenz Natter to
execute his first work of visual propaganda for British
liberty, a three-dimensional iconographic representation of
the Mayhew sermon. Natter was an extremely skillful gem
engraver. Hollis commissioned him to do a cameo representing British liberty. The gem is lost, but three later pictures
of the work allow us to study its symbolism closely. A
sketch of the gem (fig. 3) accompanied the following
description:

> A Description & Drawing of the Britannia triumphans,
> a Cameo composed and engraved in the Year 1754, by
> Laurence Natter, originally of Biberach in Swabia,
> and now in Vine-Street, Piccadilly, London.
> Lithographer. [6]

The Subject

> This Cameo reppresents the Figure of Britannia set-
> ting in full-front in a Chair of State, with a Staff
> in her right hand on which is the Cap of Liberty,
> and leaning upon her left arm on an elbow of the
> Chair, taking slight hold of some of her Robes with
> that Hand. Behind her on one side, is a Victory
> crowning Her with laurel with the right hand, and
> carrying a palmbranch in the left. On her right
> Side, is a Shield with the Brittish Arms, supported
> by a Lyon. At the Bak of these, is a Trophy with
> so much of the usual armour and Insignia, as the
> Circumstances of the Stone would admit, and as
> at a distance appears a Pyramid. On her left

Fig. 3. "Britannia victrix." Drawing, attributed to
Lorenz Natter. London, 1754. 22 1/2" x 17 3/16".
Houghton Library, Harvard University

side before the Victory is a British Genius that
pours out Fruits & Flowers from a Cornu Copia
upon the Ground, where there is carelessly lying
an ax, the Emblem of Power and Justice. Under
the Feet of the Britannia are these two letters
L.N. being the initial letters of the Engravers
Name. Beneath these is this Inscription
IAN.30.1648.

As this Cameo is remarkable among other
Respects for the Beauty & number of the Colors,
which consist of no less than five distinct
Divisions, and required the utmost skill of the
Artist on that Account to adapt them with suitable
advantage to the dignity of his subject, without
hurting the regularity or ease of the general
Composition, it will therefore be proper to give
a minute detail of the Uses that were made of
them, thereby to explain more fully and clearly
the Drawing which is hereto annexed.

Explanation of the Colors

The Head & Wings of the Genius, and the great
Robe that covers the Lap & Knees of the Britania,
marked with strong Diagonal Lines in the large
drawing, are of the uppermost and deepest brown
Color, as see Line 5. in the small drawing that
shews the depth & divisions of the stone.

The Tunica being closer to the Body, and the
brown Color being therefore thinner, it appears
Yellow. The staff from the ground to the hand is
yellow likewise.
The Head and Arms of the Britannia, the drappery
which she holds in her left Hand, her feet, the
footstool, one point of the Chair, the shield of
the British Arms, and the whole body of the
Genius (the Head and Wings as before mentioned,

excepted) are White, answering to line 4.
The Chair, the upperpart of the Staff with the Cap
of liberty, the Lyon that supports the Arms, the
Ground on which the feet of the Britania rests,
the Cornucopia, and the Ax upon the Ground, are
of the thick brown Color answering Line 3. The
Laurel & Palm-branchs in the Hands of the
Victory appear yellow, the brown Color being
nearer the white in those places & consequently
more transparent. The Pyramid, The Trophy with
its Insegnia, the Victory, and the Ground on
which are engraved the words IAN.30.1648. are
all white answering to Line 2.
At the Back of the whole Composition is a fine
brown transparent Color, which serves as the
Ground to it, and answers to Line 1.

But to form an exact & thorough Idea of this
singular and valuable Gem, the curious Lovers
must have recourse to the Original itself.

NB. Although in working this Cameo the
Ground unavoidably became very thin, Yet the
Artist ventured to engrave an Intaglia on the
Revers of it, reppresenting the Bust of Algernon
Sidney, in which the face is three-quarters
shewn. Round the Bust are these words. GVILTY!
DO YOU CALL THAT GUILT? This Intaglia was
taken from a drawing of Mr. Vertue's, after an
excellent original painting in Oyl by Justus ab
Egmondt now at penshurst.

Hollis then commissioned an Italian artist, Giovanni
Baptista Cipriani, to make a print of the gem. Cipriani's
drawing (fig. 4) for his print differs from the Natter gem in
some details. Cipriani's etching (fig. 5) after his own
drawing also differs in at least one important detail--the
use of tridents rather than spears as the decorative device
on the stiles of Britannia's throne. However, since the

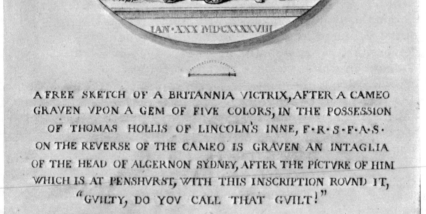

Fig. 4. "Britannia victrix." Drawing, Giovanni
Baptista Cipriani. London, 1769. 32" x 22 5/16".
Houghton Library, Harvard University

Inside the image:

IAN · XXX MDCXXXVIII

A FREE SKETCH OF A BRITANNIA VICTRIX, ETCHED AFTER A
CAMEO GRAVEN VPON A GEM OF FIVE COLORS, WHICH IS IN THE
POSSESSION OF THOMAS HOLLIS OF LINCOLN'S INNE, F·R·S·F·A·S·
ON THE REVERSE OF THE CAMEO IS GRAVEN AN INTAGLIA OF
THE HEAD OF ALGERNON SYDNEY, AFTER THE PICTVRE OF HIM
WHICH IS AT PENSHVRST, WITH THIS INSCRIPTION ROVND IT,
"GVILTY, DO YOV CALL THAT GVILT!"

I·B·C   MDCCLXX

Fig. 5. "Britannia victrix." Etching and engraving,
Giovanni Baptista Cipriani, after a drawing by Lorenz
Natter. London, 1770. 24 7/16" x 18 1/8". Houghton
Library, Harvard University

etching was made with the approval of Hollis, it may be that
he continued to develop the symbolism and so permitted
Cipriani in 1770 to express its final form even though it
differed from the actual cameo. On this assumption, we will
examine the symbolism of Britannia victrix as of 1770 in its
fully developed and final form (fig. 5).

In the center of the round field sits an enthroned female
figure dressed in a chiton and sandals. In her right hand she
holds a pole supporting the pilleus libertatis, the cap of
liberty awarded to ancient Roman freed slaves as a symbol of
their new status. The throne is decorated with two tridents
instead of arrows. To the left, beneath a military trophy a
rampant lion clasps an oval shield bearing the crosses of
Saint Andrew and Saint George. To the right is a winged
female figure holding a wreath over the central figure's head
and in her other hand a palm. At her feet stands a winged
child holding a cornucopia. At the very far right is an ax.
Beneath the whole is inscribed the date "IAN XXX MDCXXXXVIII. "
Below the picture is an inscription identifying the object portrayed as a cameo of five colors representing a "Britannia
victrix." The text also states that on the reverse of the cameo
is engraved an "intaglia" portrait of Algernon Sidney "after
the picture of him which is at Penshurst, with this inscription round it 'Guilty, do you call that guilt?'"

I have been unable to find any earlier example of the image
of Britannia with the pilleus libertatis as an attribute. This
also, I believe, is the earliest use by Hollis of what he later
called "British Liberty." Creating here a symbol that was
essentially taken from the British sestertius of Antoninus
Pius of A.D. 143-44, Hollis later developed it further and
used it very freely, especially as a stamp on the bindings
of the books he sent to Harvard for what has been called
his "library of Liberty."

The central figure represents British liberty, but the
description of the first drawing specifically states that she
is "Britannia triumphans." Are there any clues as to of
what or whom she is the victorious conqueror and the nature
of her weapon? The military trophy is used normally to
signify war on land. The lion is a usual symbol of England

(as in the royal arms). A rampant lion was used as the
figurehead of ships of the Royal Navy from the reign of
James I, and from 1703 to 1727 the style was fixed by regu-
lation. "To some extent [the] practice continued well down
to the 1760's," says M. V. Brewington in his Shipcarvers of
North America.[7] Since it was contemporary practice, Hollis
may well have had its naval meaning in mind when he placed
the lion next to a trident--a frequently used symbol of
Britain's sea power. Thus, on the left the intended symbolism
would be an allegorical statement of Britain's armed power on
both land and sea. On the right hand the winged figure of a
woman is a normal emblem of Victory. She places the crown
of victory on triumphant Britannia's head. The winged child
carrying a cornucopia is probably no more than a supporter
for one of Victory's attributes. Ripa wrote:

> Per la vittoria si dipinge una donna alata, che nella
> destra tiene un cornucopia, & nella sinistra un ramo
> di palma. E qui sono le due sorti di bene, che porto
> seco la vittoria; cioe la fama overo l'honore, e la
> ricchezza, & l'una, e l'altra per ragione di guerra,
> si toglie per forza di mano all'inimico.[8]

The attribute of the cornucopia usual in Victory's hand
is replaced by a wreath. That Hollis was aware that the
right hand normally holds a cornucopia is indicated by a
passage in his diary in which he says:

> 1759. June 1. Visiting in the morning. - Settled the
> intire disposition of a medal on the taking of Louis-
> bourg with Signor Cipriani; which is to be executed
> by Mr. Kirk. On the face. The head of Britannia,
> after my own antique paste, with the Cap of Liberty
> and Trident on each side of it, and these words
> round it O·FAIR·BRITANNIA·HAIL. On the reverse the
> figure of a Victory just lighting on the ground with a
> garland cornacopea in her right hand, and a trophy
> with a shield on which are the French fleur de lis
> in her left hand.

The cornucopia is transferred to a supporter while the left
hand holds, as it should by precedent, a palm. British
liberty is victorious on land and sea and as a result achieves
fame and wealth. But who is the vanquished and what was
the weapon with which he was conquered? The date on the
cameo is our clue. On January 30, 1648, Old Style,[9] King
Charles I, who had previously been tried and found guilty by
Parliament, was executed. The place was the Banqueting
House at Whitehall; the instrument used was an ax. We now
have all the pieces. The people of Britain are shown triumphant in the cameo; they were renowned and rich because of
their resistance to and execution of an unjust king. The
cameo is a monument commemorating the date of the execution of Charles I. It illustrated--and enriched--the imagery
of Mayhew's arguments on the celebration of that day and
was executed as "a standing memento that Britons will not
be slaves; and a warning to all corrupt counselors and
ministers, not to go too far in advising to arbitrary despotic
measures."[10]

John Baptist Jackson and Giovanni Baptista Cipriani

The text below the etching of the Natter-Hollis cameo
points out that the now lost gem of 1754 was decorated with
a carved copy of a portrait of Algernon Sidney then at
Penshurst. The next link between Hollis and Mayhew was
forged by means of that portrait. Hollis was interested in
Sidney because he considered him to be one of the greatest
English political theorists in the Commonwealth vein. Professor Robbins has written of that violent republican:
"During the American Revolution Sidney's Discourses was
more of a Bible to the revolutionaries than any of the other
works of his century. Milton only excepted."[11] On July 24,
1754, Hollis purchased from the famous antiquarian George
Vertue a drawing made after a painting at Penshurst showing
Sidney at the age of forty-one. The painting was attributed
to an artist who probably was the Belgian known today as
Justus van Egmont (ca. 1601-74). Hollis's biographer,
Archdeacon Blackburne, stated that his hero had hired an

artist to make a woodcut after the portrait.[12] In a copy of
Sidney's Discourses now at the Houghton Library, Hollis
wrote: "that the memory of so excellent a person might be
still better preserved and extended, he [Hollis] caused a
print to be made from it ... by the ingenious Mr. Jackson
of Battersea" (fig. 6). John Baptist Jackson was an English
artist about whom we now know a great deal thanks to the
work of Jacob Kainen.[13] Trained in France and Italy he produced magnificent chiaroscuro woodcuts and designed wall-
paper and printed calicoes.[14] He was patronized by both
Hollis and his friend Thomas Brand (later known as Brand-
Hollis).

Impressed with the revolutionary thought of Jonathan
Mayhew, Hollis, who was most cautious in opening a human
relationship, decided to make contact with his new hero by
sending him copies of the portrait and writings of the earlier
rebel. On February 28, 1755, Jasper Maduit, an acquaintance
of Hollis and later the agent of Massachusetts in Great
Britain, wrote Mayhew:

> Rev'd Sir,
> At the request of a Gentleman lately returned
> from his travells, & has brought home a confirm'd
> Sence of English Liberty I have put on board [as]
> Capt. Edwd Cahill Directed to you a box, containing
> some prints of that great stateman Algernon Sidney,
> also a set for Hayward [sic] College, & a Sidney
> bound, as a present to your self. Some of these
> prints are sent to Connecticut & the other provinces
> which may have their use, & increase the English
> abhorrence of a French Government which may take
> place in all the colonys if they don't write and
> support the Virginians.[15]

So, by this curiously indirect pictorial means, opened by
the return thrust of Hollis and his prints, the Mayhew-Hollis
dialogue began.

Having tried one print maker, Hollis decided to try
several more, developing what in the art world today is

Fig. 6. "Algernon Sidney." Woodcut, John
Baptist Jackson, after a painting by Justus van
Egmont. London, 1754. 35" x 22 5/16". Houghton
Library, Harvard University

described as a "stable" of etchers, engravers, die cutters, and designers--all in the cause of the propagation of English liberty. Of these the most important was a Florentine named Giovanni Baptista Cipriani, one of a considerable number of Italian artists who immigrated to England in the eighteenth century. In 1755 he left for England in the company of his friends Joseph Wilton, the sculptor, and William Chambers, the architect. It is not known when Cipriani began to work for Hollis; but in 1759, the year Hollis's known diary opened, he was busily employed, and he continued to be chief draftsman and a major print maker in the liberty campaign until 1770, when the diary closed, and perhaps until Hollis died in 1774.

Natter was the first staff artist, but he was given only a few commissions, and his character was commented on unfavorably in the diary. Isaac Gosset was credited with at least two commissions of waxes and remained an acquaintance of Hollis. Only one print was done by Jackson on commission, so far as I have been able to discover. But Cipriani was employed time and time again, always as draftsman and frequently as etcher of at least the portrait part of the "Liberty prints."

Cipriani's fully recorded career as draftsman to Hollis began in 1759, when together they went to call on Arthur Onslow, Speaker of the House, at his home in Surrey. Cipriani did a drawing after an oil portrait of Milton "as a youth" owned by the Speaker. He went on to do one of Milton as a child, as an adult, and finally as "Victorious over Salmasius." But Milton was not Hollis's only Commonwealth hero. He still remained faithful to Algernon Sidney.

On September 13, 1759, Hollis recorded the purchase of his second portrait of Sidney. He visited an engraver named Yeo in his "appartment in the Tower." From him Hollis bought several proof impressions in wax from seals cut by the well-known seventeenth-century die cutter Thomas Simon. Among them was a profile portrait of Sidney. When Andrew Millar, the publisher, visited Hollis on September 20 to discuss a new edition of Sidney's political writings, Hollis showed him a drawing by Cipriani after the wax proof by Simon. On July 15, 1760, Hollis noted that he had promised

Millar 500 impressions of the etching that he proposed
Cipriani should make of his Sidney drawing. Sometime between November 19, 1760, and January 2, 1761, the etching
was completed. Hollis recorded his satisfaction with the
result on the latter day. On May 28 one "Mr. Gardner" was
paid for engraving the inscription under the etching (fig. 7).
The etching was never used by Millar. Hollis distributed it
only as a liberty print. Instead Hollis commissioned the
currently fashionable engraver James Basire, William
Blake's master, to engrave a copy of Cipriani's etching. The
engraved version was acceptable to Hollis, and on January 5,
1763, he paid Basire for 500 impressions which he had
delivered to Millar as a gift. Millar accepted them and in
the same year issued <u>Discourses Concerning Government by
Algernon Sidney with his Letters Trial Apology and Some
Memoirs of his Life</u>. Hollis had several copies (the number
is not recorded in the diary) bound in red morocco and decorated with his stamps which Cipriani had probably designed.
One such copy was sent to Harvard College--to which he also
presented a copy of the Cipriani etching of Sidney in a red
morocco bound set of the liberty prints. Thus, Harvard was
given all three of the Hollis prints of the great republican.

To show that there was great interest in Sidney in Massachusetts one need only point out that one of his most famous
lines was adopted as the Commonwealth's motto. The text
cut under John Baptist Jackson's woodcut of Sidney was taken
from Viscount Molesworth's <u>An Account of Denmark</u>, in which
he tells us that when Sidney was ambassador to Denmark,
the French ambassador:

> had the Confidence to tear out of the book of Mottos
> in the King's Library, this Verse, which Mr. Sidney
> (according to the Liberty allowed to all Strangers)
> had written in it:

> Manus haec inimica Tyrannis
> Ense petit placidam sub libertate quietem.

Though Monsieur Terlon understood not a Word of

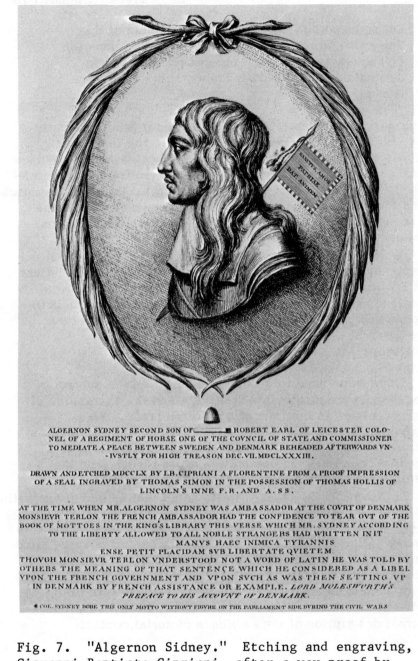

ALGERNON SYDNEY SECOND SON OF⬛⬛⬛⬛ ROBERT EARL OF LEICESTER COLO-
NEL OF A REGIMENT OF HORSE ONE OF THE COVNCIL OF STATE AND COMMISSIONER
TO MEDIATE A PEACE BETWEEN SWEDEN AND DENMARK BEHEADED AFTERWARDS VN-
-IVSTLY FOR HIGH TREASON DEC.VII.MDCLXXXIII.

DRAWN AND ETCHED MDCCLX BY I.B.CIPRIANI A FLORENTINE FROM A PROOF IMPRESSION
OF A SEAL INGRAVED BY THOMAS SIMON IN THE POSSESSION OF THOMAS HOLLIS OF
LINCOLN'S INNE F.R.AND A.SS.

AT THE TIME WHEN MR.ALGERNON SYDNEY WAS AMBASSADOR AT THE COVRT OF DENMARK
MONSIEVR TERLON THE FRENCH AMBASSADOR HAD THE CONFIDENCE TO TEAR OVT OF THE
BOOK OF MOTTOES IN THE KING'S LIBRARY THIS VERSE WHICH MR. SYDNEY ACCORDING
TO THE LIBERTY ALLOWED TO ALL NOBLE STRANGERS HAD WRITTEN IN IT
MANVS HAEC INIMICA TYRANNIS
ENSE PETIT PLACIDAM SVB LIBERTATE QVIETEM
THOVGH MONSIEVR TERLON VNDERSTOOD NOT A WORD OF LATIN HE WAS TOLD BY
OTHERS THE MEANING OF THAT SENTENCE WHICH HE CONSIDERED AS A LIBEL
VPON THE FRENCH GOVERNMENT AND VPON SVCH AS WAS THEN SETTING VP
IN DENMARK BY FRENCH ASSISTANCE OR EXAMPLE. *LORD MOLESWORTH'S
PREFACE TO HIS ACCOVNT OF DENMARK.*

✳ COL. SYDNEY BORE THIS ONLY MOTTO WITHOVT FIGVRE ON THE PARLIAMENT SIDE DVRING THE CIVIL WARS

Fig. 7. "Algernon Sidney." Etching and engraving,
Giovanni Baptista Cipriani, after a wax proof by
Thomas Simon. London, 1761. 27 1/8" x 17 5/16".
Houghton Library, Harvard University

Latin, he was told by others the Meaning of that
Sentence, which he considered as a Libel upon the
French Government, and upon such as was then
setting up in Denmark by French Assistance or
Example.

The motto is also found under the Cipriani print. As early
as 1918 Chester N. Greenough pointed to the fact that the
Hollis books and prints in Harvard Hall contained many uses
of the motto, and suggested that it was probable that Professor John Winthrop, the second Hollis Professor of Mathematics
and Natural and Experimental Philosophy, a member of the
committee appointed to create a new seal for the Commonwealth in 1775, suggested the motto.[16]

As late as 1824, Adams was writing to Jefferson about the
importance of Sidney, and he had quoted his motto in letters
of 1774 and 1775. Sidney was part and parcel of the New
England mind of the eighteenth century, and Hollis in both
books and pictures did more than a little to put him there.

The Stamp Act and The London Chronicle

There is no need to go into any detail on the subject of
the disgust aroused by the Stamp Act and the expression of
that revulsion in the form of acts of violence. What
has never been published is an account of Thomas Hollis's
efforts to fight the act by publishing anonymously both
against it and also in celebration of its repeal, and the
effects his squibs had on eighteenth-century art.

On November 18, 1765, Hollis noted that he had given William
Strahan, the famous printer, copy to be inserted in the London
Chronicle, Strahan's newspaper. It took the form of what was
known in the sixteenth and seventeenth centuries as a "blind
emblem," that is, a motto in Latin without an accompanying
picture. The emblem, by rule, consisted of a picture united
with a motto in such a way that each was unintelligible
without the other. Instead of a picture, Hollis supplied a
verbal description of the emblem's pictorial content:

> TO WHOM IT MAY CONCERN, MEN OF ENGLAND, THE
> COLONIES, BRETHERN. Consider well the Reverse
> of a Dutch Medal, struck in their early troubles.
> "Two earthen Vases, floating in the Waters.
> Inscription. Frangimur si colidimur.

I have been unable to discover the medal to which Hollis refers. However, the ultimate source of the symbolism is the
Emblemata of Andrea Alciati, the early sixteenth-century inventor of the emblem book. In the edition of 1577 published
at the Plantin Press, the emblem is Number 65. The picture
shows two pots floating down a river side by side. The text
explains that one of them is metal and the other clay. The
motto is "Aliquid mali propter vicinum malum" (Evil comes
from an evil neighbor).

One would not think today that the phrase "Frangimur si
colidimur" would make very effective propaganda against the
Stamp Act. Indeed I suspect there are few people today who
would know that the words mean "We will break if we collide,"
much less be able to see that it is a warning of future revolution. But our ancestors' minds were different from ours.
In the Colonies, Hollis's blind emblem inspired two pictorial
ones. Edwin Wolf, 2nd, Director of the Library Company of
Philadelphia, has pointed out to me that Isaac Hunt published in 1775 a political pamphlet which used the motto in
translation ("If we strike we break") and placed it below a
woodcut of two pitchers floating in the sea. The title of the
pamphlet is a summary of its contents: The Political Family:
or a Discourse pointing out the Reciprocal Advantages, which
flow from an uninterrupted Union between Great-Britain and
her American Colonies.

In Boston an engraving appeared which is even more interesting, both because it is visually more complex and also
because it was made by Paul Revere, a man who, as we have
seen, as a boy at least is said to have been punished for
going to hear Mayhew and who engraved a posthumous portrait of him apparently based on another by Richard Jennys,
Jr. Revere's use of the Hollis squib was published as a
frontispiece to Edes & Gill's North American Almanack

for 1769 in November of 1768 at the time of the occupation
of Boston by the British troops (an event which brought forth
from Revere a view of the event and later in 1770 the famous
Massacre print which Hollis republished in London).

Edes & Gill's own text describes both the picture and its
allegorical-political signifance:

> Two Female Figures. The principal, richly decorated,
> is seated on a Throne with an Imperial Diadem on her
> Head, and a Spear in her left Hand. The other Figure
> exhibits a Virgin with a Civic Crown, in the utmost
> Agonies of Distress and Horror. The Cap of Liberty
> falling from the Spear of one, and tottering to fall from
> the other. The Label of one, is Collidimur; of the other
> Frangimur. Two Ships are represented to View in a
> Tempest in the Instant of dashing to Pieces against one
> another, and sinking between the Rocks of Sylla and
> Caribdis. In the Interim are seen two Arch Angels,
> flying as 'on the Wings of the Wind.' The Label of
> the one is, "Shall not the Lord of all the Earth do
> Right.' The other is, 'The Fool' only 'hath said in
> his Heart there is no God.' After all, in a Glory, is
> inscribed these Words, "The Lord GOD Omnipotent
> reigneth, let the Earth rejoice!'

When the Stamp Act was repealed, Hollis used the London
Chronicle to publish another squib that had surprising consequences. The story has been twice in print so there is no
need to do more than summarize it here.

In his diary Hollis wrote under the date of March, 1766:

> This Evening the following advertisement appeared in
> the L. Chronicle, which had been drawn up by me of
> some time, preparatory to the repeal of that [the
> Stamp] act "March 18, 1766. Englishmen, Scottish-
> men, Irishmen, Colonists, Brethren, Rejoice in the
> Wisdom, Fortitude of one Man, which hath saved
> You from Civil War & your Enemies! Erect a Statue
> to that Man in the Metropolis of your Dominions!

Place a garland of Oak leaves on the Pedestal
and grave in it Concord."

The Pitt Statues and Lord Botetourt

As R. T. H. Halsey stated: "Under date caption of
March 18, 1766, and for many months thereafter the London
Chronicle printed at the head of its columns the following
remarkable leader: . . ." He then proceeded to quote the
passage as printed, which we have above transcribed from
the Hollis diary. He went on:

> It is interesting to note that the same packet
> which carried the news of the repeal of the Stamp
> Act to New York bore copies of the above-mentioned
> number of The London Chronicle and that the day
> following its arrival a subscription for the erection
> of a statue of William Pitt was opened by prominent
> citizens of New York. Popular sentiment, however,
> demanded that this monument be paid for by public
> funds, which were immediately voted. . . .
>   The making of this tribute was intrusted to
> Joseph Wilton, a well-known English sculptor who
> had recently executed a statue of Pitt for the city
> of Cork, having been selected by Pitt himself for
> this work. Wilton had already been engaged to
> make a statue of Pitt voted by the Assembly of
> South Carolina. . . . While still in the sculptor's
> studio, these statues, by the thoughts they awakened,
> were unquestionably responsible for a large alle-
> gorical mezzotint scraped by Charles Willson
> Peale while an art student in London.[17]

What Halsey did not know was that it was Hollis who
planted the squib in the London Chronicle, that the sculptor
Wilton was an intimate both of Cipriani and Hollis, that
Hollis was at this time (and during the last four years of
his life) an ardent admirer and friend of Pitt, and that there
is a direct use of a Hollis liberty print in the picture of
Pitt by Peale.

It is perhaps an amusing coincidence that a third standing English statue erected in eighteenth-century America was
also tied to the Hollis circle. The statue in question is a
portrait of Lord Botetourt, the former Governor of Virginia,
by Richard Hayward. It was erected in 1773 in Williamsburg.
Hayward had used as the basis of his posthumous portrait a
wax made by Isaac Gosset (1713-99). Gosset had been employed by Hollis to make the wax reliefs of "English
Worthies" for Leiden University and appeared at his house
for a visit from time to time after that as recorded in the
diary. Further the allegorical theme placed on the pedestal
was the same one recommended by Hollis for Pitt--"Concord."
On the base Hayward carved a figure of an Indian maiden
(America) extending an olive branch to Britannia, who holds
out another to America in turn. Between them stands an
altar from which rise flames. The altar is garlanded and on
it, surrounded by the leaves (unfortunately not oak), is inscribed the single word "CONCORDIA." There is no proof,
of course, that the Hollis squib inspired the design. That
the parallel existed is absolutely certain. In the case of
our next example, there is absolute proof in the form of the
use of a Hollis print as a source for two American paintings
and an American print.

The American Dissenting Painter

In 1764 Thomas Hollis was asked by the husband of the
well-known writer, Catherine Macaulay, to design a portrait of her. Catherine Macaulay was a bluestocking, much
admired by George Washington (and by Hollis), renowned
for her Whig study of the British people's struggle for
liberty. Her husband had decided that an appropriate
frontispiece to the second volume of her History would be
her portrait. When consulted, the Apostle of British Liberty
turned to his numismatic collection. From it he chose a
silver coin minted during the height of power of Marcus
Junius Brutus, the murderer of Julius Caesar, or--as Hollis
saw it--the Republican executioner of Caesar the tyrant.
One side of the coin showed a procession of two togaed

men escorted by two lictors and was marked "Brutus"
(fig. 8). The obverse bore the head of a jeweled woman inscribed "Libertas" (fig. 9). This, then, was Liberty as
coined for the executioner of the first of the two tyrants
with whom Hollis was obsessed. When Hollis designed
Mrs. Macaulay's portrait, he had Cipriani portray her as
the Libertas of Brutus and had him draw below the picture
of the historian's profile a small vignette of the reverse of
the coin that was his source (fig. 10). Earlier in 1761,
Hollis had used the same coin as a source for part of a
picture of Britannia which he had Cipriani paint in grisaille
(now lost) and after which he had him do an etching (a copy
of which he sent to Harvard in 1764) (fig. 11). The main
figure in the picture of Britannia was based on an ancient
Roman painting of Roma reproduced in Turnbull's A Treatise
on Ancient Painting (1740). But, among other changes,
Hollis introduced in the border of Roma-Britannia's robe a
procession of figures taken from the coin of Brutus. He also
changed the design of the coin by having the figures march
in procession to an altar clearly indicated as dedicated to
the goddess of Liberty. A sketch documenting this change
exists among the Cipriani drawings recently acquired by the
Houghton Library (fig. 12).

In 1765, during the Stamp Act crisis, the diary shows
that Hollis came to identify William Pitt with Brutus icono-
graphically just as he had previously identified Mrs.
Macaulay with the Libertas of Brutus. Under the date of
November 3, 1765, Hollis wrote proposing a Pitt portrait
medal in exactly the way he had designed Mrs. Macaulay's
portrait based on the coin of Brutus:

A Head in profile, the hair of which is disposed
exactly after the Intaglia of Marcus Brutus, on root
of emerald, which was in the collection of the late
celebrated Antiquary Baron Stosch, & is at this
time in the Cabinet of the King of Prussia.

Late in 1766, Charles Willson Peale, sponsored by
several wealthy Americans, including Hollis's correspondent

Fig. 8. Reverse of coin of Marcus
Junius Brutus. Rome, ca. 44 B.C.
Silver. Collection of the author

Fig. 9. Obverse of coin of Marcus
Junius Brutus. Rome, ca. 44 B.C.
Silver. Collection of the author

Fig. 10. "Catherine Macaulay." Engraving, James Basire, after a drawing by Cipriani. London, 1767. 27 5/16" x 20 5/16". Houghton Library, Harvard University

O·FAIR·BRITANNIA·HAIL

DRAWN AND ETCHED MDCCLX BY I.B. CIPRIANI A FLORENTINE FROM A PICTVRE
PAINTED BY HIMSELF IN THE POSSESSION OF THOMAS HOLLIS F.R.AND A.SS.

Fig. 11. "O Fair Britannia Hail." Etching, Giovanni
Baptista Cipriani. London, 1760. 30 5/16" x 22 1/4".
Houghton Library, Harvard University

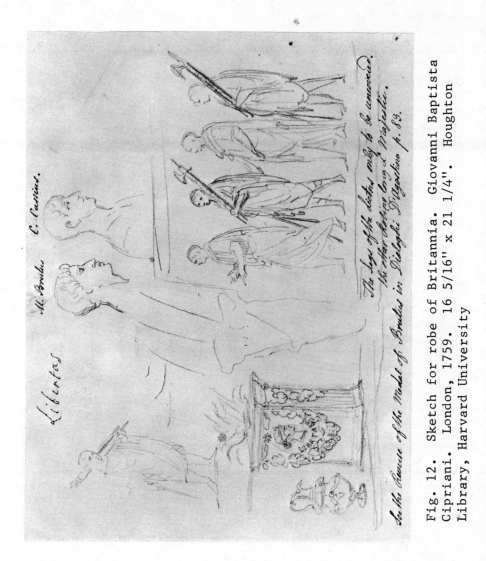

Fig. 12. Sketch for robe of Britannia. Giovanni Baptista
Cipriani. London, 1759. 16 5/16" x 21 1/4". Houghton
Library, Harvard University

William Allen of Pennsylvania, sailed to England in hopes
of making his fortune and also of perfecting himself as a
painter. We have little artistic evidence of Peale's activities in England; but thanks to the careful research of
Charles Coleman Sellers, we have some direct knowledge.[18]
We know that he studied with Benjamin West. We also know
that he undertook to do a large portrait of William Pitt. That
he produced two versions of the painting, that he "scraped"
a mezzotint after the painting, and that when he published
the print in 1768 it was accompanied by a printed text explaining it at least in part are also established facts. The
print is rare (fig. 13). The accompanying printed explanation is more so:

<u>A Description of the Picture and Mezzotinto</u>
<u>OF MR. PITT, done by</u>
<u>Charles Willson Peale, of Maryland</u>

The Principal Figure is that of Mr. PITT, in a
Consular Habit, speaking in Defence of the Claims
of the American Colonies, on the Principles of the
British Constitution.
    With MAGNA CHARTA in one Hand, he points
with the other, to the Statue of British <u>Liberty</u>,
trampling under Foot the Petition of the Congress
at New-York. Some have thought it not quite proper to represent Liberty as guilty of an Action so
contrary to her genuine Spirit; for that, conduct-
ing herself in strict Propriety of Character, she
ought not to violate, or treat with Contempt, the
Rights of any one. To this it may be sufficient
to say, the Painter principally intended to allude
to the Observation which hath been made by
Historians, and Writers on Government, that the
<u>States which enjoy the highest Degree of Liberty</u>
<u>are apt to be oppressive of those who are sub-</u>
<u>ordinate, and in Subjection to them</u>. Montesquieu,
speaking of the Constitution of Rome, and the
Government of the Roman Provinces, says, "<u>La</u>

Fig. 13. "Mr. Pitt." Mezzotint, Charles Willson
Peale. London (?), 1768 (?). 22 7/8" x 14 3/4".
The Henry Francis du Pont Winterthur Museum

Liberte croit, dans le Centre et la Tyrannic aux
Extrimetes:" And again, "La Ville ne sentoit point la
Tyrannie, qui ne s'exercoit que sur les Nations
Assujettis." And supporting Mr. Pitt, in his
Oration, to point, as he does, at the Statue, it
makes a Figure of Rhetoric strongly and justly
sarcastic on the present faint Genius of British
Liberty, in which Light, Gentlemen of Reading and
Taste have been pleased to commend it. The Fact
is, that the Petition of the Congress at New-York,
against Acts of meer Power, adverse to American
Rights, was rejected by the House of Commons,
the Guardians, the Genius, of that Liberty,
languishing as it is.

An Indian is placed on the Pedestal, in an
erect posture, with an attentive Countenance,
watching, as America has done for Five Years
past, the extradordinary Motions of the British
Senate. He listens to the Orator, and has a
Bow in his Hand, and a Dog by his Side, to shew
the natural Faithfulness and Firmness of America.
It was advised by some, to have had the Indian
drawn in a dejected and melancholy Posture: And,
considering the apparent Weakness of the Colonies,
and the Power of the Parent Country, it might not
perhaps, have been improper to have executed it
in that Manner; but in Truth the Americans, being
well founded in their Principles, and animated
with a sacred Love for their Country, have never
disponded.

An Altar, with a Flame is placed in the Foreground, to shew that the Cause of Liberty is sacred,
and, that therefore, they who maintain it, not only
discharge their Duty to their King and themselves,
but to GOD. It is decorated with the Heads of
Sidney and Hampden, who, with undaunted Courage,
spoke, wrote, and died in Defence of the true
Principles of Liberty, and of those Rights and
Blessings which Great-Britain now enjoys: For,

as the Banner placed between them expresses it,
SANCTUS AMOR PATRIAE DAT ANIMUM. A Civic
Crown is laid on the Altar, as consecrated to that
Man who preserved his Fellow-Citizens and Sub-
jects from Destruction!

The View of W_____H_____ is introduced in the Back Ground, not meerly as an elegant Piece of Architecture, but as it was the
Place where _____ suffered, for attempting
to invade the Rights of the British Kingdoms: And
it is observable, that the Statue and Altar of
British Liberty are erected near the Spot where
that great Sacrifice was made, through sad
Necessity, to the Honour, Happiness, Virtue,
and in one Word, to the Liberty of the British
People.

The Petition of the Congress at New-York, and
the Representation of W_____H_____ point
out the Time, and almost the Place, where the
Speech was delivered.

The chief Object of this Design will be answered, if it manifests, in the least, the
Gratitude of America to his Lordship. It will,
with Tradition, unprejudiced by the Writings of
Hirelings, who are made to glide in with the
courtly Streams of Falshood, be the faithful
Conveyance to Posterity of the knowledge of
those Great Things which we, who are not to
be imposed on by "the busy Doings and Undoings"
of the envious Great, have seen.

What is important about the text is not so much what it
says as what it does not say. The theme of the painting
was the justification of resistance to tyrants who violate
the British constitution by putting themselves above the
law. In 1768 it simply was not healthy to state such ideas
directly while living in England. Hollis lived in constant
paranoid fear, and Peale did his best to present his political ideas pictorially, but, at the same time, to present

them in such a way that it would be very difficult to prove
in a court of law that he was subversive. It must be remembered that the man with whom Peale was studying, West,
was very close to the king and was, in fact, George III's
favorite living painter.

West had produced a highly "Romanized" portrait of Mrs.
Macaulay's brother and John Wilkes's friend, Alderman John
Sawbridge, dressed in a toga. There was, therefore,
nothing eccentric in Peale's decision to do the same in
putting Pitt into Roman costume but in "Consular habit."
But, as Peale's printed explanation points out, Pitt was not
portrayed merely as a Roman. My thesis is that the painter's
intention was to dress him as Brutus. A contemporary portrait of Pitt by Hoare (fig. 14) shows him as he actually
looked and as he was portrayed in Copley's splendid history
painting of Pitt's death in the House of Lords. As Halsey
pointed out in 1918, Peale shows him as he was represented
by Joseph Wilton.[19] Wilton portrayed him as a Roman with
short hair and bangs and a long robe like that "Robing long
and Majestic" specifically noted in the Cipriani sketch for
figures identified by the sketch and the diary as Brutus and
Cassius. Wilton's friend Hollis in 1765 had suggested in
his diary that Pitt be identified with Brutus, the executioner
of Caesar. I have been unable to find the image of Brutus
mentioned by Hollis in the diary; but it happens that a
coin of Brutus owned by Hollis was frequently used by him
in his bindings and also at least once in his liberty prints.
The reverse of the coin is decorated with a liberty cap
on each side of which are two daggers. Underneath is
printed "EID MAR" commemorating the Ides of March, the
day of Caesar's assassination. The obverse bears a portrait of Brutus with hair cut short and with bangs which
resemble the hair in Cipriani's sketch, Wilton's bust, and
Peale's print. Like the Hollis Brutus portrayed on the border
of the Hollis-Turnbull-Roma-Britannia's robe and in the
sketch for it, the Peale Pitt stands before an altar dedicated
to Liberty and sacrifices not to Liberty alone, but to British
liberty. Like the Hollis Brutus and Wilton's Pitt, Peale's
Pitt is in a habit which is both "long and Majestic" and

Fig. 14. "William Pitt." Mezzotint, Richard Houston, after a painting by W. Hoare. London, n.d. 12 3/4" x 10". Collection of the author

"Consular." In the background is a classical building which
the accompanying text identifies ambiguously as "W_____
H_____." The building shown in the print is Inigo Jones's
Banqueting House in Whitehall. The reader will remember
that Jonathan Mayhew in 1750 published a sermon celebrating
an event of January 30, 1648/49, which occurred in Whitehall and that in 1754 Hollis and Lorenz Natter produced a
cameo of Britannia triumphans which celebrated the event.

My argument here is that the theme of the justified execution of regal tyrants had come full cycle in Peale's painting.
Mayhew preached his sermon in Boston in 1750. Hollis and
Natter gave it iconographic expression in England in 1754.
Then in 1768 Peale, an American, gave it a new iconographic
expression in England in two paintings and a print based on
two statues by Wilton that had been ordered by Americans
inspired by a squib planted anonymously by Hollis in the
London Chronicle. If I am right, the relations between art
and literature, and between Great Britain and the Colonies,
need the closest possible scrutiny because of their extraordinary intricacy.

That I am right is indicated by two pieces of evidence.
My argument to this point is frankly based on largely circumstantial evidence. But I wish, before resting my case, to
present two pieces of evidence of a link between Hollis and
Peale. The altar before which Pitt stands in the print is
decorated with two heads, those of two heroes of British
liberty--Hampden and Sidney. There is no necessary connection between those two men and Hollis. It is interesting
that two American Whigs other than Peale invoked the Brutus-
Sidney-Hampden association. John Adams wrote to James
Warren in June 1774: "There is one ugly reflection, Brutus
and Cassius were conquered and slain. Hampden died in
the field, Sidney on the scaffold, Harrington in jail, etc.
This is cold comfort. Politics are an ordeal among red hot
ploughshares."[20] Josiah Quincy made the association of
Brutus with the two English Commonwealthmen even more
clear-cut: "America hath in store her Bruti and Cassii,
her Hampden's and Sidneys, patriots and heroes, who will

form a band of brothers: men who have memories and feel-
ings, courage and swords."[21] There is then nothing unusual in the association of Brutus with Sidney and Hampden
for an eighteenth-century American Whig.[22] What is unusual is Peale's association of Pitt with Brutus. As we
have seen, that had been done in his diary by Hollis.

Finally, one last piece of evidence. The reader will
remember that Hollis commissioned three portraits of
Algernon Sidney, as well as sending one edition of his
writings to Mayhew and patronizing the publication of
another. There is no way of telling whether Peale used the
Cipriani or Basire version, but the altar before which Pitt-
Brutus stands in Peale's engraving is decorated by Peale
with the same head of Sidney that Cipriani had drawn after
Thomas Simon's seal of which Hollis bought a wax proof
from Mr. Yeo in his "appartment in the Tower" in 1759. And
across Sidney's shoulder lies a banner bearing the same
words inscribed by Simon, a second motto of Sidney's,
"Sanctus amor patriae dat animum"--May the sacred love
of the Fatherland [always] animate [the soul] (see fig. 7).

Conclusion

I have attempted to the best of my ability to analyze two
pictures of Anglo-American origin--Cipriani's etching of
Natter's cameo and Peale's "Pitt"--and to show their relationship to the Massachusetts-London and Mayhew-Hollis
axis. This illustration of the interplay of English and
American art will, I hope, convince my readers that
American art and politics of the eighteenth century are in
large part the product of an intricate dialogue between
Britain and her Colonies.

NOTES

1. The author wishes to acknowledge his gratitude to
Dr. William H. Bond, Librarian of the Houghton Library,
and his staff, for making this study possible. Mr. Arthur
A. Houghton, Jr., was the donor of the manuscript of the
Hollis diaries and the Cipriani drawing discussed here.
Without the generosity of Mr. Houghton and the kindness
of Dr. Bond and his staff this study would have been im-
possible.

2. Charles W. Akers, "Life of Jonathan Mayhew" (Ph.D.
dissertation, Boston University, 1952).

3. Ibid., p. 98.

4. Paul Revere and the World He Lived In (Boston, 1942),
p. 33.

5. Untitled bound volume of sermons in possession of
the author.

6. Dr. William H. Bond has kindly brought to my attention
that the use in this manuscript of the word "lithographer" does
not refer to Senefelder's invention of the early nineteenth
century. Dr. Bond points out that this usage, presumably of
1754, is not quite like any in the Oxford English Dictionary.
In a letter to the author of June 22, 1970, he goes on as
follows: "It apparently means an engraver on stones, in this
case on a cameo, while the nearest definition to it in the
OED is a person who carves inscriptions on stone."

7. (Barre, Mass., 1962), p. 2.

8. Translation: Victory is portrayed as a winged woman
who holds a cornucopia in her right hand and a branch of
palm in her left. The two kinds of benefits brought by
Victory are fame (or in truth, honor) and riches. By means
of war, both are seized through force of arms from the enemy.

9. The legal year changed on March 25 rather than
January 1 until the shift to New Style when the act passed
by parliament in 1750 and put into effect in 1752 made it
necessary in all legal and public affairs to use January 1
as the beginning of the year. Hollis and Natter on the
cameo were using Old Style dating.

10. Bernard Bailyn, ed., Pamphlets of the American
Revolution (Cambridge, Mass., 1965), p. 247.

11. Caroline Robbins, The Eighteenth-Century Commonwealthman (Cambridge, Mass., 1961), p. 46.

12. [Francis Blackburne], Memoirs of Thomas Hollis,
Esq. F.R.A.S.S. (London, 1780), II, 487.

13. Kainen, John Baptist Jackson: 18th-Century Master
of the Color Woodcut, United States National Museum,
Smithsonian Institution, Bulletin 222 (Washington, 1962).

14. Francina Irwin, "Scottish Eighteenth-Century Chintz
and Its Design," Burlington Magazine, CVII, no. 750 (1965),
452-58.

15. Akers, p. 238.

16. Chester N. Greenough, "Algernon Sidney and the
Motto of the Commonwealth of Massachusetts," Proceedings
of the Massachusetts Historical Society, LI (1918), 259-82.

17. Halsey, "America's Obligation to William Pitt, Earl
of Chatham," Bulletin of the Metropolitan Museum of Art,
XIII (June 1918), 138-43.

18. Sellers, Charles Willson Peale (New York, 1969).

19. Halsey, p. 139.

20. Caroline Robbins, "Algernon Sidney's Discourses
Concerning Government: Textbook of Revolution," William
and Mary Quarterly, 3d ser., IV (July 1947), 295.

21. Ibid.

22. A second example of the pairing of an eighteenth-
century radical Whig with Hampden and Sidney is to be found
in a mezzotint after Robert Edge Pine, the English painter
who came to the United States and produced the most accurate reconstruction we have of the act of signing our
Declaration of Independence. The sitter was Hell-Fire Club
member, cross-eyed John Wilkes--another Hollis hero who
plays a large part in the diary (fig. 15). You will note that
as attributes Pine has included a clearly labeled portrait of
Hampden and an equally clearly labeled copy of Sidney's
writings--perhaps the Hollis-sponsored edition. Like
Peale, Pine was certainly identifying a contemporary radical
Whig with two of his Commonwealth-Revolution of 1688
predecessors--and, interestingly enough, the same two,

Fig. 15. "John Wilkes." Mezzotint, James Wilson, after
a painting by R. E. Pine. London, 1764. 12" x 10".
(see footnote 22). Collection of the author

Sidney and Hampden. It would seem that Peale's British
parallel was Pine. Both produced pictures expressing the
Commonwealthman point of view about contemporary heroes
of the radical Whig movement. Both used Hampden and
Sidney as the vehicle of visual propaganda. And finally,
to move beyond the preliminaries to the events of the open
war for independence itself, both became visual historians--
painters of the history of the American Revolution. Together
they constitute a radical Whig of English origin and his
American contemporary painting pictures which express the
"arts of dissent."

The finished relief print, "The State House, Boston,"
from a modern zinc line photoengraving of the original
(which was drawn by John Warner Barber and engraved on
wood by S. E. Brown, ca. 1840). Printed here on a
Washington hand press, by Darrell Hyder and Elizabeth
Harris at the Winterthur Print Conference, 1970

PRINTS AND SCIENTIFIC ILLUSTRATION IN AMERICA

Charles B. Wood III

JAMES SMITHSON, the father of the Smithsonian Institution, once said that "the man of science is of no country, the world is his country, all mankind his countrymen."[1] The early history of science in America is but an extension of the history of science in Europe, and it must be viewed against that background. The same is true for American scientific illustration. Although the subject is treated here with little or no reference to European developments, "American" illustration was closely related to and usually followed similar developments in England and Europe. There are no studies of American scientific illustration known to me.[2]

Science in the eighteenth century was considered a branch of philosophy and in the broadest sense an aspect of social history. It was not compartmentalized as it is today into the various sciences--there were only two broad categories: natural history and natural philosophy. Into the former fell botany, zoology, and geology; into the latter physics, chemistry, and astronomy. Some persons, such as physicians, were in fact both natural historians and natural philosophers, being versed in such related fields as chemistry and anatomy, botany and materia medica.[3] Into these two broad categories there blends imperceptibly the closely related area of technology--essentially the practical application of scientific knowledge. In the eighteenth century there was hardly any distinction between science and technology--indeed, all scientific study was justified on the grounds of its usefulness to society. One need only leaf through the early volumes of the publications of the American learned and scientific societies to see how closely related they were. Although my primary concern here

is scientific illustration, I will consider briefly a few
eighteenth-century illustrations of technology.

With a few exceptions, book illustration in America prior
to about 1800 was rudimentary. The two kinds of graphic
techniques used throughout the eighteenth century in this
country were the woodcut and the copper engraving. The
woodcut, or relief print, so very sympathetic in use with
type face, and perhaps the most "graphic" of all media, was
singularly unsuited to the exact and precise nature of scientific illustration. This shortcoming can be seen elsewhere in
this volume in the paper by Richard Holman illustrating the
astronomical woodcuts by John Foster published in 1675.
Copper or line engraving, on the other hand, was well suited
to scientific illustration. It was a technique which depended
to a very large degree on the skill and proficiency of its
practitioner. During the entire eighteenth century, copper
engraving was far and away the most widely used medium for
book illustration, both in Europe and America. It was during
this period that scientific publishing--and illustration--really
got its start in this country.

Among the earlier American scientific copper engravings
are those found in the journals of the two major learned societies,
the American Philosophical Society at Philadelphia and the
American Academy of Arts and Sciences in Boston. These are of
particular interest because in most cases they are completely
native products drawn and engraved by Americans and used to illustrate articles written by Americans, a fact of some importance in this period when so many American books were simply
straight reprints of English originals. Volume I of the
Transactions of The American Philosophical Society, published
in 1771,[4] includes several astronomical plates drawn by David
Rittenhouse and engraved by Henry Dawkins to illustrate John
Ewing's piece on the 1769 transit of Venus. It also contains
several technological plates, including an illustration of a file-
cutting machine, unsigned but presumably also engraved by
Dawkins. One of the pronounced characteristics of almost all
eighteenth-century American technical illustration was a de-
ficiency in perspective. This can be seen again and again; it

is clearly apparent in Dawkins's file machine and also in the plates of Oliver Evans's <u>Millwright's Guide</u> (Philadelphia, 1795). Paul Revere could do no better; the plate of a hemp mill, engraved in 1765 for Edmund Quincy's <u>A Treatise of Hemp Husbandry</u>,[5] shows again a lack of knowledge of drawing in perspective. Just as is true today, models were frequently made to supplement the illustrations; another plate in the same volume of the <u>Transactions</u> shows a design by Richard Wells for a machine for pumping water from vessels at sea; the model for this has survived and is in the collections of the American Philosophical Society.[6]

The subsequent volumes of the <u>Transactions</u> have a number of illustrations of interest; Volume II, published in 1786, contains five plates engraved by James Poupard, including two illustrating Dr. Franklin's stove. These were not the first illustrations of Franklin's famous fireplace; an account of it was originally published with a fine folding engraved plate in Philadelphia in 1744.[7] Volume III, published in 1793, contains an attractive plate, engraved with considerable skill but un-signed, illustrating a botanical piece by Benjamin Smith Barton. This was among the earliest botanical prints executed in America, although there had been a number of finely illustrated books on American flora and fauna published in England during the earlier eighteenth century, one of the finest of which is Mark Catesby's celebrated work on the natural history of the Carolinas.[8] Six years later, in 1799, Volume IV of the <u>Transactions</u> included a well-executed engraving of a mouse-like animal called the American jerboa engraved by John Vallance (fig. 1). The author of the accompanying account, once again the prolific Barton, makes an interesting comment on this illustration:

> I am of the opinion, with the late M. deBuffon, that elaborate descriptions of animals are by no means necessary when we are enabled to give accurate re-presentations of these animals. The drawing which accompanies this paper has been made with great care, all the proportions being preserved with the most scrupulous nicety. My description, therefore, shall not be long.

Dipus Americanus.

American Jerboa.

Fig. 1. "American Jerboa." Engraving by John
Vallance, used with an article by Benjamin Smith Barton
in the <u>Transactions of the American Philosophical
Society</u>, IV (Philadelphia, 1799)

As with the botanical plate, this engraving too is an early example of its genre.

The same volume contains a handsome engraving of one of the favorite subjects of eighteenth-century American naturalists, the Crotalus durissus, or rattlesnake, executed by R. Scot. According to some writers of the period, this deadly serpent had the faculty of enchanting and attracting birds, squirrels, rabbits, and frogs; others thought that the snake inspired small animals with terror "to such a degree that they are from that moment deprived of their senses, attacked, as it were, with insanity";[9] still others said that these animals were violently affected and suffocated by a vapor and fetid emanation which the reptile diffused upon everything around it.[10] By the end of the eighteenth century most of these myths had been laid to rest, but interest in the rattlesnake continued; we will see him again shortly.

Turning briefly to the early volumes of the Memoirs of the Boston-based American Academy of Arts and Sciences we find several more noteworthy scientific and technical engravings. The first volume, published in 1785,[11] contains a fine plate of an air pump and a press (fig. 2). The air pump, incorporating several improvements, was designed and constructed by the Reverend John Prince, the famous instrument maker of Salem.[12] The case, or press, so very interesting to the student of the decorative arts, is not mentioned at all in the article. One gets the impression that it simply was not considered worth mentioning, and indeed, to the reader of 1785 interested in the design of the air pump, it was not. We cannot determine who drew the original draft; perhaps Prince himself did. The engraving is not signed, and it is not known if this particular air pump and its press were actually built and have survived to the present.[13] The second volume of the Memoirs, published in 1804, contains an interesting unsigned plate of "four remarkable fishes" caught near the Piscataqua in New Hampshire by William Peck of Kittery in 1794. This again is an early attempt to illustrate and describe American fish; the first complete book on American fish, actually the fishes of Massachusetts, unillustrated, was not published until 1833.[14] Finally, in Volume III, part 2 (1815),

Fig. 2. An air pump and press designed and constructed
by Rev. John Prince of Salem. Plate from <u>Memoirs of
the American Academy of Arts and Sciences</u>, I (Boston,
1785)

we find a most interesting kind of scientific illustration, a plate with a movable part. This engraving illustrates an attempt "to display at one view all the annual cycles of the equation of time in a complete revolution of the suns apogee." The movable paper disc rotates parabolically around an axis, the point at which it is attached to the larger plate with a piece of string. Earlier engravings with movable flaps or volvelles were not unknown in Europe and England in the sixteenth, seventeenth, and eighteenth centuries; they were used to illustrate and teach astronomy,[15] anatomy,[16] and perspective.[17]

Before turning our attention to new developments we should note in passing a few of the more important illustrated scientific books (as opposed to periodicals or journals) of the eighteenth century. One of the key works in any such discussion must be the first American illustrated medical book, William Smellie's An Abridgement of the Practice of Midwifery (Boston, 1786), with thirty-nine plates engraved by John Norman (fig. 3).[18] The quality of the illustrations here is rudimentary at best, due not so much to the limitations of the medium as to the limitations of the engraver; John Norman was not a craftsman of inordinate skill.

One of the most ambitious publishing undertakings in eighteenth-century America was the famous Dobson Encyclopaedia (18 vols., Philadelphia, 1790-97). All the plates (over five hundred) were reengraved in Philadelphia; this lengthy process gave employment to nearly every competent engraver in the city, and helped put the trade of engraving on a sound economic basis.[19] The production of the great Encyclopaedia marked a high point in eighteenth-century American publishing and signified, as Lawrence C. Wroth says, "the end of printing in America as a household craft and the beginning of its factory stage of development."[20] But, as with the Smellie book, this was a straight reprint of an English original and not, strictly speaking, a scientific book. The field of natural history was one of the few areas where there was significant original scientific publishing in eighteenth-century America. In order to collect his specimens, the naturalist made field trips; the records of

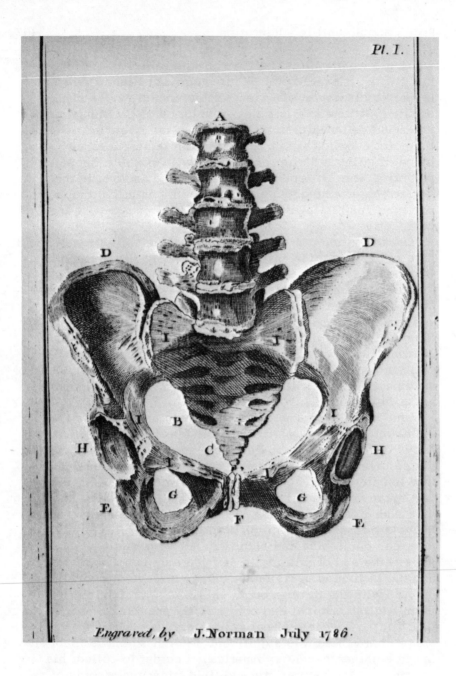

Pl. I.

Engraved, by J. Norman July 1786.

Fig. 3. Engraving by John Norman from William Smellie's An Abridgement of the Practice of Midwifery (Boston, 1786), pl. 1

these travels, often of great popular interest, frequently contained fine botanical and zoological illustrations. One of the earliest such works with plates published in America was William Bartram's Travels through North and South Carolina (Philadelphia, 1791).[21] The engravings here, in contrast to the John Norman plates, are quite skillfully done; they are not signed, but we can attribute them to the important Philadelphia engraver James Trenchard, after drawings by Bartram, on the basis of the frontispiece which is signed by Trenchard. The plate of the great soft-shelled tortoise of East Florida (fig. 4) is representative of the high quality of the illustrations. The careful observation and accurate representation is quite apparent and indeed is the underlying purpose of all illustrations made by and for scientists.

In summary, then, we must conclude that there was little important printed scientific illustration in eighteenth-century America; certainly little of international importance. This was not due to a lack of interest in science; it was simply that America was too young to be overly concerned with such matters. Science, then as now, was an international discipline, and the centers of scientific learning were London and Paris. Thus, in this light, it is not surprising that there were no American editions of Franklin's immensely and internationally important Experiments and Observations on Electricity published during the eighteenth century, although it went through five English and three French editions and was translated into German and Italian as well.[22] By the early nineteenth century, however, the picture gradually began to change, as ever-increasing numbers and kinds of scientific illustration appeared. It is to these that we now turn.

So far we have been concerned only with the slow and painstaking process of copper engraving. The opening of the nineteenth century saw rapidly expanding activity in all areas of scientific endeavor, especially in the natural and earth sciences, and faster and more accurate means of illustration were needed. The use of color and the development of new graphic techniques, primarily aquatint and lithography, marked the first half of the new century. The application of hand-brushed coloring to monochrome copper engravings is the earliest of these new techniques. Its primary

Fig. 4. "Turtle." Engraving attributed to James Trenchard, after a drawing by William Bartram for his Travels through North and South Carolina (Philadelphia, 1791)

and earliest scientific use was to further the accuracy of natural history illustrations. Although a few scattered instances could doubtless be found dating from the eighteenth century, one of the first and certainly one of the most important instances of this technique is found in Alexander Wilson's American Ornithology (Philadelphia, 1804-14), the first book published in America on American birds and the first great American color-plate book.[23] Through it, as Edwin Wolf, 2nd, has pointed out, American ornithology was elevated to a science.[24] A friend and unofficial student of William Bartram, Wilson was well qualified for his work on birds; he made all of the drawings himself and is said to have studied drawing, etching, and coloring with his friend Alexander Lawson, who made the engraved plates for the Ornithology.[25] The illustrations did, however, have their faults, from both aesthetic and ornithological points of view. Most of them are over-crowded-- in one instance two owls, a hawk, a thrush, and a bat are included in the same composition (fig. 5)! Nevertheless, this was an important book and in its day won international recognition; the illustrations achieved a degree of scientific accuracy both in line and color that surpassed all previous efforts. Wilson's relative obscurity today is due largely to the fact that his book was completely overshadowed some twenty years later by the great work of John James Audubon.

The color in Wilson's "Birds" was applied by hand; in 1818 the first book with plates printed in colors appeared. This is one instance where we can point to a historical "first" with certainty; this development has been well documented by historians of printing, particularly, in this case, by Stanley Epstein.[26] It is important at this point to make a clear distinction between printed and hand coloring. Epstein has defined them nicely: "Color plates or color prints may be defined as impressions printed in more than one color. They are to be distinguished from colored plates, wherein monochrome impressions have been painted with at least one additional color, either applied freehand or controlled by stencil or otherwise."[27] The earliest attempt in America at color printing seems to have been made by Benjamin Dearborn in Boston about 1812; his isolated experiment involved the application

John Dewey Library
Johnson State College
Johnson, Vermont

Fig. 5. Engraving by Alexander Lawson after a drawing by Alexander Wilson for his <u>American Ornithology</u> (Philadelphia, 1808-14), V-VI, pl. 50

of three colors to a typographically printed woodblock.[28]
Since it does not fall into the category of scientific illustration and since it apparently had few repercussions in the
graphic arts we can pass it by without comment. The first
American book with intaglio color plates (actually aquatints)
was Dr. Jacob Bigelow's American Medical Botany published
in Boston in three volumes in six parts in 1817, 1818, and
1820 (fig. 6). The plates in Volume I were printed in monochrome and colored by hand; all of Part I, Volume I, was done
in this way, and its plates all show a smooth gradation of
tone, an overall softness, and a high degree of finish--all
qualities which are characteristic of hand-colored engravings.
But this method proved too slow, and necessity forged a new
invention (or more accurately the reinvention of the aquatint
process as developed earlier in France). The advertisement
to Part I of Volume II states that "the style of engraving is
wholly new in this country and is one which has been successfully attempted only by the first artists of France." Dr.
Bigelow's own account tells the story in some detail:

> In 1818, I began to publish a work on American Medical
> Botany, to consist of six half-volumes with colored en-
> gravings. My attachment to botany and exaggerated
> estimate of therapeutics led me at that time to attach
> greater value to such an enterprise than I have since
> done. At any rate, I involved myself in the difficult
> responsibility of investigating the whole subject of
> furnishing sixty plates and sixty thousand colored en-
> gravings, which were to be engraved in outline and
> the impressions separately colored by hand.
>
> At that time the state of the arts was low and im-
> perfect in this country, and I soon found that I had
> greatly overrated the ability of my artists and under-
> rated the time and labor necessary to oversee the
> proceeding of the work. I experienced a considerable
> struggle between the pride which forbade the abandon-
> ment of the undertaking and the apparent impossibility
> of carrying it to completion. At that period both litho-
> graphy and photography were unknown. I came to the

Fig. 6. Intaglio color engraving (aquatint) from
Jacob Bigelow, American Medical Botany (Boston, 1817,
1818, 1820), I, pl. 48

conclusion that the only mode of extricating myself from the difficulty was to invent some new mode of printing the impressions at once in colors from the copperplates. After many trials and experiments a tolerably successful mode was discovered, which consisted in engraving the plates in aqua tinta thus producing a continuous surface, to the parts of which separate colors could be applied, and the surplus wiped off in different directions, so as not to interfere with each other. In this way the simple plates, or those with few colors, could be delivered from the press complete, without requiring to be re-touched. But those which had small or insulated spots were obliged to be finished with the pencil.

The principal difficulty was found in the surface of green leaves, which required a pigment suffi-ciently viscid to cause the constituent points or dots to adhere, or become fused together, and at the same time sufficiently transparent to admit the requisite shading, which was deepened in the proper places by lining or stippling as in common engrav-ings. After many trials, a compound of gamboge and Prussian blue ground in nut oil was found to answer the purpose sufficiently well, and a work-man could strike off a hundred complete copies in a day. Although these copies had a respectable appearance, and were sufficient for all scientific purposes, yet from the neutralizing effect of this oil they wanted the brilliancy of water colors laid on by the pencil. The aquatinting of colors, when duly improved, I have no doubt would have passed into profitable use, had not the invention of litho-graphy soon afterwards superceded its employment.[29]

Bigelow's work was well received and was given high praise by New England reviewers, one even making a favorable com-parison of Bigelow's color plates with those of Francois Andre Michaux's great work on the forest trees of North America.[30]

It reported "a conviction of the greater accuracy of the
figures in the Medical Botany, inferior as they certainly are
to those of Michaux in brilliancy of coloring, and in that
graceful, lively, finished representation of verdant nature
which evinces the perfection of modern art in Europe."[31]

In contrast to Bigelow's book is William P. C. Barton's
Vegetable Materia Medica, published in Philadelphia between
1817 and 1819; this contained the earliest intaglio colored
botanical plates produced in America (fig. 7). As did Bigelow,
Barton had difficulty in supplying the great number of plates
needed; he initially thought that the book would have a small
subscription and that he could color all the plates himself;
eventually he had six people coloring for him, and still could
not meet the demand. But he stuck to the time-honored method
of hand coloring. Indeed, he even went so far as to state
that:

> it is the next thing to impossible to present true imi-
> tations of plants by mere colored copperplates--that
> is to say, by impressions from engraved copper, in
> printing which, one, two, three or even more colors
> are put on the copper. Nothing comes near to nature
> and consequently nothing is faithful but colors laid
> on the colored (i.e. monochrome) impressions, by
> the pencil, under the direction of persons well
> acquainted with the real hues of plants.[32]

The two books are compared in a contemporary review:

> Bigelow's work comprises most of the plants figured
> in Barton's Materia Medica and many more beside;
> and although the prints of the latter derive a superior
> freshness from the circumstance that their colors
> were put on by the hand, whilst the former came
> colored from the plates, still the greater finish
> and fidelity of the figures in the Medical Botany
> entitle them to a higher regard than those of the
> Materia Medica.[33]

Fig. 7. Hand-colored intaglio engraving by William
P. C. Barton, for his <u>Vegetable Materia Medica</u>
(Philadelphia, 1817-19), pl. 42

The reviewer was perceptive (or perhaps he was just a
Bostonian favoring the efforts of a fellow Bostonian); in any
event the color-printing process was to have far-reaching
significance. With the constantly growing demand for all
sorts of color-plate books and the need for quicker means of
supplying these illustrations, the practice of hand coloring
began to die away in the late 1830s; the development of the
steam press and the chromolithograph in the 1840s and 1850s
killed it completely.

This brings us to the medium of lithography. The first
American lithograph is generally agreed to have been a landscape by Bass Otis published in the <u>Analectic Magazine</u> for
July 1819;[34] the first American scientific illustrations in the
new technique, as far as I can determine, were geological
sections executed by Barnet and Doolittle of New York and
published in Volume IV of the <u>American Journal of Science and
Art</u> in 1822.[35] The editors made specific mention of the new
plates:

> The great recommendation of lithography is the com-
> parative cheapness and dispatch, with which designs
> are executed by it; we may perhaps be able hereafter
> to speak with more precision upon these points. All
> the drawings in the present number are printed on stone
> by Messrs. BARNET & DOOLITTLE whom we are happy
> to introduce to our readers as artists in this compara-
> tively new department. Having availed themselves in
> Paris of a regular course of practical instruction, they
> have brought to this country, not only the skill but
> the peculiar materials and press necessary to the
> execution of the art and are now establishing them-
> selves in New-York. The designs in this number
> are, by no means, presented as <u>chef-d'-oeuvres</u> in
> lithography, but merely as accurate representations
> of the objects, with sufficient neatness for designs
> of the class to which they belong. Messrs. Barnet
> & Doolittle have in their possession, a great variety
> of lithographic prints, which sufficiently evince the
> adaptedness of the art to an elegant as well as

common style of execution. The finest things done
in this way are really very beautiful; and they possess a softness which is peculiarly their own. Still,
lithography is not a <u>rival</u>, it is merely an <u>auxialiary</u>
to copper plate engraving, which, especially in the
higher branches of the art, must still retain the pre-
eminence which it possesses. But the regular introduction of lithography into this country must still be
a subject of congratulation; and we trust the American
public will give this fine art vigor by an adequate
patronage. [36]

The art of lithography did indeed thrive in America, though
curiously enough the <u>American Journal of Science and Art</u> gives
us no further information about it. The medium was particularly well suited to the exacting requirements of scientific
illustration because the artists themselves could draw directly
on the stone rather than having to go through the intermediary
of the engraver, in which process something was always lost,
no matter how skilled the engraver. Among the earliest botanical lithographs in America were those published in New York
in 1822 in James Edward Smith's <u>Grammar of Botany</u>. [37] The
preliminaries state:

> The publisher feels a becoming gratification in inform-
> ing the readers of the work that the beautiful and
> highly appropriate drawings, which so highly embellish
> it, are specimens of American lithography. They are
> from the pencil of Mr. Stansbury, and were executed
> by the lithographic press of Barnet and Doolittle of
> this city.

What would appear to be one of the earliest uses of lithography
for medical illustrations appeared in Sir Anthony Astley Cooper's
<u>Lectures</u>, published in Boston in 1825 and 1828. The third
volume includes two plates illustrating hip disease; they were
drawn by William Pendleton and printed by John Pendleton,
Boston's pioneer lithographer. [38]

All the lithographs mentioned thus far have been in monochrome; by the third decade of the nineteenth century the use

of color was becoming widespread. Philadelphia quickly became the center for lithographic artists and printing firms, and
together they established a sort of mass-production system of
color illustration. The best artists sketched birds and animals
in habitat and transferred their originals to stone. The lithographic presses produced the print, which was then taken over
by the "lady-colorers" with the artist's sketch as a guide.

One of the foremost publications of the day, with attractive
plates of reasonable scientific accuracy, was the Cabinet of
Natural History, begun in 1831. Published by the landscape
painter Thomas Doughty, it is not surprising that the Cabinet
had handsome color plates. Doughty himself contributed
twenty-three illustrations to the first year's output; each of
his prints was specifically signed "from nature and on stone
by T. Doughty." The coloring was obviously executed with
skill and care; uniform high quality and an allover color
harmony suggest that the Doughty establishment was carefully
supervised. In addition to the considerable degree of accuracy
of the bird and animal drawings (fig. 8), Doughty's plates are
valued for their landscape and habitat backgrounds. But they
are prized most highly for their expressive and severely honest
view of nature. As Edgar P. Richardson has said in his
Painting in America:

> Doughty began to paint because of an intense love of
> nature. He was an enthusiastic hunter and fisherman,
> who found something in the wooded hills and lonely
> streams of this country that had to be expressed. His
> art never lost the impression of its origin. Each of
> his pictures is built out of the emotion of communion
> with nature. [39]

Doughty's was but one of many similarly illustrated publications of the thirties--natural history, horticulture, agriculture,
views, Indian portraits--a vast array of subject matter came
before the brushes of the lady colorists. All this collaboration between artist, publisher, lithographer, and colorist was
not without its cumulative effect in spurring on a new and far-
reaching process of printing in color.

Fig. 8. "Wild Turkey from Nature." Color lithograph
by M. E. D. Brown for <u>Cabinet of Natural History</u>
(Philadelphia, 1831), III, pl. 1

We have already seen the pioneer efforts of Jacob Bigelow, but we have not mentioned at all the many and varied experimental developments in color printing in France and England.[40] These were important in the overall picture, but we cannot go into them here; suffice it to say that the groundwork for color printing in America was laid by those lithographers working here who had been trained in England and on the Continent. Peter S. Duval of France, the Rosenthals from Poland, William Sharp and Thomas Sinclair, both Englishmen, all contributed to the development of the chromolithograph.

Before that was achieved, however, there were several intermediate achievements which we should note in passing. The first of these was the so-called tint stone. This was a second stone, inked in a contrasting tint, usually tan, and impressed over the entire surface; the effect was to soften the original tint. The next step was the lithotint, the laying of several tints from one stone to paper.[41] This was accomplished by the application of chemical inks (neutral tints--not colors), brushed into the original design and impressed once, in flat tones. It was common practice for lithotints to be finished with colors applied by hand. One of the finest examples of the lithotint process was John Edward Holbrook's <u>North American Herpetology</u>, originally published in four volumes in Philadelphia, 1836-38, with a five-volume second edition in 1842 (fig. 9). The history of this book is complex; it is related fairly reliably in Whitman Bennett's checklist of American color-plate books.[42] Volume IV of the original edition is so extremely rare that its existence has been denied. "If a correct four volume first edition could be assembled," Bennett tells us, "it would be extremely valuable, the only limit being the fact that the public prefers birds and flowers to snakes and turtles. It is ten times rarer, right and complete, than the giant folio Audubon."[43] It is indeed a handsome and beautiful book, describing and illustrating the reptiles inhabiting the United States. The plates were drawn on stone by prominent lithographic artists of the day, including George Lehman, Albert Newsam, J. H. Richard, and James Queen; they were printed by Duval. A few plates have the specific imprint "Lithotint by J. H. Richard." In addition to serpents, there are turtles, frogs, alligators, and lizards. The conventions of

Fig. 9. "Rattlesnake." Lithotint printed by Peter S. Duval for John Edward Holbrook, North American Herpetology (Philadelphia, 1836-38)

modern scientific illustrations have been observed throughout;
two views, always taken from the same point, lateral and reverse (anal), and a uniform scale (fig. 10). In sum, Holbrook's
Herpetology is one of the greatest American color-plate books
of natural history and a major contribution to the development
of modern scientific illustration.

Finally, we come to the lithography actually printed in
colors, the so-called chromolithograph. The actual term
"chromo" has come to mean, in general, the bright and garish
multicolored prints produced in quantity on steam presses from
mid-century on. But technically speaking, so far as I can
determine, it is correct to call all lithographs printed in colors
by this term. The chromo was printed from a series of stones,
each with a different color. The earliest illustrations printed
in this manner are difficult to identify positively, but a work
that appeared in 1841 is certainly a contender for the honor.
Morris Mattson's The American Vegetable Practice, published
in Boston in that year, has colored illustrations which, the
author informs us, in his preface:

> have been procured at great expense, and were executed
> by a new process, invented by Mr. Sharp,[44] recently of
> London, being the first of the kind ever issued in the
> United States. The different tints were produced by a
> series of printed impressions, the brush not having
> been used in giving effect or uniformity to the color-
> ing. Connoisseurs in the arts have spoken of them in
> terms of admiration, and Mr. Sharp will no doubt suc-
> ceed in bringing his discovery to a still greater degree
> of perfection.

Sharp's plates occasionally betray their origin by the failure
of each separate color to register precisely. In the "White
Pond Lily" (fig. 11) one can see--in the original print if not
in the photograph--three separate colors around the edges of
the leaf. Other plates that show faint traces of faulty registration are the "Purple Lady's Slipper" and the "Bittersweet."
As in many of the plates we have seen, these have a considerable degree of beauty and aesthetic appeal quite apart from

Fig. 10. "Turtle." Lithotint printed by Peter S. Duval for John Edward Holbrook, North American Herpetology (Philadelphia, 1836-38)

White Pond Lily.   Nymphaea Odorata.

W. Sharp Lith del.   Sharp Michelin & Co ?

Fig. 11. "White Pond Lily." Chromolithograph by
William Sharp for Morris Mattson, <u>The American
Vegetable Practice</u> (Boston, 1841)

their scientific purposes; it is not surprising that interest in these early books of science and natural history has soared in recent years. Early American science is still a relatively unexplored field, and there is room for all manner of research and study. Perhaps some diligent scholar will undertake a really thorough and systematic study of American scientific illustrations--it will be a rich and rewarding study. I have only scratched the surface.

NOTES

1. Paul H. Oehser, Sons of Science (New York, 1949), p. 9.

2. Letter to the author, from Whitfield J. Bell, Jr., Nov. 17, 1969.

3. Whitfield J. Bell, Jr., Early American Science: Needs and Opportunities for Study (Williamsburg, Va., 1955), p. 9.

4. A detailed account of the publication and reception of this first volume is given in Brooke Hindle, The Pursuit of Science in Revolutionary America (Chapel Hill, N.C., 1956), pp. 141-45.

5. Illustrated in Clarence S. Brigham, Paul Revere's Engravings (Worcester, Mass., 1954), pl. 4, pp. 16-17.

6. Described and illustrated in Robert P. Multhauf, Catalogue of Instruments and Models in the Possession of the American Philosophical Society (Philadelphia, 1961), p. 46 and fig. 17.

7. Benjamin Franklin, An Account of the New Invented Pennsylvania Fire-Places Wherein Their Construction and Manner of Operation Is Particularly Explained (Philadelphia, 1744).

8. The Natural History of Carolina, Florida, and the Bahama Islands (London, 1731-43). Catesby has been called "a pioneer in the field of scientific illustration . . . he not only made the drawings for his book but studied etching so that he could make the plates himself " (Bruce R. Voeller and Paul F. Cranefield (Three Centuries of Botany in North America, an Exhibit [New York, 1967], p. 10.)

9. American Philosophical Society, Transactions, IV (1799), 363.

10. Ibid., p. 367.

11. Details of publication are given in Hindle, pp. 266-67.

12. For notes on Prince, see David P. Wheatland and Barbara Carson, The Apparatus of Science at Harvard, 1765-1800 (Cambridge, Mass., 1968), passim. According to Wheatland "a detailed study of the man, his ideas, and his products" remains to be written. See also Silvio A. Bedini, Early American Scientific Instruments and Their Makers (Washington, 1964), pp. 24-25.

13. I am indebted to Miss Rodris Roth for informing me that the Smithsonian Institution owns an eighteenth-century American air pump and press but not, apparently, this one. The Library Company of Philadelphia also owns one; see Edwin Wolf, 2nd, and Robert C. Smith, "A Press for Penn's Pump," Art Quarterly, Autumn 1961, pp. 227-48.

14. Jerome V. C. Smith, Natural History of the Fishes of Massachusetts (Boston, 1833).

15. Thomas Harrington, Science Improved; or, the Theory of the Universe (London, 1774).

16. Anothomia oder Abcontersectung eines Weydes leybg (Strasbourg, 1538), folio broadside of female figure with superimposed movable flaps showing various parts of the anatomy. I am indebted to Timothy Trace of Peekskill, N.Y., for this reference.

17. Joseph Moxon, Practical Perspective; or, Perspective Made Easie (London, 1670).

18. On Norman, see Samuel A. Green, Remarks on the Boston Magazine . . . and John Norman, Engraver (Cambridge, Mass., 1904), and Charles H. Hart, "Some Notes concerning John Norman, Engraver," Proceedings of the Massachusetts Historical Society, XXXVIII (1904). On the history of the Smellie book, see K. F. Russell, British Anatomy, 1525-1800 (Melbourne, 1963), p. 26, also nos. 753-66.

19. Rollo Silver, The American Printer, 1787-1825 (Charlottesville, Va., 1967), p. 153.

20. The Colonial Printer (Portland, Maine, 1938), p. 294.

21. The interesting story behind the publication of this important book is told in Hindle, pp. 310-11.

22. I. Bernard Cohen, Benjamin Franklin's Electrical Experiments (Cambridge, Mass., 1941).

23. The full and very interesting story of the publication of this great book is given in Elsa G. Allen, "History of American Ornithology before Audubon," American Philosophical Society Transactions, XLI, pt. 3 (1951).

24. Bibliothesauri; or Jewels from the Shelves of the Library Company of Philadelphia (Philadelphia, 1966), p. 66.

25. According to G. C. Groce and D. H. Wallace, The New-York Historical Society's Dictionary of Artists in

America, 1564-1860 (New Haven, 1957), p. 388, Lawson "won international recognition" for his work on the plates for Wilson's "Birds." Lawson himself made a comment on the state of engraving in America in 1794 which sheds useful light on our present topic: "Thackara and Vallance were partners when I came to Philadelphia. I engraved with them two years. They thought themselves artists, and that they knew every part of the art; and yet their art consisted in copying, in a dry, stiff manner with the graver, the plates for the Encyclopaedia, all their attempts at etching having miscarried. The rest of their time, and that of all others at this period, was employed to engrave card plates, with a festoon of wretched flowers and bad writing--then there was engraving on type metal--silver plate--watches--dog plates--dog collars and silver buttons, with an attempt at seal cutting. Such was the state of engraving in 1794" (William Dunlap, A History of the Rise and Progress of the Arts of Design in the United States, new ed. [Boston, 1918], II, 123-24; quoted in Silver, p. 154).

26. "The Earliest American Color Plates," Printing and Graphic Arts, IV (1956), 42-45.

27. Ibid., 42.

28. Emma Forbes Waite, Benjamin Dearborn," Old-Time New England, XLII (1951), 44-47.

29. George E. Ellis, Memoir of Jacob Bigelow, M.D., L.L.D. (Cambridge, Mass., 1880), p. 55 ff.

30. The North American Silva: or, A Description of the Forest Trees of the United States, Canada and Nova Scotia (Paris, 1818-19).

31. "Botany of the United States," North American Review, XIII (1821), 100-134; quoted in Epstein, p. 44.

32. Barton, second advertisement to his Flora of North America (Philadelphia, 1821), quoted in Epstein, p. 43.

33. See note 31.

34. Charles Henry Taylor, "Some Notes on Early American Lithography," American Antiquarian Society Proceedings, XXXII (1922), 68-69; Joseph Jackson,"Bass Otis, America's First Lithographer," Pennsylvania Magazine of History and Biography, XXXVII (1913), 385-94.

35. A few notes on Barnet and Doolittle are given by Taylor, ibid., pp. 69-71.

36. Pp. 169-70.

37. I have not actually seen a copy of this book, I obtained this reference from a valuable manuscript study by Emma Forbes Waite, "Development of American Lithography with Emphasis on Color Printing," 1951, deposited in the library of the American Antiquarian Society. Miss Waite's study should be edited and published.

38. On the Pendletons, see Harry T. Peters, America on Stone (Garden City, N.Y., 1931).

39. Painting in America, the Story of 450 Years (New York, 1956), p. 57.

40. See Ruari McLean, Victorian Book Design and Color Printing (London, 1963), especially chaps. 4, 5, 7, and 11.

41. McLean defines lithotint as follows: "the technique called lithotint (the name given to the process patented by Hullmandel in 1840) uses one (or more) colors in addition to black; [Hullmandel] initiated a whole series of collections of topographical sketches drawn on stone, tinted with one or more lithographic tints, and sometimes, in addition, colored by hand. The earliest plates by this method were imitations of wash drawings on tinted paper, with highlights added. Neutral tints, and not colors, were used, often with very great skill and subtelty" (ibid., p. 55).

42. A Practical Guide to American Nineteenth Century Color Plate Books (New York, 1949), p. 57.

43. Ibid.

44. William Sharp (ca. 1820-?), on whom see Groce and Wallace, p. 571.

In the demonstration of printmaking by the intaglio
process (engraving and etching), Jay Cantor inks the
plate, while Martin Weil blots the dampened paper.
This etching press was made by Karl Krause, ca. 1910,
in Leipzig, Germany.

JACOB PERKINS, WILLIAM CONGREVE, AND COUNTERFEIT PRINTING IN 1820

Elizabeth Harris

SIDEROGRAPHY, compound plate printing, and medal engraving are three early nineteenth-century printing processes which were all off the mainstream of the graphic arts and almost useless to the artist-engraver of the day. In order to put these technical oddities into their setting, two features of the period--its great inventiveness and its acute problem with counterfeit--must be considered.

The inventiveness was, at one level, a fashion for sheer novelty. So far as printing processes were concerned, a wealth of delightful and ingenious suggestions was put forward by all kinds of people for new ways of making marks. Only a few were practical. In the late eighteenth century an English engraver named Cumberland claimed to have printed from copper, silver, brass, tin foil, bismuth, pewter, plaster of Paris, paper, wood, glass, stone, seashell, tortoise shell, Pontipool ware, and carrot.[1] Thirty years later some prints made by a new process, "acrography," were greeted by an editor with the remark, "Only one of half a hundred experiments which have been submitted to us in tangible form."[2] And in 1859 a book was published in London with the express purpose of sorting out the confusion of new processes. Its title page lists 156 names of processes.[3]

Most of these processes were already forgotten a year or two after they were introduced, partly because it was difficult to persuade the printing trade to abandon its old, tried ways. The three processes we are considering owed much of their success to the fact that they were carefully placed in a field that was not served satisfactorily by the ordinary

processes--the field of security printing. Bank notes, certificates, paper seals, admission tickets, lottery tickets --all
these were printed products which represented money and
offered profit to the good counterfeiter. So long as the
genuine article was produced by the everyday process of
copper engraving any competent engraver was qualified to
forge. Many did.

One of the great drawbacks to copper engraving for bank
notes was the limited life of the copperplate. For a bank with
a large circulation a copperplate would have a printing life of
not many days. After a few thousand impressions it would be
showing visible signs of wear and would be returned to the
engraver's shop for retouching. But a retouched plate is
never the same as the original plate. A few thousand more,
and some retouchings more, and the plate would have to be
discarded. So the larger banks employed teams of engravers
continuously working on new plates and touching up old ones.
As a result there was considerable variety among notes that
were supposed to be the same; so the official engravers would
include some secret signs in the engraving to show its
genuineness--apparently accidental flaws and scratches that
could be recognized by the bank officials. Of course, it was
essential to the success of this system that the telltale signs
were not publicly known. Consequently the forger had an
easy time. Any reasonably good copy of a bank note could be
passed off for genuine, and who but a bank official could know
the difference? [4]

It was suggested in England that the rather new process
of lithography might be used for printing money, but the
committee appointed to examine the problem saw trouble there
too. Lithography, they reported, was a "discovery as applied
to the subject of forgery more to be dreaded than encouraged." [5]
So there existed a challenge to work out a printing process that
could not be copied easily. Sir William Congreve and Jacob
Perkins were two of the men who rose to meet this challenge.

Congreve was a flamboyant English baronet, engineer,
soldier, and father of many inventions, of which the most
famous was a military rocket. Among more important things
he described and patented a number of perpetual motion

machines. Perkins was a brilliant engineer from Massachusetts who, it seems, took a special delight in exposing the
inventors of perpetual motion machines. The two men met
when Perkins, after considerable success in this country,
went to England in 1819, and they quickly became rivals in
the fight against counterfeit.

Perkins had been interested in security printing for a
long time.[6] In 1799 he had produced what he called a "check
protector," "stereotype plate," or a composite plate for printing on the backs of bank notes. He was encouraged by the
Commonwealth of Massachusetts, and in the early years of
the nineteenth century the check protector was used by a
number of banks. In 1809 he improved the process. It went
like this:

A steel plate was first engraved with any intricate design.
Often Perkins used engraving machines and engine lathes to
make complicated linear patterns. The engraved plate was
then cut up into strips, and each strip was separated from its
neighbor with a strip of plain steel. The alternating strips
were clamped together and used to stamp their design onto
another plate of a softer metal. That could be used as the
printing plate, or if it was necessary to reverse the image
again, it could be transferred once again to a plate of yet
softer metal. Thus, the printed bank note would have a
striped design made up of engraved and plain bands. In
order to find out whether a note was genuine, one simply
folded the paper to bring two neighboring edges of engraved
strips together, and if it was real the lines would coincide
and make a single perfect design. If it was a fake, the coincidence would not be perfect. The counterfeiter would not
have the equipment to transfer the design on the strips; so
he would have to copy by hand the finished striped plate
and in that way he could not possibly get such perfect
coincidence. The very simple test of notes was one of the
great advantages of Perkins's plates; a note could be proved
against itself. It did not have to be compared with another
that was known to be good.

Perkins tried this technique with metals other than steel,
but steel was the best because it was hard wearing. Even

soft steel plate would last considerably longer than copper in
printing. Hard steel was better still but it was too difficult
to engrave. Perkins got around this last difficulty by juggling
with hard and soft steels, and it was this, rather than the
cutting up of plates, that became the core of his process in
its final and most successful form. In that final form, the
process came to be known as siderography, which means
"engraving on steel." The process was this:

An engraving was made either by hand or machine on a
thick plate of soft steel. The design was in reverse, just
like an ordinary engraving. The steel was then casehardened
in a furnace, but only superficially so that it would not
crack with the heating and cooling. This plate was called
the die. Next a small cylinder of soft steel was rolled and
pressed repeatedly over the now hard engraving on the die
until it picked up the engraved design, which came out as a
positive, relief design instead of a reversed, intaglio design. The steel cylinder was called the roll. Next it was
hardened in turn and rolled over a number of other plates of
soft steel to press its design down into them--once more, as
an intaglio reversed design. Finally those plates were
hardened, and they were the finished printing plates. By
this process any number of identical plates could be made,
or alternately, a single design could be repeated any number
of times on one plate (fig. 1).

In 1810 Perkins patented his process in England and,
through an agent, submitted it to the Bank of England, but it
was turned down. That Bank was not yet ready to abandon
copper engraving, although it had several times invited suggestions for alternatives from the public. There was some
prejudice among the old-school engravers against steel
engraving. In 1813, it was reported by the Bank engravers
that Perkins's steel plates were hard to engrave, that they
cracked in the hardening process, and that they lasted no
longer than copperplates.

The problem of counterfeit became more and more serious,
and in Britain the Bank of England was taking the brunt of it.
All else being equal, the wider the circulation of a bank's
notes the better the chances of a forged note going undetected.

Fig. 1. Back of note from the London Journal of Arts and Sciences, I (1820), pl. XIX.
7 1/2" x 3 7/8"

In 1801 there had been 3,000 forged Bank of England notes discovered. By 1817 the number had gone up tenfold to 31,000.[7]
It had become a matter of serious public concern, and the
general opinion seemed to be that the Bank of England had
never grappled with the problem. On the one hand it offered
great temptation to the many engravers who could only make a
meager honest living, and on the other the penalty for the
offender was unnecessarily severe--death or transportation to
the penal colonies of Australia. In 1818 the Bank was forced
to reopen a public competition for ways of defeating forgery.
It was this competition which took Perkins to England in 1819,
determined to present his process himself and thus to avoid
the failure of 1813. He submitted his process, siderography,
to the committee appointed as judges for the Bank of England.
Among the committee members was Sir William Congreve.
This was Perkins's first encounter with Congreve.

William Congreve had not been involved with printing for
as long as Perkins, nor was his interest as permanent. He
dabbled in many things. His printing process had one thing
in common with Perkins's in that the printing plate was composite. It was called compound plate printing.

A compound print was a color relief print, made in two or
more colors, which were all printed at the same time from the
composite block (fig. 2). Like Perkins's siderography, the
security lay in the way the block was made. An extra process was involved, and no engraver with ordinary equipment
could have imitated the effect of this extra process.

A thick plate of brass was cut into a stencil pattern, with
holes right through the plate. It was put face down on a
flat surface, and another softer metal was melted and poured
over the stencil plate to fill up the holes and cover the back
of it. When the two metals had cooled and solidified they
could be separated to make two perfectly fitting plates. They
were put together and patterns of lettering were engraved on
them, making the design cross the surfaces of the two metals.
When the plates were to be printed they were separated,
inked each in a different color, fitted together again, and
printed as one block--in relief like woodcuts.

Fig. 2. Compound printing. A specimen bank note engraved by Robert Branston for William Congreve, 1820s. 4 1/4" x 8 1/4". John Johnson Collection, Bodleian Library, Oxford

The printed effect was a design made up of continuous white lines crossing different colored grounds. The edges of the colors would meet exactly but never overlap. This was the feature that would be so difficult to produce by any conventional printing process. Normally each color is printed at a separate impression. It is possible to get remarkably close registration between colors, but never as close as this (fig. 3).

In spite of the fact that he was one of the judges, Congreve entered his compound printing for the Bank competition. It came to a choice between his process, Perkins's siderography, and one other. After much debate the contract was given to the third party, but neither Perkins nor Congreve considered the race to be over, and there followed a public skirmish between them in which each tried to prove the superiority of his process. Congreve opened with a booklet about his process and a set of copies of what he called "the American plan" by which he hoped to prove that Perkins's plates were not inimitable.[8] Perkins replied by saying that the imitations were a failure, and as such they provided a better advertisement than he could have thought of himself. Perkins even offered to "furnish every purchaser of Sir William Congreve's work with the original notes, free of charge, . . . desirous of giving the greatest possible publicity to Sir W.'s imitations."[9] Curiously, English popular feeling was on the side of Perkins, who had brought a party of American engravers and engineers with him while the French who were watching the episode favored Congreve. The French pointed out that their own revolutionary government had been using some transfer processes similar to Perkins's back in the eighteenth century.[10]

As it turned out, neither party ever won a contract with the Bank of England. After a few years the Bank decided that even the new process they had adopted--which was another multicolor process--was not good enough, and they reverted to copper engraving. Perkins and Congreve meanwhile had collected as much business as they needed from the many private English banks. Perkins wrote to a friend "we only wish for the honour of the thing that the Bank should at

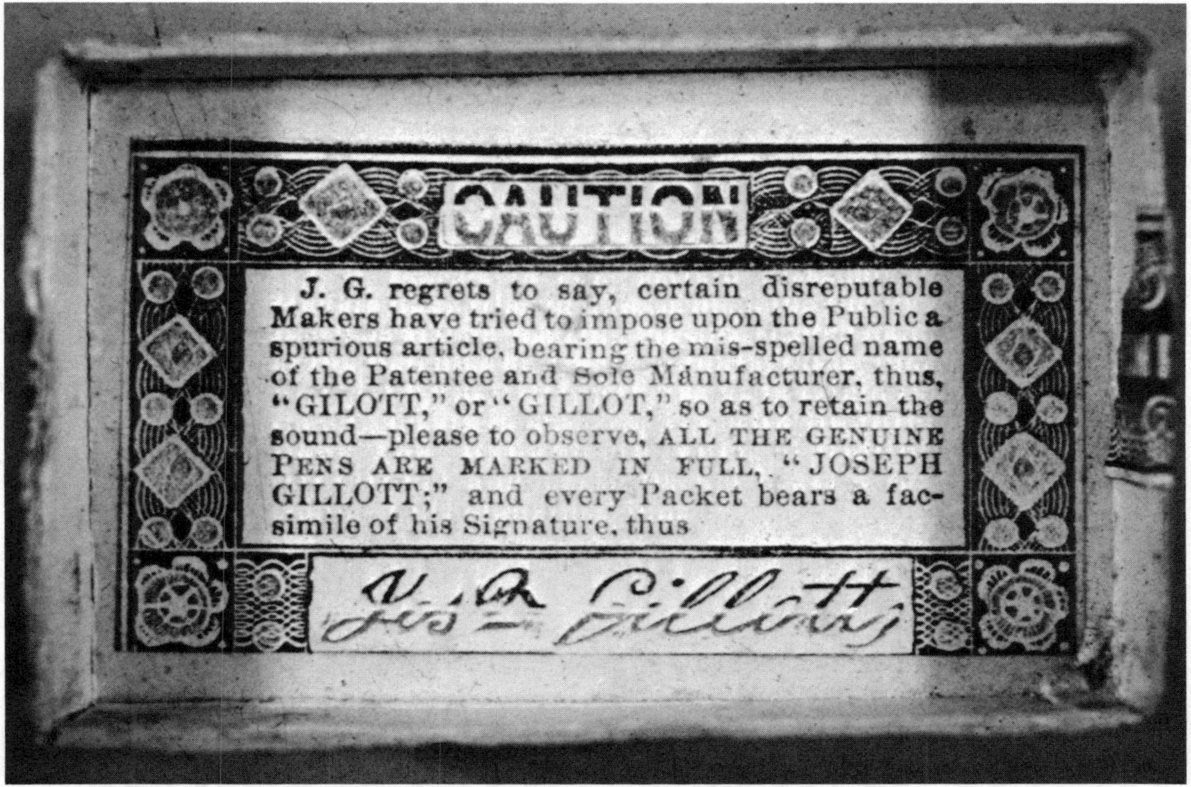

Fig. 3. Compound printed label inside a pen-nib box. Mid-nineteenth century. John Johnson Collection, Bodleian Library, Oxford

present adopt our plan as we shall make more money than we expected to by the adoption of it by them."[11] Ironically, both processes were sometimes used on the same private bank note. The face would be one of Perkins's plates and the back would be a compound print. Some years later, when both men were dead, their processes were submitted for a national postage stamp competition, and both were selected. Perkins's siderography was used for the first penny blacks, and a form of Congreve's process for the second issue of the stamped envelopes.

Technically the two processes had little in common, for siderography was an intaglio process in black and white, and compound printing was a color relief process, but they found and shared much the same market. Apart from the many banks that used them in the 1820s, they were both used for manufacturers' labels, especially patent medicines. Inimitability was one reason for the choice, but there were others. Both processes could give a virtually unlimited run on any image, since the plates could be made to reproduce or perpetuate themselves, Perkins's by transfer and Congreve's by casting. But above all, both processes allowed a motif to be repeated with variations. For example, the brass key plate of Congreve's process could have several secondary plates cast upon it; each one could then be engraved with different lettering (fig. 4). In siderography the separate elements of a design could be combined and repeated in any number of ways (fig. 5). Because of this fact both processes were used for books in series, Congreve's color prints usually for the covers and Perkins's more delicate steel engravings for the title pages. Both were used for tickets, invitations, and certificates. Compound printing, being colorful and often rather crude and broad in character, usually took care of the cheaper, more popular segment of the market, such as lottery tickets, while siderography was used for more elegant productions such as formal invitations and private bookmarks.

To bring the histories up to date, siderography is still the method used in producing postage stamps in many countries. It has been used in this country ever since 1847.

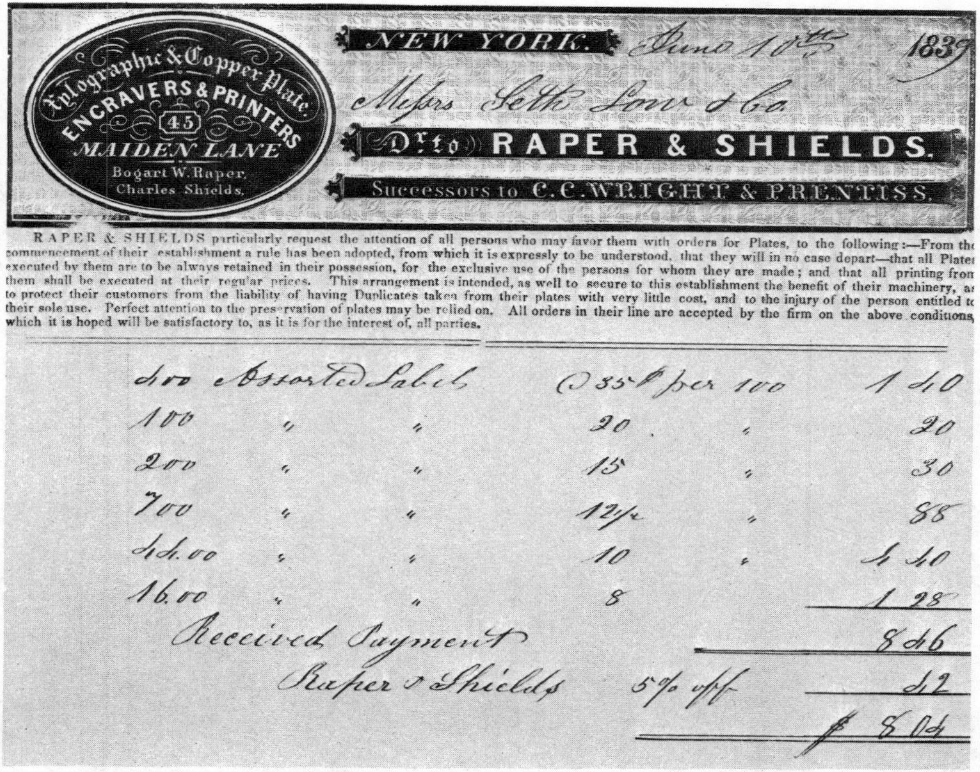

Fig. 4. Compound printed bill-heading, 1839. 1 3/4" x 7 1/2".
Warshaw Collection, Smithsonian Institution

Fig. 5. Bank note from the _London Journal of Arts and Sciences_, I (1820), pl. XIX.
7 1/2" x 3 7/8"

Compound plate printing was used in this country and Europe
in the nineteenth century. So far as I know its last stronghold was Somerset House, a government office building in
London, where it was still being used to print medicine seals
in the 1920s.[12] But even today one can see designs that owe
their form to compound printing, particularly designs which
carry the implication of authority or a seal of authenticity,
like those of warranties or token money.

Figure 6 is an example of another engraving process called
medal engraving. Technically it had nothing in common
with the other two processes, but it was another odd contemporary that found its way to bank notes as a form of security
because of its oddness.

Medal engravings were made by a machine which was a
cousin of the pantograph. A pantograph was a device on which
two connected tracing points were attached to the angles of a
hinged parallelogram in such a way that when one point was
made to trace a design, the other followed its movements
exactly, drawing an identical design of the same size or
larger or smaller. The original pattern for medal engraving
was not a drawing but a medal, bas-relief sculpture, flat
fossil, or any other design which was molded in low
relief.

The medal-engraving machine was more complicated than
the pantograph because it worked in three dimensions. The
point at the end of one tracing arm was drawn in a straight
line across the surface of the medal. The second point
followed the movements of the first but turned the rising and
falling line on to its side and traced it onto a sheet of
paper, a copperplate, or a lithographic stone. This gave a
single profile of the medal. Next, the two arms were both
moved up about a 0.01 of an inch, and a second profile was
drawn, next to the first. This was repeated all the way
across the medal until there was a series of parallel profiles
representing its whole surface. It was the difference between
each line and its neighbor that gave the illusion of depth.
Wherever a series of lines was climbing up the side of a
slope of the medal the lines would be spread apart and
would give the effect of light striking that part of the medal.

Belisarius.

Fig. 6. Medal engraving by Asa Spencer. 5 1/8" x
3 5/8". Warshaw Collection, Smithsonian Institution

As they fell down the other side of the slope the lines would crowd together to give a shaded side.

Medal engraving was not the invention of any one man. It seems that the machines were known in France in the late eighteenth century and were probably used for ornamenting metal surfaces such as watchcases, but not for printing. In 1816 the author of a turner's manual thought of making medal engravings as printing plates, and published the plates in his book together with a description of the machine.[13] At about the same time an American engineer from Perkins's circle, Christian Gobrecht, made a similar machine apparently quite independently. Two friends of Gobrecht's, Asa Spencer and Joseph Saxton, also from Philadelphia, built themselves machines. These were the beginnings, in France and in Philadelphia. In the 1820s things started to move to London. Spencer was one of the engineers who went to England in 1819 with Jacob Perkins, and he took his machine with him. He left it when he returned home three years later. Then Saxton, the other Philadelphia engineer, went to England in 1829 and built there an improved form of the machine. A French mechanic, Achille Collas, built a machine following the instructions in the turner's manual of 1816, and friends of his went to England with a scheme for engraving and publishing all the coins in the British Museum. At about the same time Spencer, now back in the States, sent some engravings to his friend Jacob Perkins in London, and suddenly a great dispute took place. It was essentially a three-cornered fight over priority and mechanical quality. Saxton, the American in England, had shown his machine to a number of people, and one of them, John Bate, quietly took out a patent in his own name. When the French arrived with their plan for engraving the British Museum collection, the English protested that such an important contract should not be given to a foreign party. Eventually it was all settled by a parliamentary committee,[14] but not before Saxton had left, "disgusted with the turn matters had taken,"[15] and had sold his machine and returned to Philadelphia where he joined the Mint.

The question of quality, which was raised during the debate, was quite an interesting one. Once you have grasped the

principle of medal engraving it seems to have the beauty and
simplicity of a great idea, but there was actually a flaw in
the theory which produced distortion in the final engraving.
As an illustration, take a round medal showing the head of
a man, full face. Since the medal is round, of course the
engraving will be round. Suppose the highest point of the
medal, the tip of the nose, is dead in the center and is 1/4
inch higher than the field. In the medal it is in the center,
but in the engraving it will be thrown 1/4 inch away from the
center. That is no help to the numismatist wanting to take
accurate measurements between points on the medal. Sometimes the distortion was bad enough to make a beautiful face
grotesque. After all, a bas-relief is already severely fore-
shortened; it is designed to be seen from the front only. If
you take an oblique view you can no longer see the fore-
shortening. The engraving machine did not even take an
oblique view. It took a series of edge-on profiles and put
them together to be read as a full-face view (fig. 7).

All three contending parties claimed to have solved this
problem. Only Saxton explained how. On his machine the
tracing arm took a path on an oblique plane across the medal.
The second arm ignored all movement up and down--which
was the movement that did the damage--and recorded only
the horizontal movement of the first arm.

The debate resolved nothing. The outcome was that each
engraver-engineer went back to his own country more determined than ever to make a success of his machine. Artists
would have little use for medal engravings, so special applications had to be found. A rather small number of albums
of medal engravings was published. Occasionally the process was used for maps, and the results were most attractive, but they were only as accurate as the relief model that
had to be made for each one. Apart from this, medal engraving was used in ways remarkably similar to those for which
the other two processes, siderography and compound plate
printing, had proved useful--ornamental borders, trade cards,
packaging, labeling (fig. 8), and all the forms of printing
that represented money--checks, bills, tickets, bank notes
(figs. 9, 10, 11). It is still used, from time to time, on bank
notes.

Fig. 7. Medal engraving showing some distortion of the
face. Engraved by "W. L. Ormsby's Pentographer."
5 1/4" x 5". Warshaw Collection, Smithsonian Institution

Fig. 8. Sheet of labels with medal-engraved borders,
printed lithographically, ca. 1850. 9" x 8 3/4".
Warshaw Collection, Smithsonian Institution

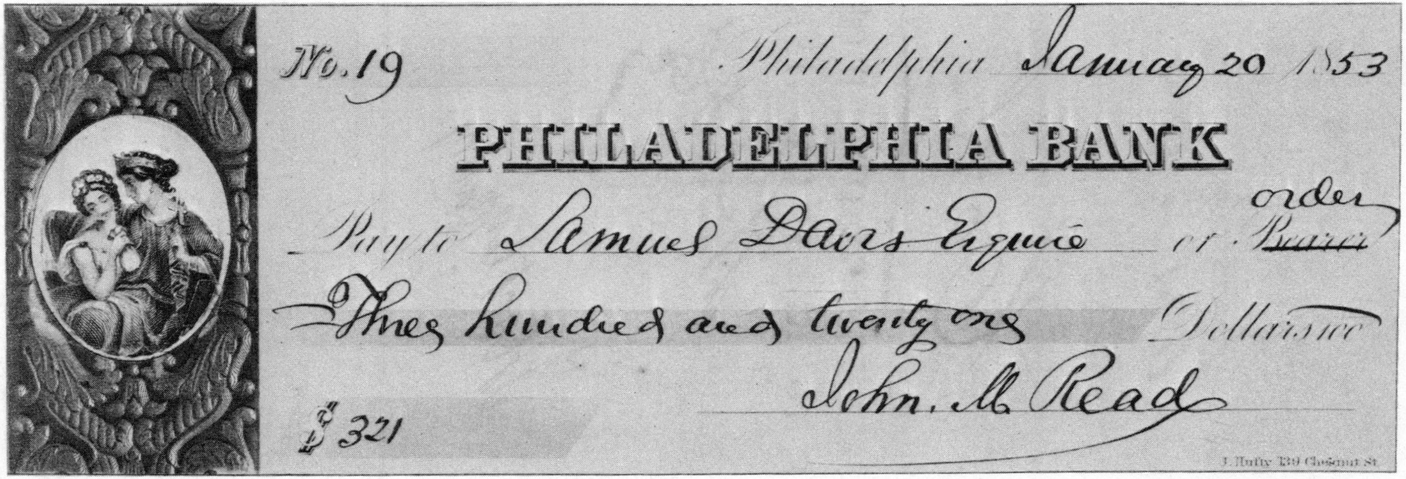

Fig. 9. Medal engraving on Philadelphia bank note, 1853. 2 3/8" x 7". Warshaw Collection, Smithsonian Institution

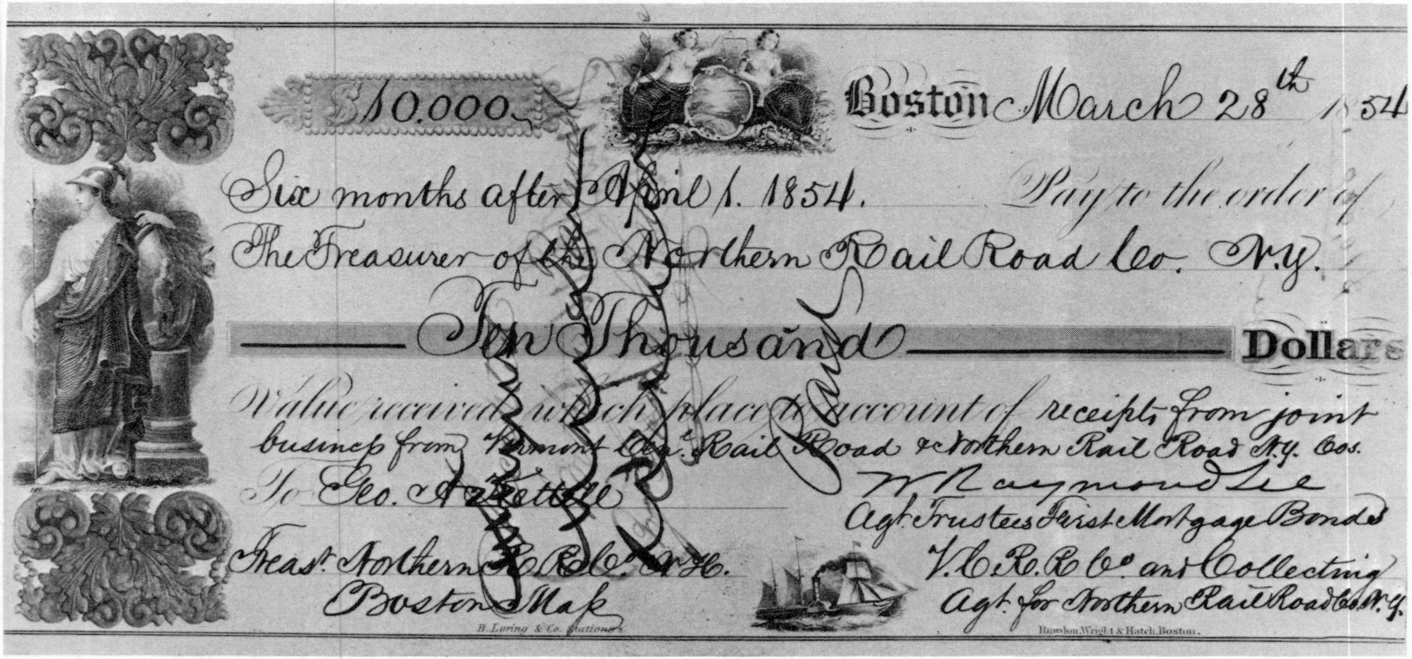

Fig. 10. Medal engraving on Boston bank note, 1854. 3 1/2" x 8".
Warshaw Collection, Smithsonian Institution

Fig. 11. Siderography. Admission ticket engraved by
Perkins, Fairman and Heath, ca. 1820. 3" x 4 1/2".
John Johnson Collection, Bodleian Library, Oxford

NOTES

1. Journal of Natural Philosophy, XXVIII (London, 1811), 56.

2. Art Union (London, 1841), p. 92.

3. [William J. Stannard] The Art Exemplar (London, [1859]).

4. The Report of the Committee of the Society of Arts . . .
relative to the Mode of Preventing the Forgery of Bank-Notes
(London, 1819) is an interesting and very readable account of
the problem. The Bank of England Note (Cambridge, 1953) by
A. D. Mackenzie tells the story from the Bank's point of view.

5. Mackenzie, p. 61.

6. Greville and Dorothy Bathe, Jacob Perkins (Philadelphia,
1943).

7. Mackenzie, pp. 55, 58.

8. William Congreve, An Analysis of the True Principles
of Security against Forgery; Exemplified by an Inquiry into the
Insufficiency of the American Plan for a New Bank Note . . .
(London, n.d.)

9. London Journal of Arts and Sciences (London, 1820),
p. 209.

10. Literary Gazette (London, 1820), p. 586.

11. Bathe, p. 81.

12. E. Denny Bacon, The Line Engraved Postage Stamps
Printed by Perkins Bacon and Company (London, 1920), p. 5.

13. L. E. Bergerson, Manuel du tourneur (Paris, 1816).

14. Report of the Select Committee of the House of Commons
on the British Museum (London, 1836).

15. Athenaeum (London, 1836), p. 706.

AMERICAN LITHOGRAPHIC TECHNOLOGY BEFORE THE CIVIL WAR

Peter C. Marzio

Introduction: The Debt to Europe

Ladies' "drawing-room" magazines and gentlemen's scholarly journals published in America before the Civil War exalted lithography as a new art for democracy. A cheap and durable printing process, it promised "pictures for everyone." As early as 1826, one magazine insisted that the "cheapness and facility of the lithographic process, the number and goodness of the impressions to be obtained from a single plate . . . show that it is a most valuable substitute for copper-plate printing in all but the highest branches of the art." Graham's American Monthly concurred. The "cheapness of lithographic prints," wrote the editor in 1832, "brings them within the reach of all classes of society," thereby serving as a principal means for developing a democratic art.[1]

While enticing, this bombastic rhetoric oversimplified the technique of making lithographs. A planographic printing process, lithography required rethinking by all printmakers. But most Americans were unwilling--perhaps unable--to devise unique approaches for drawing on stone. Their bristling enthusiasm for a "democratic art" did not lead to progress in the technology of lithography. Not one American contributed a new important idea for the design of presses or the use of stones before the Civil War.

Europe remained the source of innovation and expertise for at least seventy-five years. The thousands of lithographers who drew and printed lithographs in the United States used European manuals, Bavarian stones, and presses of English, French, or German design. Many

American lithographers were European-born and trained in
the shops of Paris or Munich. Only three patents for "improvements in lithography" were granted in America between
1830 and 1860; not one was significant. After the Civil War
the patents increased rapidly, but most dealt with methods
for using steam to power lithographic presses.[2]

Historically, Americans who have painted and drawn for
their daily bread have used the existing technology of their
society to produce their works. They rarely have made technological innovations to improve their art. Those who did invent
new machines (like Samuel F. B. Morse) had to free themselves
from their chosen professions. Lithographic promoters of
1820-60 were no exception. Their "democratic art" rested on
European technology carried to America in the 1810s and
1820s. Although they enjoyed emphasizing the uniqueness
of their own lithographs, they continually paid homage to
Europe. "In the art of lithography," wrote one American
painter in 1860, ". . . a steady advance may be witnessed;
though our works . . . cannot yet claim comparison with
those of the continent of Europe."[3]

Standardization of Lithography: Preparing the Stones

By 1820 the basic tools for making lithographs had been
determined in Germany, France, and England. The best limestones came from only one place--the Solenhofen quarries
near Bavaria. Lithographers who refused to rely on this
German resource searched their local areas for substitutes,
but all failed. The uniqueness of the Solenhofen stone may
have hurt the national pride of the French and English, but
it did not cause serious concern. As the inventor of lithography, Alois Senefelder, wrote: "All the inhabitants of
Solenhofen are quarrymen, and the entire surrounding
country seems to have a surplus of the stone, so that even
with the greatest demand no scarcity is to be feared for
centuries."[4]

The stone blocks varied from one to four inches in thickness, depending on the size of the drawing. Appleton's
Dictionary of Machines, Mechanics, Engine-work &

Engraving (1851) gave this formula: "In order to sustain the pressure used in taking impressions, a stone, 12 inches square, ought not to be less than 1 1/4 inch thick, and this thickness should increase with the area of the stone." The largest prints came from the thickest stones, protecting against cracks caused by the pressure of the scraper blade.[5]

When the stones arrived in the lithographer's shop, they were sawed to a proper size. The printing surface was then smoothed and leveled. A common abrasive, such as sand, was spread on the stone and mixed with a few drops of water. Another stone was placed on top of the first and pushed back and forth until the proper texture, or grain, was produced. It usually took more than one texture of abrasive to grind a stone, so lithographers worked their stones several times before getting the desired surface.[6]

Drawing directly on the stone with crayons, pens, and pencils, a lithographer did not need the special skills required for engraving. The drawing tools contained grease or soap, as the lithographic manuals noted, composed of fatty acids found in common items like tallow, resin, and wax. The fats reacted with the lime in the stone, producing an insoluble lime soap which received ink but repelled water. Therefore, whenever a lithographer drew on polished stone, an affinity for ink resulted (figs. 1, 2, 3).[7]

After the drawing was completed, the entire stone was covered with a solution of gum arabic and dilute nitric acid. This fixed the drawing against spreading by desensitizing the clean portions of the stone to grease. The entire surface was then washed, and the damp stone was rolled with printing ink and sent through the special press. Inking was the most crucial step, for the exact amount of ink had to be applied. This was learned only by experience. If a stone were underinked, the impression appeared too light. But if too much ink was applied, the image on the stone became blurry, and the outline had to be redrawn.

Alois Senefelder had developed this entire process by 1818. His Complete Course of Lithography (translated into English in 1819) served as the standard text for all lithographers throughout the nineteenth century. And to this

Fig. 1. Lithographers at work. From Edward Hazen, The
Panaroma of Professions and Trades (Philadelphia, 1836),
p. 175. Here lithographers are shown drawing directly
on their stones, and the variety of sizes of stones
used can be seen.

Fig. 2. Details of a lithographic drawing room. From a billhead of F. F. Oakley Lithographic Company, 1857. A lithographer appears to be examining a finished stone with his client.

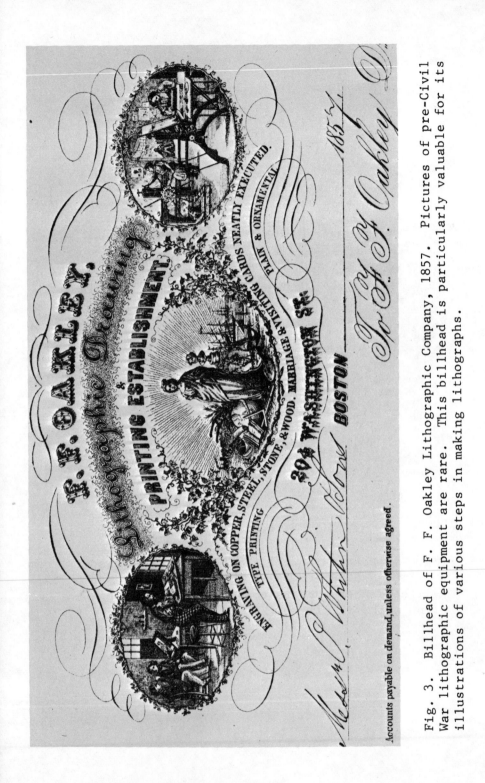

Fig. 3. Billhead of F. F. Oakley Lithographic Company, 1857. Pictures of pre-Civil War lithographic equipment are rare. This billhead is particularly valuable for its illustrations of various steps in making lithographs.

day, those who draw on stone follow the formulas established by him. Other Europeans wrote manuals which elaborated Senefelder's ideas, but not one American wrote a treatise equal even to these secondary works.

The standardization of lithography at this early date meant that the entire craft was imported to the United States. Americans received it enthusiastically, honoring it as a fixed science with a complete set of laws. Rather than attempting to improve the process, their initial reaction was to look for local stones that worked as well as the magical specimens from Solenhofen.

Bass Otis, an early promoter of lithography in the United States, worked with limestones quarried from Dirks River, Kentucky. He may have learned of these stones from the editor of the Western Review, who wrote in 1820: "Fortunately we have in Kent., the peculiar sort of stone which is made use of by the German artist . . . and it has been found to succeed admirably." The Troy Lyceum in New York owned a "compact limestone" from Indiana, and an anonymous lithographer noted with pride that his picture of a boy holding a dead rabbit was printed from "Vermont Marble." Francis Lieber's Encyclopaedia Americana advised that when German stones were too expensive, Americans could fabricate "artificial slabs" by commissioning any "intelligent potter" who could "easily imitate the density of natural stones." Stucco "composed of lime and sand, and fastened with the caseous part of milk" was held to be a suitable substitute![8]

Neither stucco nor the Vermont nor Kentucky stones printed satisfactorily, and as early as 1808 Americans began importing Solenhofen's best. "Dr. Mitchell of New York," reported the National Intelligencer and Washington Adviser, "received a lithographic stone and inks from Paris and made some experiments in this new art." By 1818 the American Philosophical Society owned a stone "imported from Munich" in order to permit its members the opportunity of unlocking the mysteries of Senefelder's discovery.

America's first major lithographic house was opened in Boston in 1825. William Pendleton and his brother John, who had studied the craft under the "first artists of France,"

imported from Paris "a good supply of the proper stone and
other materials for the pursuit of the art." The Boston
Monthly Magazine considered the Pendletons' purchase a
major step in the promotion of lithography in the United States.
Besides printing their own works, they sold some of this
equipment (with instructions) to other budding lithographers.[9]
Their various firms in Boston and New York (1825-38) also
employed most of the best lithographers in America--including
the young Nathaniel Currier.

The early professional lithographers purchased stones
directly from Europe. But by the 1830s "commission
merchants"--businessmen who purchased items for clients
at a given percentage--began dealing in lithographic equipment. Horatio Wilkes of New York City, for example, was
patronized by lithographers all along the eastern coast. In
1831 he sold to C. G. Childs of Philadelphia 218 1/2 pounds
of stone at 10 cents per pound. These were "large" stones
which Childs had to cut himself. Moreover, the deal was
"cash and carry." And Childs had to ship the load, probably
by water, to Philadelphia at his own expense.[10]

By the early 1850s at least six importers of lithographic
supplies operated in New York City. Lithographers were
cautious in dealing with these "merchants," for as Senefelder
warned in his Complete Course of Lithography, Solenhofen
stones varied in hardness, texture, and solidity. Expert
care in selecting durable stones was crucial, if the invest-
ment was to pay. Because large orders were demanded by
commission merchants, smaller firms were not likely to deal
with them. Lone lithographers probably bought equipment
from larger printing houses, paying slightly higher prices.
In addition, lithographic companies were continually going
out of business. Their capital inventories must have glutted
the market with secondhand equipment by the 1840s.

With black and white or hand-colored lithographs only one
stone was needed. But as chromolithography developed in
the 1840s, many stones were used for one print. P. S. Duval
of Philadelphia and Louis Prang of Boston pioneered this art
in America, getting their information from England and France--
particularly from the writings of Godefroy Engelmann. This

slow and involved process was described in detail by the New York Tribune on May 25, 1866:

> Upon the first stone a general tint is laid, covering
> nearly the whole picture, and as many sheets of paper
> as there are copies of the picture are printed from it.
> A second stone is then prepared, embracing all the
> shades of some other color, and the sheets already
> printed with the first color are worked over this stone.
> A third, fourth, fifth, and sixth follow, each one
> repeating the process and adding some new color,
> advancing the picture a step further until the requisite
> number of colors have been applied.

It was a tedious process which required months to complete. The most difficult part of the operation was to insure that the paper fell on each stone exactly in the proper place. A wood frame was built around each stone, and brass pins were driven into it. When the paper was laid across the first stone, the pins punctured small holes in each corner. These holes then served as guides for all subsequent impressions, insuring that every sheet fell into the same position on every stone.[12]

Chromolithography increased the need for Solenhofen stones, particularly after the Civil War. Several New York importers such as Kraus & Wimpfenheimer at 481 Broome Street and J. Birkner of 92 William Street specialized in "lithographic stones and materials." They dealt directly with the stone quarries in Bavaria, and advertised a complete inventory (figs. 4, 5). By this time, lithography was moving away from a "democratic art" and into the area of advertising. The sale of equipment became more profitable as industry used illustrations to display its wares.

Lithographic Presses: A Search for Standardization

Although the technique for preparing stones had been standardized by 1820, the search for an efficient lithographic press continued until the Civil War. Senefelder, as well as

Fig. 4. J. Birkner advertisement. The "View of Lithographic Stone Quarries at Solenhofen Bavaria" reassured Birkner's clients of high-quality merchandise. The stones at the right of the picture are perfectly layered, simply waiting to be taken from the quarry wall and placed in a lithographer's shop. The stone cutters and the factory buildings are bustling—supplying the world with Solenhofen treasures.

Fig. 5. Hermann Schott's advertisement

other Europeans, applied all their efforts--but the break-
through never occurred. The best presses of 1860 were not
discovered by a single genius; rather they evolved from the
painstaking efforts of hundreds of printers who experimented
daily.

Some of the first American lithographers worked without
a press. Good impressions could be taken by placing a sheet
of wet paper on the stone's surface, covering the print paper
with a few pieces of dry paper, and rubbing a block of hard,
sanded wood across the entire area. Senefelder followed
this method when his presses failed to work, and he explained the process in his famous treatise. When Bass Otis,
the American artist who published some of the first lithographs in the United States, experimented with drawing on
stone, he, too, probably struck his prints without a press.

The hand operation was only temporary. European lithographers tried to convert letterpresses and copperplate
presses for use with stones, but according to Senefelder,
these attempts were frustrated. Because the letterpress
printed from raised type, only a small amount of pressure was
required--far too little to make a lithograph. Attempts to
increase the pressure by adding weights only made the
stones crumble. The copperplate press worked with thin
metal sheets, and the rollers tore the lithographic paper when
a thick stone was used. So--as Senefelder decided at a very
early date--a new press for the planographic print process
had to be invented.[14]

Printing was the crucial step which Senefelder did not
master. "An exact description of all presses used hitherto
for lithography," he wrote in his treatise, "would demand a
book that would nearly equal the present one in magnitude."
Little is known about these early European presses, and only
bits of evidence survive from American accounts. When the
Analectic Magazine published its famous article about lithography in 1819, two varieties of presses were mentioned:
Senefelder's pole press and Godefroy Engelmann's press consisting of a stationary bed and a roller for applying
pressure.[15]

The first practical lithographic press, Senefelder's

invention, applied pressure with a scraper blade. A long
vertical pole with the scraper at one end was forced against
a piece of leather (called the tympan) covering the stone. A
series of levers placed great pressure on the tympan, and the
scraper was pulled across the surface by the printer. This
press simply copied the action of the human hand in the older
process (fig. 6).

With Senefelder's press great pressure could be applied
without fear of snapping the stones. Unlike the older letterpress that applied pressure over the entire stone at one time,
the scraper touched only a thin area. Senefelder estimated
that a letterpress required fifty tons of pressure to make a
lithograph. His new invention made good impressions with
only three tons applied successively across the stone. The
wooden scraper had a second advantage. It did not tug or
tear the paper as it moved across the tympan. In addition,
it was easy to exchange blades of different sizes and to replace old worn ones.

Senefelder patented his press in 1801. Numerous variations and improvements were made by several inventors, and
wooden-pole presses were illustrated in most lithographic
treatises after 1810. Since this was the most popular press
during the 1810s, it is possible that some Americans constructed similar machines in their own shops.[16]

By 1820 the principle of the pole press gave way to a new
design. Instead of having the scraper move across the stone,
the stone was placed in a bed and passed beneath a fixed
scraper blade. Leather straps attached to a winching
cylinder at one end of the press pulled the bed along on
tracks. The winch was cranked by either a lever or star
wheel--depending upon the lithographer's preference. The
lever predominated in England; the star wheel reigned in
France[17] (fig. 7).

Between 1820 and 1860 the most popular presses embodied
this new design. Most could be operated by a single pressman, but a few--especially in Germany--required two
laborers. The later types sported automatic devices for
dampening and inking the stones, and others were popular
because they printed by moving their beds either left to

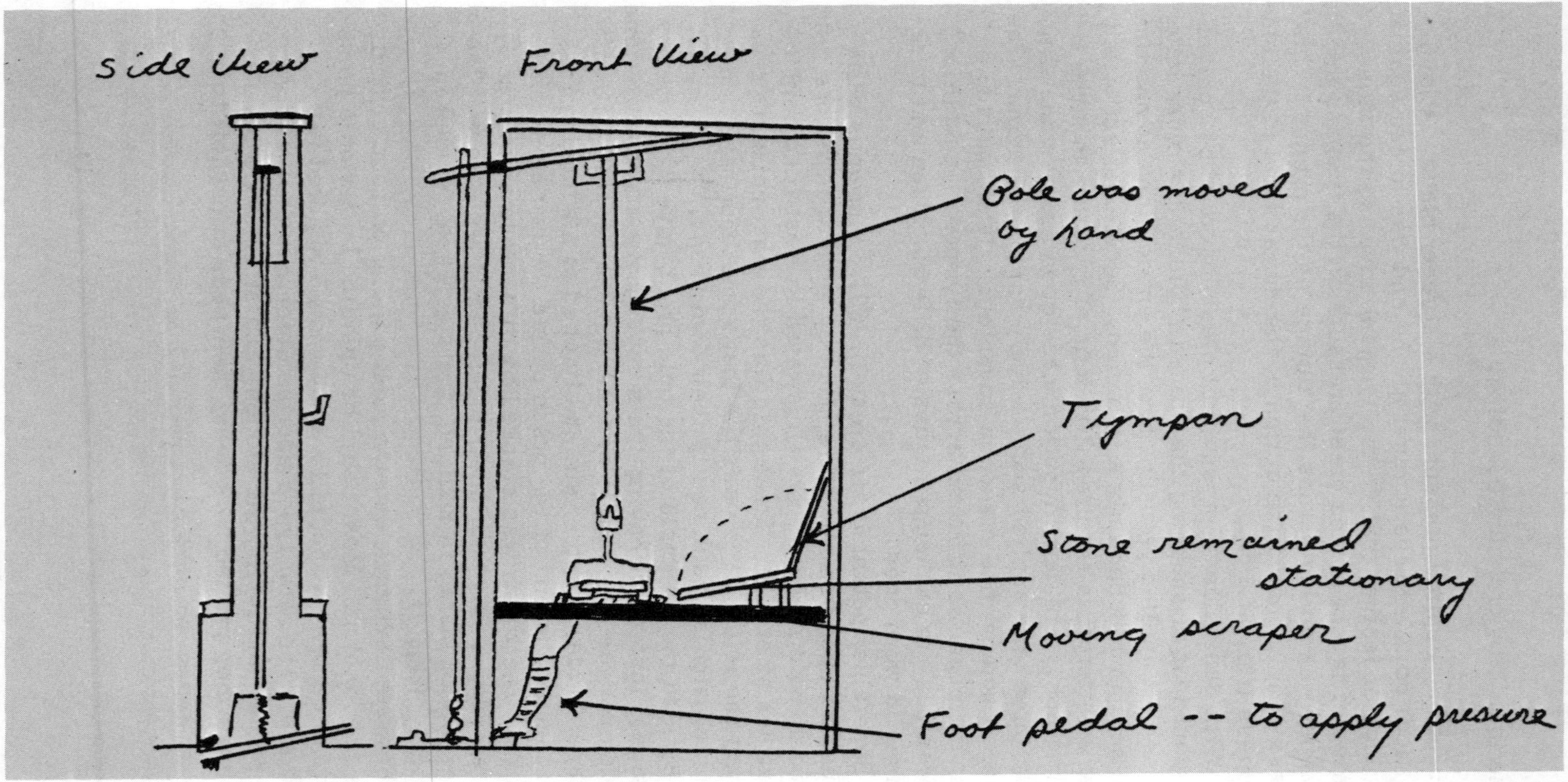

Side view   Front view

Pole was moved
by hand

Trympan

Stone remained
stationary

Moving scraper

Foot pedal -- to apply pressure

Fig. 6. Senefelder's pole press (English patent specification, no. 2518, June 20, 1801)

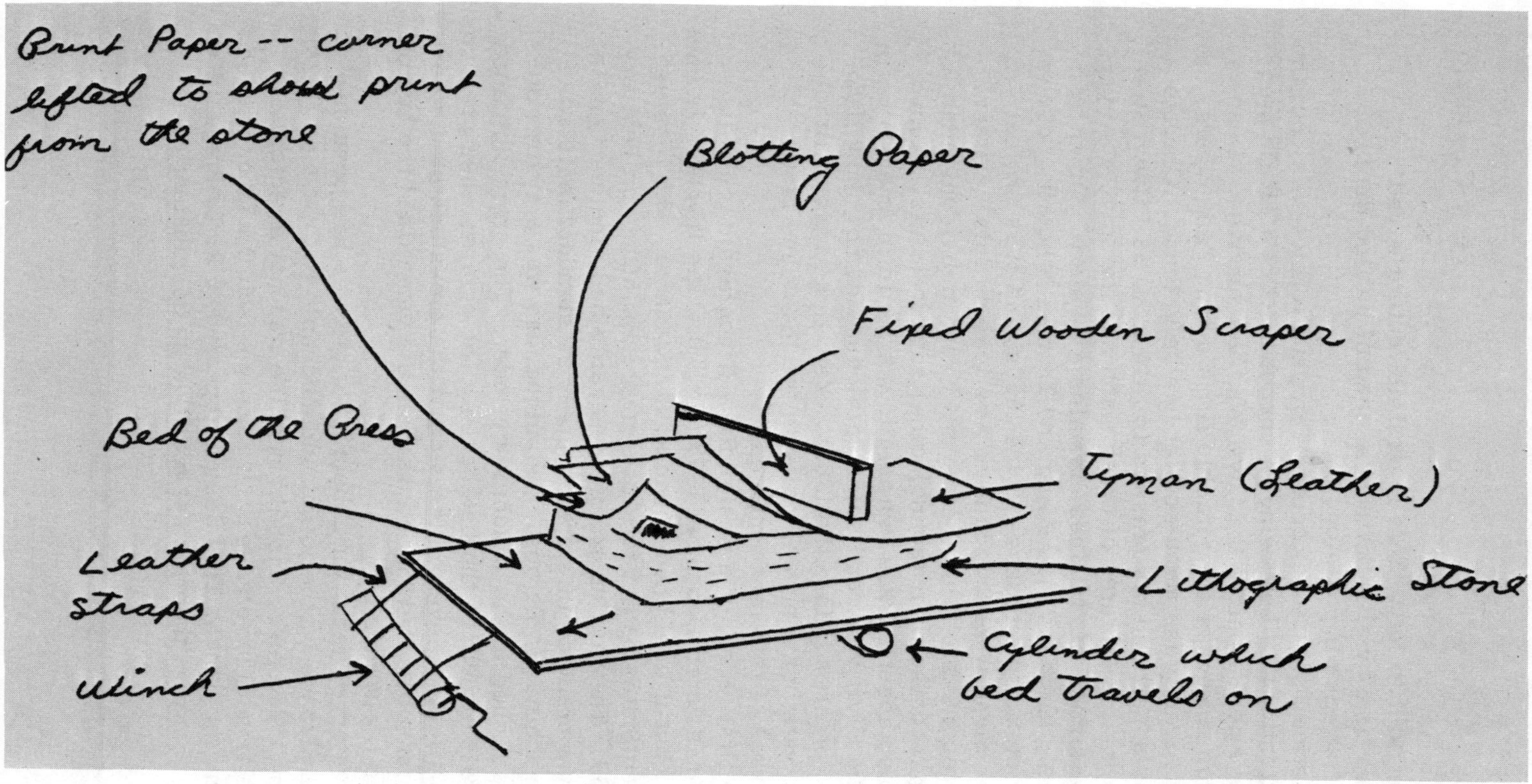

Fig. 7. Basic elements for making a lithograph with a stationary scraper and a movable bed

right or right to left. This reversible feature saved
precious time by eliminating the need of pulling the bed
back after each impression.

American presses embodied European refinements, but the
full extent of this borrowing is unknown. Not a single press
used in America before the Civil War has survived. Despite
the large number of lithographic firms during those years, only
one American press manufacturer has been found. Charles
Massey advertised his presses in 1845 from 68 Dilwyn Street,
Philadelphia. Pictures of these machines are lost, however,
and the size of his business remains a mystery. Other busi-
nessmen, such as Louis Prang and Thomas Ashcraft, both
from Boston, sold presses in the 1850s, but it is unclear
whether these were European or American models. Patent
office records are silent before 1847, and individual firms
seldom recorded their technological advancements. A long-
run lithographer's trade journal did not begin in America until
after the Civil War, and sales catalogues do not show lithographic presses before the 1860s. Yet, thousands of lithographs were being printed daily in the 1840s and 1850s--all
on presses of different vintages.[18]

The first record of a design for a lithographic press in
America is dated December 1833 (fig. 8). The inventor is unknown, but it could have been R. C. Manners, who received
a United States patent for "lithographic printing" on February
15, 1833. The wooden scraper, movable bed, leather tympan,
and lever crank on this press appear as standard features of
many machines in Europe. Its uniqueness was a system of
gears attached to the winching cylinder. The gears lightened
the strain of pulling the bed beneath the scraper when pressure
was applied. A lever on the side of the press operated a cam,
but it cannot be determined whether the cam raised the bed or
lowered the scraper.[19]

A system of gears for lithographic presses had been devised in France by the joiner and mechanic J. C. Cloue (1826).
Like the 1833 press, Cloue's machine was not a radical de-
parture from older presses. It simply eased the labor needed
to crank the winch. This design appeared in R. L. Bregeaut's
Manuel complet theorique et pratique du dessinateur et de

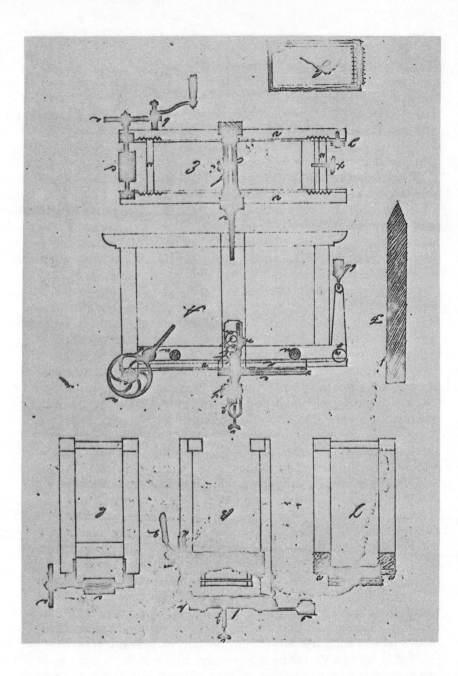

Fig. 8. Drawing of a lithographic press with a fixed
scraper and a moving bed, artist unknown, December, 1833

l'imprimeur lithographe (Paris, 1827), and it was shown at
the Paris exhibition of 1827. Although the jurors of the exhibition found the machine "ingenious," they reported that
the gear mechanism worked too slowly for any lithographer
with profits in mind. The resemblance between the 1833 and
Cloue presses, however, is strong, and the 1833 press might
have been inspired by the work of his French contemporary.[20]

A more radical change appeared in a United States
patent awarded to John Donlevy of New York City in 1847
(figs. 9, 10, 11). His only claim was for adjustable bearings
that fitted any size of axle on any type of "cylindrical roller."
It is important to keep this in mind because his patent included
detailed drawings of an entire press as well as telling comments
about the "usual form" of the component parts.[21]

Except for the carriage and scraper, the Donlevy press
was made of metal--either iron or brass. The wooden carriage
that held the stone moved on top of a roller that rested on the
adjustable bearings. A lever was attached directly to the
roller, and the carriage was moved beneath the scraper simply
by cranking the lever. Unlike many older presses, this one
did not need a winching cylinder. Pressure was applied by ad-
justing the scraper blade and the carriage. Beneath the axle
of the roller were two eccentric cams--one on each side.
These cams could raise the bed toward the scraper, insuring
sufficient pressure for a print. Donlevy labeled all these
features the "usual appendages."

The skeleton of the tympan consisted of "cast iron or
brass in the form of a rectangular frame." Leather was
stretched across this form and fastened with metal bolts
through eyelets on the frame. The scraper blade was fitted
between two pieces of metal clamped tightly together. This
scraper box, as the whole unit was called, was attached to a
solid rod that was threaded at one end. The rod screwed into
the top of the arch on the press, and it could be adjusted to
accommodate all thicknesses of stones. The scraper blade
traveled in channels, or trains, affixed to the inner surface
of the columns of the arch. The length of these trains depended upon the distance covered by the scraper. On top of
the arch just above this screw was a lever with an eccentric

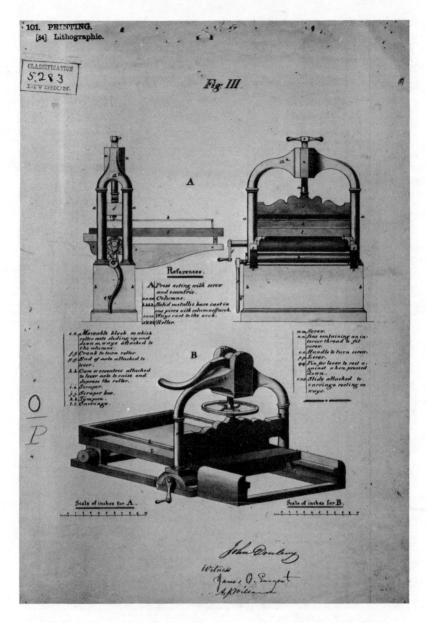

Fig. 9. Complete view of John Donlevy's lithographic press, U. S. Patent no. 5283. Donlevy's patent was the only one issued before 1860 with complete drawings of a lithographic hand press. Its great value is its modesty. Basically, this press resembled others of its day, with only a few modifications.

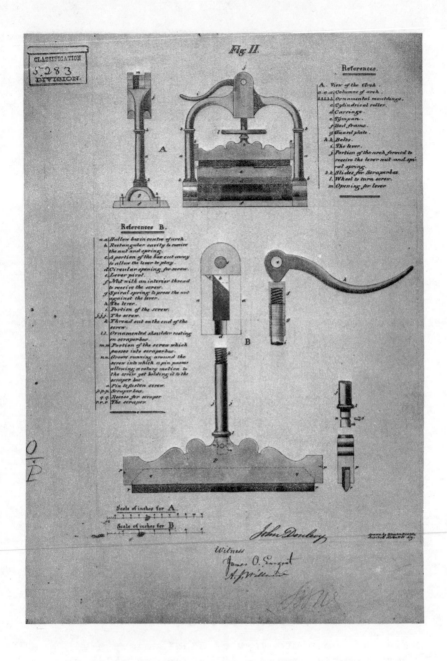

Fig. 10. View of the scraper mechanism of the Donlevy
press

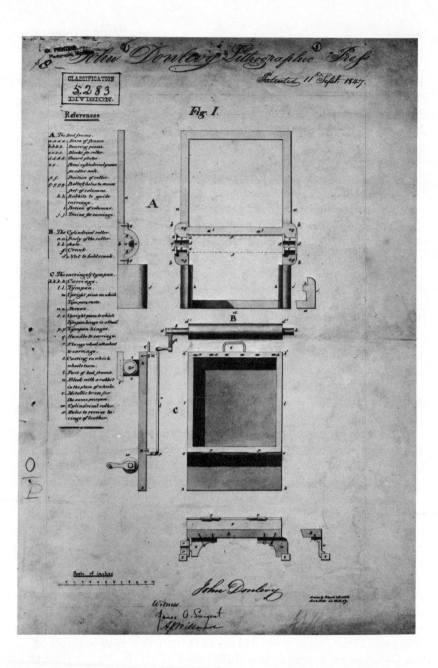

Fig. 11. View of the roller mechanism and bed of the
Donlevy press

at one end. When pushed to the "down" position the eccentric applied additional pressure to the scraper against the stone. Donlevy did not patent either the tympan design or the scraper blade mechanism. Rather, he emphasized that they were drawn in "the manner ordinarily employed in lithographic presses for which I make no claim."

Various features of this press had been established in Europe. Metal construction typified English presses as early as the mid-1820s, but France and Germany retained their wooden models until the late 1830s. The leather tympan and wooden scraper blade had been used by Senefelder at an early date, and movable carriages with stationary scrapers became common throughout Europe in the 1820s.

Two presses in particular seem to have influenced Donlevy. In 1827 Charles Motte, a French printer, received a silver medal from the jurors of the Expositions des Produits de l'Industrie for improvements in a lithographic press. He had designed a lever with an eccentric that forced the scraper against the stone. As in Donlevy's later press, Motte's scraper moved vertically within tracks on the sides of the columns of the arch. The pressure came by depressing the lever, forcing the eccentric against the screw that regulated the scraper blade. [22]

This French press was adopted enthusistically in England, and it received the highest praise of Charles Hullmandel in The Art of Drawing on Stone (London, 1824). "Its compactness and skillful engineering," he wrote, "pleased the English--a people who were used to that kind of work." Hullmandel's treatise was the bible for American lithographers. One of the earliest authoritative works to be published in English, it influenced the development of American lithography beyond all calculations. [23]

A close copy of the Motte press was manufactured by Taylor and Martineau of England. Unlike Motte's, the English model propelled the bed without the use of gears or winches: a cylinder with a serrated finish guided the bed beneath the scraper. The roller mechanism received the approbation of the Gentleman's Magazine (1822) and of C. F. Partington in The Engravers' Complete Guide (London, 1825). The simple design and the low cost promised "to extend the use of lithography . . . among amateurs and printers." These words from the Gentleman's Magazine--if read by Americans-- surely touched a responsive cord. The 1820s marked a period of search in the United States. Artists and critics were seeking a popular art form which would serve all the people. Lithography was to answer the call, but only when technology made prints of high quality and low cost feasible. The Motte press appeared to be a tool that would democratize the arts. [24]

Donlevy's patent of 1847 incorporated the key improvements of both the Motte and the Taylor-Martineau models. But he must have been aware of Hullmandel's single misgiving: neither machine applied enough pressure to print chalk lithographs. Donlevy corrected this defect by putting the ends of the roller on eccentrics. This dual system gave additional pressure, but the printer had to be careful of breaking stones.

Because of the modest claims in Donlevy's patent, one can assume that other American presses were similar. The double-pressure feature, not common to European presses, may be a distinguishing characteristic of American presses, and if so, it surely predated 1847, because Donlevy treated it as typical of lithographic presses. [25]

Nine years after Donlevy's patent, a large Philadelphia firm, Wagner and M'Guigan, published an interior view of their printing room "containing upwards of forty presses" (fig. 12). Although the picture lacks explicit detail, the presses appear to be of the type manufactured by the Glasgow firm of M. McCulloch & Co. They are side-lever presses with a self-acting tympan, and according to advertisements, they could print up to a third more pictures than any other press in a given amount of time. The end of the tympan closest to the scraper was fixed to the end of the bed. Cords, pulley wheels, and a counterweight held the other end in an upright position. As the bed traveled beneath the scraper blade, a cylinder in front of the scraper pressed the tympan into a horizontal position. In cranking the bed back, the counterweight forced the tympan up to its original station. [26]

Fig. 12. Interior view of Wagner and M'Guigan's pressroom. Containing almost forty presses of the most modern type, Wagner and M'Guigan's pressroom was a center of constant activity. Fashionably dressed couples stroll the center of the floor, while young men transport the heavy lithographic stones on little carts to the pressmen.

Unlike the Donlevy press, McCulloch's machine operated with a single-pressure system. A series of eccentrics brought the bed up to the scraper blade. In the Wagner and M'Guigan advertisement it is unclear which system of eccentrics was used. Several had been developed, and all worked efficiently.

The McCulloch press was larger and heavier than Donlevy's. It stood on cast-iron legs designed for long, hard use. At least four standard bed sizes were sold: 14 inches at £11 11s.; 16 inches at £12 12s.; 18 inches at £13 13s.; and 20 inches at £14 14s. Larger, custom models could be ordered.[27]

The cast-iron construction, single-pressure system, and self-acting tympan made this side-lever press a favorite among English and--apparently--American lithographers. Related in basic principles to Donlevy's it was more efficient and faster. First advertised in the earlier 1840s, it was still in wide use during the late 1860s. Comparing it to the star-wheel press, an Englishman, C. Straker, wrote in the Instructions in the Art of Lithography (London, 1867):

> The French . . . press . . . is preferred by some for working drawings and colours, where nicety of register and regularity of impression are required; but being a slower and a more expensive machine, it does not, in our opinion, possess equivalent advantages.
>
> The English, or Side Lever, is the press invariably working in this country, and any results can be obtained by it.

At least forty side-lever machines were operating in Philadelphia in the mid-1850s.[28]

Like the French and Germans, American lithographers also used the star-wheel press. Invented in 1805 by Hermann Joseph Mitterer, the director of the Feiertagschule lithographic press, the star wheel became a standard machine in most European firms. Numerous changes and improvements appeared through the 1860s, mirroring the development of the lever press: a fixed scraper blade, a self-acting tympan, eccentric cams which raised the bed against the blade, and a mechanism which returned the bed automatically after each printing.[29]

By 1825 German, French, and English lithographers were using the star wheel for their top-quality work. The major advantage over the lever press was that the star wheel permitted greater pressure to be applied to the stone. This was crucial for printing chalk lithographs and taking impressions from large stones. The star wheel was slower than the lever press, however, and not as suitable for job printing (i.e., calling cards, letterheads, and advertisements).

Pictures and evaluations of these presses appeared in encyclopedias as well as most handbooks of lithography. American lithographers must have been aware of the star wheel, particularly those who worked for firms employing French or German printers. The only picture, however, is dated ca. 1856-1857 and comes from a billhead of the F. F. Oakley Printing Establishment (fig. 13).

Francis Oakley operated a lithographic company in Boston for at least eight years, 1856 to 1863. He employed Benjamin F. Nutting--an artist, a drawing teacher, and a lithographer--and produced works of high quality. The star wheel symbolized this workmanship.

It is important to note that an iron lever press accompanied the star wheel on Oakley's bill. With the exception of the tympan, this lever press operated exactly as those shown in the Wagner and M'Guigan advertisement. Also, the lever press is placed in the foreground of the print, emphasizing that big, commercial orders were preferred.

It is impossible to determine the exact type of star wheel press pictured on Oakley's billhead. It does not correspond exactly to any known European presses, and the drawing lacks sufficient detail to determine just how it worked. A fixed scraper beam which could be raised or lowered by a screw can be seen. The star wheel apparently was attached directly to the roller which brought the bed beneath the scraper. Most European presses had the wheel at one end of the press and operated the bed with gears or straps. As with Donlevy's lever press, however, Oakley's star wheel is

Fig. 13. Star-wheel and lever presses from F. F. Oakley's billhead. This star-wheel press, the only one I have found in the United States, was slow and cumbersome to operate, as the awkward position of the printer indicates. The lever press in the foreground was a modern type for the 1850s. The printer is shown inking the stone and preparing it for the press, while a workman in the background appears to prepare new stones for the presses. The prints above his head are being dried before being sent to customers.

located closer to the middle along the side of the machine.

From the early 1830s the French and German star wheels raised the bed to meet the scraper with a series of eccentrics operated by a pedal. Although Oakley's pressure system is not shown, a beam running along the floor through the center of the press can be seen. Perhaps a pedal with levers and rods was attached to this piece. The material used to construct the Oakley star wheel is also unknown. Eugene Brisset, the most successful manufacturer of starwheel presses in Europe, sold both iron and wooden models through the 1860s. Although the style of Oakley's model suggests wood, Donlevy's patent indicated that iron was common in American presses.

Operating either the lever or star-wheel presses was an inefficient, time-consuming business. The heavy stone had to be fixed to the bed and tightened to prevent any shifting. The scraper had to be adjusted to the proper height so that when the bed was raised just the right amount of pressure was applied. After the stone was inked very carefully and the paper laid across it, the tympan was lowered. Pressure from a lever or pedal was applied, while a handle or star wheel cranked the stone beneath the scraper. When the entire print was made, the pressure was released, the bed drawn back, and the tympan lifted from the stone. The print was then peeled off, and the entire operation repeated.

The most efficient lithographers produced only 200 to 250 prints per 12-hour workday. It was a cumbersome process, more awkward and slower than working a letterpress. As one writer noted, lithography "will never supercede printing with types for books and papers . . . [;] the work has been and is a very slow business." As late as 1860 The New American Cyclopedia condemmed the apparatus used in making lithographs as having the "appearance of clumsiness and imperfection." Godefroy Engelmann, an enthusiastic promoter of lithography in Europe, calculated that an experienced printer spent 36 seconds producing a lithograph. Most of this production time depended on the speed and efficiency of the workman. When letterpress was linked to the steam engine in the early 1800s, it made the lithographic machines appear archaic.[30]

As early as 1818 Alois Senefelder perceived the problem:

> I am only too well aware . . . of a grave defect
> in lithography, which is that the beauty and even
> the number of impressions depend mainly on the
> skill and industry of the printers. A good press
> is necessary, to be sure; but even with the best
> a poor workman will produce nothing but trash,
> because in this respect lithography is far more
> difficult than any other printing-process. I
> shall not admit that lithography has made a great
> step toward the utmost perfection until the erring
> work of the human hand has been dispensed with
> as much as possible and the printing is done
> almost entirely by machinery.[31]

Unlike some print processes--such as etching--the inking
and printing of lithographs was not considered part of the
creative process. There was only one correct procedure.
The test of a good printer was the ability to make one print
from a stone look like every print from that stone. But
because the hand-operated press required so much human
labor, the prints varied in quality and were limited in
quantity. An automatic machine would correct the "erring
work of the human hand," and it would meet the demands
of the art promoters who sought to make prints for everyone.

The first commercially successful steam press was
patented by a Mr. Sigl in Austria on May 30, 1851. Numerous
powered lithographic machines had been invented during the
1840s, but these had proved impractical. The Sigl press
operated with lithographic stones, mechanical inking and
damping devices, and an automatic system that delivered
and removed the paper. Bigger and faster machines followed,
some using stones but others adopting "impression cylinders"
and zinc plates. This all belongs to the second half of the
nineteenth century and is beyond the scope of this paper.[32]

Edward Young, in his enthusiastic history, Leading
Pursuits and Leading Men (Philadelphia, 1856), stated that
P. S. Duval was operating a steam press as early as 1846.

Neither the Philadelphia City directories for 1846 and 1847
nor the advertising blurbs in local newspapers, however,
verify Young's statement. A successful steam press would
have made good advertising copy. But not until the early
1850s did Duval begin to advertise the steam press on his
prints. And not before 1856 did several firms, including
Wagner and M'Guigan as well as Duval, make a concerted
effort to inform the public of their new powered machines.
Duval may have been experimenting with steam at an early
date, and he was one of the first lithographers to employ it
successfully, but Young's date seems premature.[33]

Even as late as July 25, 1852, the Scientific American
lamented that all:

> lithographic presses are worked by hand; not one
> has been made, so far as we know, self-acting,
> to be driven by steam power. The man who in-
> vents an improvement in the lithographic art,
> whereby the printing press will be self-acting
> and capable of being driven freely by steam
> power, will confer a benefit upon a most beauti-
> ful branch of the printing art, for which he should
> be highly honored and richly remunerated.

The hand press still predominated in 1860. As one writer
observed, "Other results are . . . attained . . . by the use
of machinery worked by steam, which to some extent is applied to this process." Not a single patent was issued in
the United States for a lithographic steam press before 1861.
During the next thirty years, the Patent Office was flooded
with applications, but not one inventor claimed the idea of
harnessing steam for lithography. Patents for "Improved
Lithographing Power Presses," automatic inking and damping
devices, special carriages which adjusted to stones of
various sizes, and speedier methods for printing with a power
press were issued.

Ten years after the Civil War, the steam press triumphed.
Richard Hoe, the largest manufacturer of printing presses
during the 1870s and 1880s, advertised at least five powered

models. The largest weighed 12 1/2 tons and was powered by a one-horsepower engine. It cost $7,200 delivered.[34]

As the Scientific American predicted, the steam press revolutionized the lithography business. The 1870 census in Philadelphia recorded thirty different manufacturing firms valued at a total of $509,200. Their inventory included 294 printing presses--both hand and powered models. The power machines used thirty horsepower, indicating that at least fifty steam presses were in operation. As an 1874 lithograph by Louis Prang and an advertisement by J. H. Bufford demonstrate, the hand press was not discarded (figs. 14, 15). The demand for fine artwork, the need for proofing, and the heavy investment in hand presses made these older machines necessary. And as late as 1881, R. Hoe and Co. sold six different hand models ranging from $175 to $485.[35]

Despite the endurance of the hand models, a faster, more efficient press was the dream of all lithographers. Before 1860 they built their businesses simply by purchasing more and more hand presses: the larger firms owned forty or fifty of them. This growth simply multiplied the inefficiency. A large, automatic machine would standardize the printing process and make lithography a threatening competitor of the letterpress. By the late 1870s Americans turned their attention to this challenge. American inventors considered speed the essential ingredient. They wanted lithography to be profitable; so they sought to standardize the printing process just as Senefelder standardized the preparation of stones.

Portable Lithographic Presses

Alois Senefelder invented the first portable press sometime before 1819. Improvements were made by other lithographers in France, England, and Italy--all recommending these smaller presses for those persons who "draw their own designs and wish to go through the whole of the process themselves."[36]

American lithographers used European manuals, so they were aware of the search for convenient, light presses.

Fig. 14. Lithograph by Louis Prang, 1874. As both figures 14 and 15 show, the steam press did not replace the hand machines immediately. Both types were used even after the Civil War.

Fig. 15.   Advertisement by J. H. Bufford

American magazines hailed lithography as a popular art
which was cheap enough for anyone. They insisted that
anyone who could draw could also produce a lithograph.
Inexpensive, simple printing presses should have captured
the attention of every art promoter in the United States. But,
curiously enough, American sources failed to mention the
existence of the portable presses.

The French and German models were made of wood. They
were simple machines that could be made without a knowledge of joinery, and Americans could have built their own
presses from descriptions in the European handbooks. Henry
Bankes, Lithography (1816); C. Ridolfi and F. Tartine,
Memoria sulla litografia (1819); L. J. D. B., Coup-d'oeil
sur la lithographie (1818); Rancourt de Charleville, Manuel
theorique et pratique du dessinateur et de l'imprimeur
lithographes (1819); and J. H. M. Poppe, Die Lithographie
oder Steindruckerei (1833) provided detailed examples.

In 1822 Rudolph Ackermann, a prosperous publisher and
promoter of lithography in England and Germany, shipped a
press to Stephen Elliott in Charleston, South Carolina. In
all probability it was a duplicate of Senefelder's portable
press which Ackermann presented to the English Society of
Arts in 1819. Ackermann's gift to the Society was a small
box with a scraper, a clamp mechanism for holding the
stone, and a tympan hinged to one side. The scraper moved
across the stone, being pulled by straps attached to a
winch. Pressure was applied by closing the tympan and
lid tightly over the stone and the printing paper (fig. 16).[37]
Elliott was a southern gentleman famous for work on the
flora and fauna of South Carolina. He might have used the
press for reproducing drawings of plant specimens while
working on his monumental treatise, A Sketch of the Botany
of South Carolina and Georgia (1816-24).

English models were advertised in America, but unlike
those from the Continent, these were made of iron. Albert
Waterlow manufactured the most popular press: he claimed
a sale of 2,000 between 1850 and 1859. This "improved
autographic press" consisted of a bed which moved between
two cylinders. A lever at the side of the press was used to

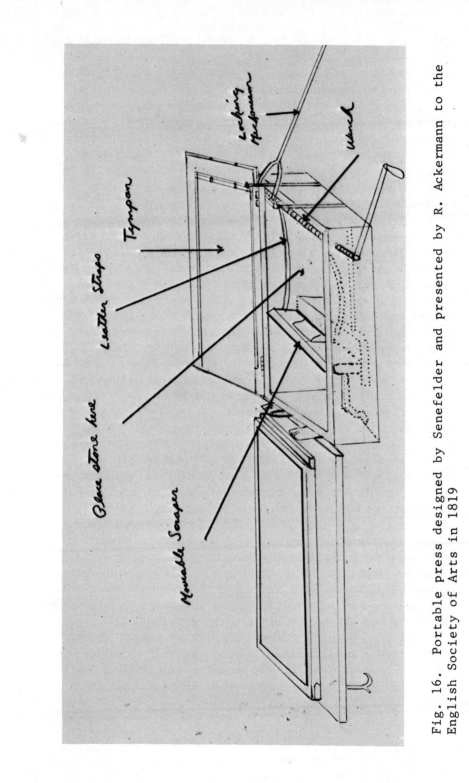

Fig. 16. Portable press designed by Senefelder and presented by R. Ackermann to the English Society of Arts in 1819

apply pressure, and a handle attached to the lower cylinder
pulled the bed through the rollers (fig. 17).

"Simplicity" characterized the Waterlow press. Its purpose was "to enable any person of ordinary intelligence to
perform all the operations of this form of lithography without
being compelled to seek the aid of a professional printer."
Office work, calling cards, even fine lithographs could be[38]
done. The Waterlow made "Every Man His Own Printer."

The number of Waterlow presses sold in America is unknown,
but the democratic message of the advertisements surely
caught the eyes of many. The Waterlow model could serve
as an office duplicating machine or an artist's personal
press. Its mobility also made it attractive. As late as 1884
James S. Pettit, the drawing instructor at the West Point
Military Academy, cited the fact that General Sherman's army
carried a lithographic press on the march from Atlanta to the
sea. Each day reconnaissance sketches and reports were
given to the lithographer. Working through the night, he
drew and printed enough copies for all the officers. Pettit
failed to describe the type of hand press used in the Civil
War, but it was probably similar to the Waterlow.[39]

Conclusion

The development of lithographic technology falls into
three periods. The first dates from 1800 to 1820 when a few
artists, intellectuals, and aristocrats tried to learn both
the advantages and limitations of lithography. They gave
little thought to selling pictures or creating a popular art.
By 1820 they had discovered the best method for preparing
and inking the rocks from Bavaria, but they had failed to
crack the problems of a workable press. Lithography arrived
in the United States near the end of this period. Americans
accepted the European solutions and proceeded to make lithographs just as the artists did in Munich or Paris.

The second period, 1820 to 1855, witnessed the spread
of lithography to all classes. Artists as well as business-
men tried to use lithographs to reach all the people. These
democratic pictures were produced by slow, unreliable

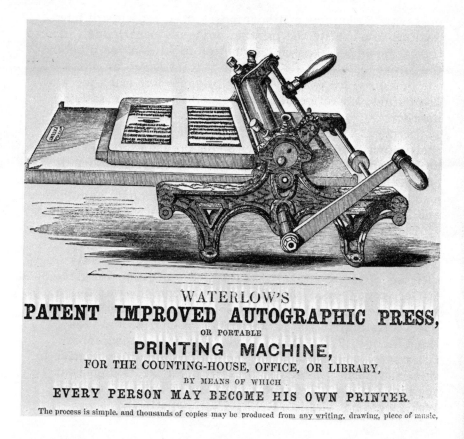

WATERLOW'S
PATENT IMPROVED AUTOGRAPHIC PRESS,
OR PORTABLE
PRINTING MACHINE,
FOR THE COUNTING-HOUSE, OFFICE, OR LIBRARY,
BY MEANS OF WHICH
EVERY PERSON MAY BECOME HIS OWN PRINTER.
The process is simple, and thousands of copies may be produced from any writing, drawing, piece of music,

Fig. 17. Waterlow's "Autographic Press." From Waterlow, Every Man His Own Printer (London, 1854). The Waterlow was used as an office duplicating machine as well as convenient press for fine art work. Its style suggested the elaborate designs which would characterize presses by the 1880s.

presses. So European lithographers tried a series of new
designs to expedite the printing process. Americans followed
the European lead, often lagging ten to fifteen years behind
the latest innovations. Even the fastest American press--
the type used by Wagner and M'Guigan--was much too slow.
The daring, inventive genius of American mechanics lay
dormant.

During the third period, 1855 to 1890, Americans applied
their technological abilities. Steam presses foretold great
profits, and Senefelder's dream of a completely automatic
press was realized. For various reasons--of which total
mechanization is only one--the artistic emphasis vanished,
and lithography became the medium for American business.

Through all three stages the debt to Europe was immense.
Today, museum curators who take pride in their "American
Collections" of lithographs see these prints differently from
citizens of the nineteenth century. A craft that was developed
in Germany, France, and England, lithography was an
import--a fact which few nineteenth-century Americans for-
got. Artistically, the genre scenes of Currier and Ives,
the Kelloggs, P. S. Duval, and other large lithographic
firms seem so American that the entire craft seems native to
this land. But technically these popular prints document
the fact that profit-minded artists and printers of the New
World were not blind to Old World innovations.

Notes

1. "Lithography," United States Literary Gazette, IV
(June 15, 1828), 226; "Lithography," Graham's American
Monthly Magazine (Aug. 1832), p. 359. See also Peter C.
Marzio, "The Art Crusade: A Study of American Drawing
Books and Lithographs, 1830-1860" (Ph.D. dissertation,
University of Chicago, 1969).
2. Harry T. Peters, America on Stone (Garden City,
N. Y., 1939), and John Thomas Carey, "The American
Lithograph" (Ph.D. dissertation, Ohio State University, 1954),
give useful biographies of American lithographers. Subject-
Matter Index of Patents for Inventions Issued by the United
States Patent Office from 1790-1873, Inclusive (Washington,
1874), II, "Lithography."
3. "Fine Arts," Eighty Years' Progress of the United
States (New York, 1861).
4. Alois Senefelder, The Invention of Lithography,
trans., J. W. Muller (New York, 1911), p. 101.
5. "Lithography," Appleton's Dictionary of Machines,
Mechanics, Engine-work & Engraving (New York, 1851),
II, 212.
6. See, for example, Senefelder, pp. 101-09,
"Lithography," Appleton's; "Lithography," The New York
American Cyclopedia (New York, 1860); "Lithography,"
Encyclopaedia Americana (Boston, 1856); J. G. Heck,
Iconographic Encyclopaedia (New York, 1851), IV, 172-77.
7. Ibid.
8. "Lithography," History of American Manufacturers
(Philadelphia, 1860), I, 252; Carey, p. 30; Western Review
I (1820), 59-60; "Lithography," Encyclopaedia Americana;
Analectic Magazine, XIII (1819), 67-68.
9. National Intelligencer and Washington Advertiser,
Jan. 8, 1808; Early Proceedings of the American Philosophical
Society . . . Entry May 7, 1819 (Philadelphia, 1884), p. 487;
"Lithography," Boston Monthly Magazine, I (June 1825),
378-84. Boston Atheneum, Oct. 31, 1825. Carey gives an
account of conflicting views about the Pendletons.
10. Henry Inman to C. G. Childs, New York, March 19,

1831 (Historical Society of Pennsylvania); <u>New York City</u>
<u>Directories 1829-30, 1930-31</u>.

    11. Senefelder, pp. 101-09.

    12. See also Heck, IV, 172-77.

    13. Michael Twyman, "The Lithographic Hand Press
1796-1850," <u>Journal of the Printing Historical Society</u>,
no. 3 (1967), pp. 5-6.

    14. <u>Ibid</u>., p. 5.

    15. Senefelder, p. 153. <u>Analectic Magazine</u>, II, 70.
"The Germans take the impression on paper, by means of a
wooden roller, wrapped round with buff leather, and attached
to the end of a long stick, of which the other end is attached
to take the impression." Engelmann's press was described
as consisting "of a hollow table, terminated at one end by
an upright frame, supporting a roller, which by means of a
winch may be made to traverse along the table from one
extremity to the other."

    16. Twyman, pp. 4-16.

    17. <u>Ibid</u>., pp. 9-10.

    18. I have searched in all the major depositories in
Washington, Baltimore, Philadelphia, and New York. Also,
I corresponded with more than forty libraries and historical
societies in other cities. For the most part, material concerning lithography before the Civil War has vanished. Only
the lithographs remain.

    A useful source on sales catalogues is Lawrence B.
Romaine, <u>A Guide to American Trade Catalogues, 1744-1900</u>
(New York, 1960). Also see <u>Smithsonian Subject-Index for</u>
<u>Trade Catalogues</u>. Thomas MacKellar, <u>The American Printer</u>
(Philadelphia, 1878); Douglas C. McMurtrie, ed., <u>The</u>
<u>Invention of Printing: A Bibliography</u> (New York, 1942);
E. C. Bigmore and C. W. H. Wyman, <u>A Bibliography of</u>
<u>Printing</u> (New York, 1945).

    <u>The Lithograph</u> was the first trade journal for
lithographers, but only two issues appeared: Jan 1 and
March 1, 1874. <u>Boston City Directory, 1825-1860</u>.

    19. Manner's patent was destroyed by fire, and it was
not renewed when the Patent Office was reorganized. The
press dated December 1833 appears to be a draft for a

Patent Office application. It comes from the Columbia University Typographic Collection, Book arts--Printing Presses, L to S.

20. Twyman, p. 25.

21. John Donlevy, United States Patent No. 5,283 (Sept. 11, 1847).

22. Twyman, pp. 23-25.

23. Ibid.

24. Ibid.

25. Donlevy's patent is more useful than others. His random discourse about "typical features" helps to answer the question of whether or not patents reflect the machines which were being used during the nineteenth century.

26. Twyman, p. 35.

27. Ibid.

28. Ibid., pp. 33-34.

29. Ibid., pp. 16-21.

30. "Lithography," New American Cyclopaedia; Twyman, p. 41; "Lithography," Scientific American, July 25, 1852, p. 357; "Lithography," Art Union, Oct. 1845, p. 322.

31. Senefelder, pp. 153-54.

32. Twyman, pp. 41-50.

33. Edward Young, Leading Pursuits and Leading Men (Philadelphia, 1856), p. 232; Carl M. Cochran," James Queen Philadelphia Lithographer," Pennsylvania Magazine of History and Biography, LXXXII (April 1958), 144.

34. "Lithography," Scientific American, p. 357; "Lithography," New American Cyclopaedia; R. Hoe & Co.'s Catalogue of Printing Presses (1881), pp. 31-34 (copy in the Franklin Institute).

35. Lorin Blodget, The Industries of Philadelphia (Philadelphia, 1877), "1870 Census-Lithographers" (copy in the Library Company of Philadelphia); Hoe Catalogue, p. 34.

36. Twyman, pp. 37-41.

37. W. J. Burke, "Rudolph Ackermann, Promoter of the Arts and Sciences," Bulletin on the New York Public Library, no. 38 (1934), p. 948; Joseph Ivor Waring, History of Medicine in South Carolina (Charleston, 1964), pp. 211-12.

38. Every Man His Own Printer; or, Lithography Made
Easy (London, 1854), pp. iii-vi. The operation of an
"autographic press" is described in "Lithography,"
Appleton's Dictionary of Machines.

39. Jas. S. Pettit, Modern Reproductive Graphic
Processes (New York, 1884), p. 39.

Jerome Kaplan inks the leather roller for printing
by the planographic method, or lithography, as Bruce
St. John and Wendy Shadwell look on.

THE GRAND TRIUMPHAL QUICK-STEP; OR, SHEET MUSIC COVERS IN AMERICA

Nancy R. Davison

THE introduction of lithography in America revolutionized the production of popular prints of all kinds. A simple and direct method of making multiple copies, lithography was to be a primary process for reproducing maps, caricatures, book illustrations, advertisements and trade cards, prints of current events, portraits, pictures for American parlors, and sheet music covers during the second quarter of the nineteenth century. Another new printing process, wood engraving, became important in the illustration of books, magazines, newspapers, and advertisements during this time.

Both new methods were part of a rapid expansion of the publishing industries in America. The population was grow-ing. More and more people were learning to read in the public schools, and these people demanded books. More efficient presses, cheaper papers, and improved transporta-tion and distribution facilities filled this need. Music books, both secular and religious, and sheet music also found a ready market, as more people learned to read music.

Interest in music had been strong in the New World since its settlement. This interest could not really be cultivated and encouraged on a larger scale until the people had come to terms with the land, and had established ways of living that gave them enough leisure to pursue such activities. In colonial and federal times formal education in the arts of music was reserved for the elite, although everyone sang,

and singing schools were popular. In 1826, however, the
same year that the Pendleton brothers began lithographing
covers for sheet music in Boston, Lowell Mason arrived in
that city. Noted for his hymns and songbooks, Mason is
also remembered for the establishment of a program of
systematic musical instruction in the public schools of
Massachusetts and elsewhere, and for his emphasis on the
works of European composers.

The piano or pianoforte business grew rapidly during this
period of increasing prosperity. Families that could not
afford pianos often bought melodeons, or reed organs.
Guitars were also very popular. Sheet music publishers
began to appear in Boston, New York, and Philadelphia
during the 1790s. Many of these late eighteenth-century
music dealers also taught music and sold musical instruments. The songs they published included patriotic and
topical tunes as well as popular imports from England and
the Continent. Scored for several voices, voice and instrument, or instrument alone, these early pieces of sheet
music were printed from engraved plates and were rarely
equipped with illustrations.

Illustrated sheet music covers became popular and
feasible with the development of lithography, both in
America and in Europe. The use of lithographic illustrations on sheet music began in France and Germany during
the early nineteenth century and reached England by 1820.
European and English designs for sheet music strongly influenced American draftsmen and lithographers, particularly
during the 1850s. Many of the earlier American music sheets,
however, were fairly free of these influences. Although New
York and Philadelphia lithographers printed many illustrations for sheet music, Boston publishers and lithographers
were major producers of both music books and sheet music.
This paper will be primarily concerned with sheet music
published in Boston.

The first dated, lithographically illustrated sheet music
cover in America was issued in Boston in March 1826.
Printed by the Pendleton brothers, "The Log House" was
composed by Anton Philip Heinrich and illustrated by David

Claypool Johnston (fig. 1). Heinrich, a Bohemian banker
and musician, came to Philadelphia around 1818. He had
tremendous enthusiasm for America and for the possibilities
of developing a truly American musical idiom based upon
the land itself and upon native Indian melodies. Seeking
inspiration for his music, he visited the Indians in Bardstown, Kentucky. Heinrich's comment on this visit, "After
many storms and wanderings of life--found a temporary
asylum in this remote Kentucky cell. APH Bardstown
1818," was inscribed upon the chimney of the log house by
Johnston.

"The Log House," subtitled "A Sylvan Bravura," is
described on the cover as "No. 19, of the Sylviad by A. P.
Heinrich. To His Log House." Following four flourishing
lines of introduction the verse reads:

> Far in the West an endless wood
> Sighs to the rushing Cat---aracts flood!
> 'Twas there an humble log-house stood
> To Fa-------me un-known;
> There first, lov'd minstrelsy I woo---d
>   and woo-----'d a-lone.

Unfortunately, Heinrich lacked the talent and the technical
skills to become a great American composer, and his
"Sylviad" and "Columbiad" have been forgotten. Yet his
attempt was noteworthy. He was the first of many, im-
migrant and native alike, to try to develop a body of
national American music.

D. C. Johnston in his illustration for "The Log House"
was not as concerned with the Americanness of his product
as Heinrich was. Nevertheless, his drawing is almost
completely devoid of European influences, and it incorpor-
ates two images that recur in American popular art--the
log cabin and the ragged Negro musician.

The log cabin is familiar to Americans as the birthplace
of Abraham Lincoln and as a symbol of the man of common
origin. Johnston's "Log House," however, is a slave
cabin, not a pioneer cabin. Pioneer cabins are usually

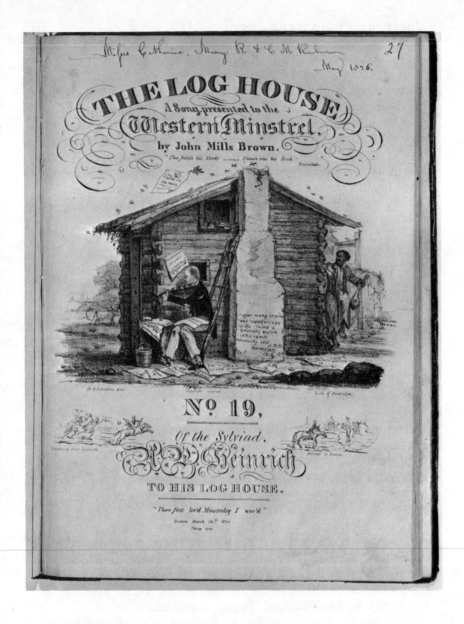

Fig. 1. "The Log House." Boston: 1826

located either on a farm or in the woods, but this dwelling
is flanked by a pillared mansion and several other planta-
tion buildings. The chimney is cracked, rats dance on the
window sill, and the whole scene serves as a backdrop, a
stage setting, for the musician with his intent face and
tapping foot. The grinning Negro with his gourd banjo re-
appears on music covers during the mid-century heyday of
the black-face minstrel shows. His ragged clothes, wide
grin, and musical instrument are attributes of the stereotype.

David Claypool Johnston was active as a caricaturist
and painter from about 1820 to the 1860s. He began his
artistic and theatrical career in Philadelphia around 1819.
His arrival in Boston in 1825 coincided with the establishment of the Pendletons' lithographic business. Johnston
soon became acquainted with William and John Pendleton
and their new process. His first lithograph, a small landscape, was published in the Boston Monthly Magazine of
December 1825. Three months later "The Log House" was
printed.

Johnston did several other sheet music covers during
the next fifteen years. One of these, "Coal Black Rose.
New Version," departs from the standard format. The illustration, etched around 1830, is printed inside the
sheet music folder just above the first three lines of the
song. Most pieces of illustrated sheet music printed
after 1826 carry a lithograph on the cover, and the music
begins on the next page. Few music sheets had engraved
or etched illustrations, although the music itself was
printed from engraved plates until the 1850s. Johnston's
music sheets are humorous and well drawn. "The School-
master," with his pigtail, ferule, and class of obstreperous
little boys, and "The Total S'iety," a temperance meeting
where the speaker just happens to have a bottle of something in his pocket as he passes out the pledges, are
among his best efforts.

Johnston was one of many skilled artists who worked
for the Pendletons and their successors. Fitz Hugh Lane,
later highly regarded for his marine paintings, began

working in the Pendleton shop in 1832. According to his
fellow apprentice Benjamin Champney, "F. H. Lane . . .
did most of the views, hotels, etc. He was very accurate
in his drawing, understood perspective and naval architecture perfectly, as well as the handling of vessels, and was
a good, all-round draughtsman."[1] He also did sheet music
illustrations during the 1830s and early 1840s. A few were
printed by Pendleton, but several were lithographed by
Thomas Moore, Pendleton's successor in Boston. One of
these is a view of the Salem Mechanick Light Infantry
mustered on the Salem Common about 1837 (fig. 2). A few
civilians survey the martial scene from the shelter of the
McIntire Arch while the captain addresses his men. Another
volunteer militia company appears in the illustration for
"Captn. E. G. Austin's Quick Step" and/or "A Yankee Ship
and a Yankee Crew," published by Parker and Ditson in
Boston in 1837. The volunteers, complete with brass band,
march over a small hill somewhere near Boston Harbor. Behind them, among other boats in the harbor, floats the
U.S.S. Constitution. Behind her, visible between the
masts, is the Massachusetts State House. "The Song of
the Fisher's Wife," printed by Sharp & Michelin and published in 1840 by Oakes & Swan, is a marine lithograph of
a different kind. The Fisher's Wife sits quietly on the
shore, watching the boats below. This delicately drawn
vignette is framed by two nautical still-life designs composed of anchors, starfish, shells, and nets. The full-
page illustration is backed by a buff tint. An innovation
of the middle 1830s, the use of such a background color
was common thereafter.

Although some artists, such as Lane and Johnston, developed their skills at home, it was common for young
artists to serve an apprenticeship with an engraver or a
lithographer and then, funds permitting, go to Europe for
further training. Benjamin Champney and Robert Cooke
followed this pattern. They both worked for Thomas Moore
during the late 1830s and then shared a portrait studio in
Boston. They sailed for Paris in 1841. Cooke died a few
months later, but Champney eventually became known for

Fig. 2. "Salem Mechanick Light Infantry Quick Step."
Salem, Mass.: Ives and Putnam, ca. 1836

his portraits and landscapes. Compared to the prolific
Robert Cooke, Benjamin Champney illustrated only a few
pieces of sheet music. Among these are "We Were Boys
Together. A Ballard . . . by Henry Russell," 1841, and
"The Old Sexton" also written by Henry Russell in 1841.
The illustrations for both songs have an atmosphere of
serene, English melancholy. The two old men who "were
boys together" share a park bench and discuss events of
long ago. "The Old Sexton" leans on his spade "Nigh to
a grave that was newly made" and reflects upon years of
digging graves.

Robert Cooke drew many covers for music written for
and dedicated to various volunteer militia companies. He
also illustrated such pieces as the "Shawmut Quick Step"
by T. Bricher and "The Pirate's Serenade" composed by
J. Thomson of Edinburgh. Cooke's lithograph for the
"Shawmut Quick Step" shows a quiet rustic view of two
Indians in a canoe paddling past a settlement of tepees.
The three peaks of the "trimountain" on the Boston or
Shawmut peninsula are barely visible in the background.
The title character of "The Pirate's Serenade" has come
a-wooing, complete with guitar and rope ladder. He sings
con spirito:

> My Boat's by the Tow'r, My Barque's
>   in the Bay;
> And both must be gone, ere the dawning
>   of day.
>
> . . . . .
>
> And this night or never my Bride thou
>   shalt be.

His boat and his barque are visible in the bay below. The
whole scene is very Mediterranean, and was probably
borrowed from a European sheet music cover, as was often
the case.

Winslow Homer also began his career as an apprentice
to a lithographer. He entered the employ of John H.
Bufford about 1854 or 1855 and left early in 1857. Although

Homer's apprentice work is often hard to identify, since
Bufford discouraged apprentice signatures and much of the
work was copy work, ten illustrated sheet music covers
have been definitely attributed to him. Among these are
pictures for "Minnie Clyde," "The Wheelbarrow Polka,"
and "Rogers Quick Step"(fig. 3). "Rogers Quick Step" is
one more example of a number dedicated to a volunteer
militia company, in this case the Boston Light Infantry.
The captain with his matching shako and moustache is not
presented in a completely dignified manner. David
Tatham suggests that Homer had his tongue firmly in his
cheek when he drew the lithograph from W. L. Champney's
design.

John H. Bufford, Homer's first employer, began his own
career as an apprentice draftsman and lithographer in the
shop of William Pendleton of Boston. The lithograph he
drew for "Rangers' Trip to Westborough or Lion Quick Step"
was done during this period (fig. 4). Although the "Rangers'
Trip" commemorates the activities of yet another volunteer
militia company, Bufford de-emphasized the Rifle Rangers
in his picture in order to make a visual pun. A lion domi-
nates the cover, and the inscription reads in part, "Per-
formed for the first time on their visit to the Lyon Farm by
the Brigade Band at the opening of the Rail Road to
Westborough--November 15th 1834." The railroad in
question is barely visible in the background. The vignette
Bufford drew for "The Winnisimmet Quick Step" is not as
original as the "Rangers' Trip" illustration. Done in 1840,
this view of Boston and Charlestown is borrowed from an
engraving after a design by W. H. Bartlett entitled
"Boston, & Bunker hill. (From the East)." The fore-
grounds of the two prints differ. Bufford eliminated a few
cows and added some people, but the views are similar in
the perspective and placement of landmarks, such as
Beacon Hill and the Bunker Hill Monument. Even boats in
the harbor are the same in position and detail.

From 1835 to 1840 Bufford worked for lithographers
such as Nathaniel Currier, another former Pendleton

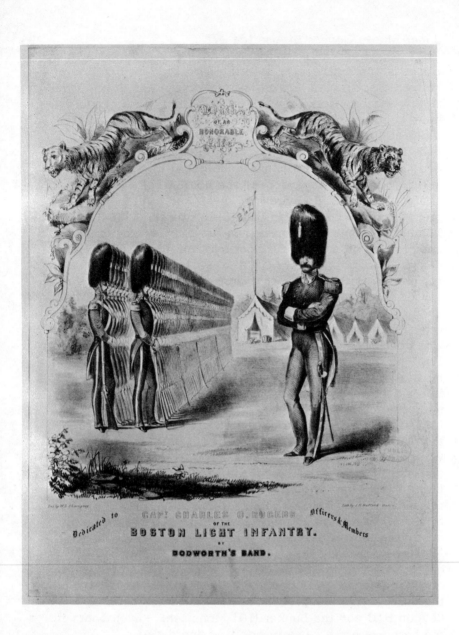

Fig. 3. "Rogers Quick Step." New York: H. B.
Dodworth, 1856

Fig. 4.   "Rangers' Trip to Westborough or Lion Quick Step."   Boston: C. Bradlee, 1834

apprentice, in New York City. He returned to Boston in 1840
and joined the lithographic firm of B. W. Thayer & Co.
Bufford drew several lithographs for Thayer, among these illustrations for sheet music, but he gradually became more
involved in the business side of lithography, the printing,
publishing, and selling of lithographs.

John H. Bufford & Co. is listed in the 1845 Boston City
Directory. The shop continued to do business at various
addresses until about 1911. Bufford trained artists and lithographers in turn as he had been trained by William Pendleton.
Alexander J. Davis and Joseph E. Baker, an especially prolific
illustrator of sheet music covers during the 1850s and 1860s,
were among the artists who worked for Bufford. Francis
D'Avignon and Leopold Grozelier were also employed in his
shop. They were among the many European artists and lithographers who worked in America.

New York and Philadelphia were also major centers of
lithographic activity. The firms of Nathaniel Currier and,
later, Currier and Ives were, of course, of great importance
in the history of American lithography. They printed lithographs
for sheet music along with their general work, but these were
of secondary interest to the company. The illustrations for
"Charter Oak! Charter Oak Ancient and Fair" and "The
Handsome Man" are among those printed by Currier.

In Philadelphia the major lithographers included the
French lithographer Peter S. Duval and his various associates,
and Thomas S. Sinclair, who was born in Scotland and trained
in lithography in Europe. Both Duval and Sinclair did a great
deal of experimental work with color printing and chromolithography. Philadelphia lithographers printed many book illustrations and special items as opposed to the more general
work produced in New York and Boston. Compared to these
cities, Philadelphia printers seem to have produced only a
small number of lithographs for sheet music.

Long-lived, stable lithographic establishments, such as
those of Bufford, Currier and Ives, Duval, and Sinclair were
the exception rather than the rule. Lithographers contracted
and dissolved partnerships and business arrangements with
surprising fluidity. Many firms were in business for only a

few years. Others moved to California in 1849. Some took up
engraving, while others found new partners and continued
making lithographs. Lithographers were often involved in
other business enterprises on the side and frequently quit
lithography altogether to take up something completely
different. Oddly enough, the Pendleton brothers followed or
perhaps established this pattern of instability.

  The story of the career of the brothers Pendleton,
collectively and individually, is confused before 1825. One
or both were trained as engravers, and William Pendleton
was working with Abel Bowen in a Boston "copperplate printing" company in 1825. Abel Bowen, incidentally, was the
first successful wood engraver in Boston and one of the first
in the country. John Pendleton brought lithographic supplies
and one or two men trained in the art of lithography to Boston
from Europe around 1825. Although Pendleton's Establishment
printed lithographs in Boston from 1825 to 1836, John Pendleton left the company around 1830 and moved south to "set up
the first lithographic plant" in Philadelphia.[2] The firm of
Pendleton, Kearny and Childs lasted only a year or so, but
the third partner, Cephas G. Childs, remained interested in
lithography. For a time he and the painter Henry Inman published lithographs as "Childs & Inman," and it was this firm
that persuaded P. S. Duval to come to the United States.
Pendleton in the meantime established a lithographic house in
New York. He sold this shop to Currier & Stodart in 1834,
and left the printing business. William Pendleton remained
in Boston, but in 1836 he sold the business to his bookkeeper,
Thomas Moore, and "seems to have gone into bank-note
engraving."[3]

  Almost all of the lithographic houses, large and small,
printed sheet music covers. The larger firms, such as
Currier & Ives, produced large numbers of prints that would
appeal to mass audiences. The Pendletons, however, and
many of the smaller firms executed prints on commission for
limited audiences. An advertisement which appeared in the
Boston Directory of 1830 gives a fair idea of the type of work
produced by these firms:

PENDLETON'S ESTABLISHMENT, No. 1
Graphic Court, Washington St. Engravings
of every description, executed on Steel &
Copper. . . . Copper Plate Printing, In all
its branches, particularly attended to.
Every description of LITHOGRAPHIC
DRAWING & PRINTING executed with
dispatch, & always in the most superior
style. Particular attention paid in the
execution of Lithographic copies of
Portraits, Miniatures, Views of Public and
Private Edifaces.----Also Maps, Surveys,
& Plans of all kinds [.] Machinery--
Specification-Drawings for Patents--
Business and Invitation Circulars--
FacSimiles--Shop Bills, &c. &c.

Lithographic stones and supplies and instructions for
"Artists & Amateurs" are also available. The bill continues:

Always on hand, an extensive
collection of ENGRAVINGS & LITHOGRAPHIC
PRINTS, American & Foreign, including a
great variety of small subjects particularly
adapted for Scrap Books, Tables, Boxes &c.
A constant stock of PLATE & LITHO-
GRAPHIC MUSIC, including all the latest
novelties produced in Philadelphia, New York
& Boston.

Many firms, including the Pendletons and J. H. Bufford,
produced both engravings and lithographs. The mention of
"A great variety of small subjects particularly adapted for
Scrap Books, Tables, Boxes &c." is interesting for it tells
how the smaller single-sheet lithographs were used. Large
folio-sized lithographs such as those produced by Currier &
Ives were obviously suitable for framing and hanging in one's
parlor, but the smaller ones were apparently treated differently. The pieces of "Plate & Lithographic Music" were

kept and bound for future use. These bound volumes of sheet music often contained supplementary material on the rudiments of music.

The Pendletons are important in the history of lithography in America not only because they were the first commercially successful lithographers in this country but because they "Succeeded in interesting and launching a large group of artists and lithographers who were major and minor figures in the history of American lithography."[4] In the course of their work, they also began the large-scale production of litho-graphed sheet music covers.

Artists sometimes published lithographs. F. H. Lane, who worked for the Pendletons, joined forces with John W. A. Scott, another famous former Pendleton apprentice, to produce lithographs under the imprint "Lane & Scott's Lith." during the middle 1840s. Both men later became known for their marine paintings, and Scott painted portraits as well. Their prints are hard to find, but the one Lane & Scott lithograph in the Boston Public Library is an illustration for the song "He Doeth All Things Well."

The music-publishing business in the early days was as changing and unstable as the lithography business. Partner-ships and locations changed frequently. Men combined other trades and the selling of other commodities with the selling of music.

Prior to the Revolutionary War, sheet music and music books were sold in bookstores and by subscription. William Arms Fisher in his history of the Oliver Ditson Company notes that:

> It was not until the close of the century that music-shops, under the names of "magazines" or "emporiums," began to appear, but the constant removal of these early music and book-shops and the frequency with which they changed hands suggest a somewhat pre-carious existence for the pioneers.[5]

As an increasingly stable and prosperous society evolved, people could afford to spend some time and effort on their music.

Music making was a fashionable and respectable form
of recreation. As the demand for sheet music and musical
instruments grew, the music trades prospered. Thousands of
single-sheet copies of popular songs were sold every year.
Although some music sheets sold for as much as a dollar,
the usual price was twenty-five to fifty cents each. These
music sheets were expensive for the day and a luxury, but
people who owned pianos and melodeons would pay the price.
Besides, pieces of sheet music were one of the few presents
a young man could give to a young lady without offending the
proprieties. A well-drawn, well-printed cover helped to sell
the music, but plain scores were also available, and sold for
somewhat less. Cheaper still were the penny-a-piece song
sheets which named the tune to be sung and gave new verses.

Baltimore was an important city in music publishing
during the second quarter of the nineteenth century. George
Willig, Jr., bought out an earlier music company in 1823,
which he and his sons ran until 1910. John Cole and his
sons formed another early music publishing company in
Baltimore. Cole, an Englishman, began his endeavors in
1799, and the business ended with his death in 1855. One of
his sons, George F. Cole, published music in Charleston,
South Carolina, from 1847 to 1859.

Music publishers active in New York during the early
nineteenth century included Thomas Birch, whose company
flourished from 1820 to the 1890s. George Melksham Bourne
published music for only five years, from 1827 to 1832, but
his catalogue included many songs illustrated by John Pendleton's company. George Endicott, the lithographer, is listed
in the <u>New York City Directory</u> of 1834-1836 as a "Lithographer,
Music Dealer and Depository of the Fine Arts." In 1839 he
advertised as a "Lithographer, Pianofortes, Music" dealer,
although for most of his sixty-odd year career he was listed
as a lithographer and engraver. His company produced a
large number of "music titles" along with the general lithographs. Joseph F. Atwill published sheet music in New York
from 1833 until 1849, when gold was discovered in California.
From 1850 to 1859 he published music in San Francisco.

In Boston, John Ashton & Co., Henry Prentiss, and

Charles H. Keith augmented their sales of music with the sale
of umbrellas up to about 1845. Boston, thanks to Lowell
Mason and his hymn writing and music teaching, was a publishing center for religious and school music. Oliver Ditson,
perhaps the most vigorous music publisher of the nineteenth
century, was based in Boston, although he set up many sub-
sidiary companies in other cities.

In Philadelphia, George Willig, father of Baltimore's
George Willig, Jr., established one of the early music-
publishing houses. This business lasted from 1794 to 1856,
when it was absorbed by Lee & Walker. Lee & Walker,
established in 1845, was in turn taken over by Oliver Ditson
of Boston in 1875. Another long-lived Philadelphia firm was
managed by the Klemm brothers from 1818 to 1881.

Music publishers were active in most American cities of
any size. Many firms were in business for only a few years,
but a number of them published music for forty years or more.
Large firms, such as Oliver Ditson & Company, bought out
many smaller companies. Catalogues, plates and stones used
for printing sheet music, and the rights to individual songs
were included in the transfers.

Sheet music was immensely popular, and some songs went
through many editions. "The Old Arm Chair," written by
Henry Russell and copyrighted in 1840, was printed in at
least twenty-three editions. The cover illustration remained
essentially the same, but some copies are signed by F. H.
Lane, others by B. Champney, and some are not signed at
all. Another song, "The Bird at Sea," appeared in four
editions with five different illustrations. Artists and lithographers constantly borrowed and stole ideas and designs
from each other and from European sources. Lithographs made
for other purposes often appeared, unchanged, on sheet music
covers.

Of the many possible categories of sheet music lithographs, a few stand out as particularly pleasing or interesting. Volunteer militia companies were often subjects for
sheet music covers. Several of these such as the "Salem
Mechanick Light Infantry Quick Step" have been discussed
already (fig. 2). (A quick step is a military march in quick

time--120 steps per minute.) These particular lithographs
commemorate the activities of some of the volunteer companies.
Other sheet music covers, such as "Hall's Quick Step" and
"Hewitt's Quick Step," feature a single standing figure,
usually the captain of the unit, who models the uniform of
the company. Other militia covers included "The New York
Light Guards Quick Step" printed by N. Currier's Lith. in
1839 and "North-End Forever or Hull Street Guards Quick Step"
lithographed in Boston around 1838 (fig. 5). Many of these
military lithographs double as city views, another popular
subject for sheet music illustrations.

City views were often used as advertisements. "The
National Guards Quick Step" not only shows the National
Guards marching along Court Street, Boston, but it also
features the establishment of "Henry Prentiss, Importer and
Manufacturer of all kinds of Musical Instruments, No. 33
Court Street . . . . " The illustration for "The Return Quick
Step" is an elegant view of Charles Bulfinch's Tontine
Crescent on Franklin Street, Boston. "The Carrier Dove, an
admired ballad sung with great Applause at Niblo's Garden
by Miss Watson" in 1836 is decorated with a lithograph of
the dove flying over "lower New York, Brooklyn and the bay"
(fig. 6). The "north front of Mercantile Row with a N.E.
distant front of the Bangor House" in Bangor, Maine, is
shown on the cover of "The Bangor March." City views on
sheet music covers are numerous and deserve further study.

Political songs were very popular, especially during
election years, and the lithographs on their covers were
effective propaganda. "There is the White House Yonder or
The Fremont Campaign Song" of 1856 combines a portrait of
the candidate, John D. Fremont, with vignettes of his past
in the great West and, hopefully, his future in the White
House. The portrait was copied from a photograph, a practice that became increasingly popular in the 1850s and 1860s.
Eventually sheet music covers would be printed by photoreproduction processes, but during this earlier period photographs and daguerreotypes were used only as models. The
concept of the negative had not yet been developed, and
each exposure resulted in a unique picture on a prepared

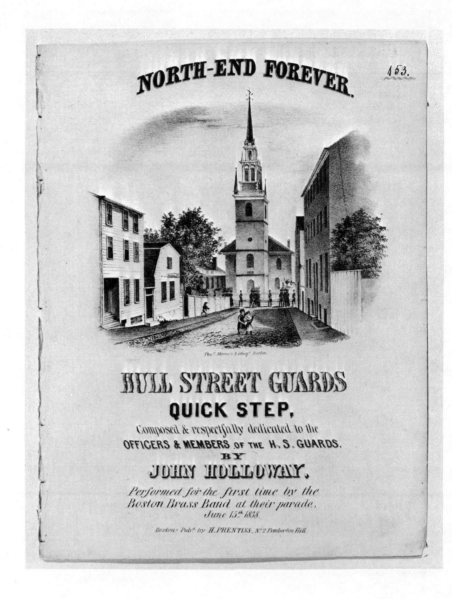

Fig. 5. "North-End Forever: Hull Street Guards
Quick Step." Boston: H. Prentiss, 1838

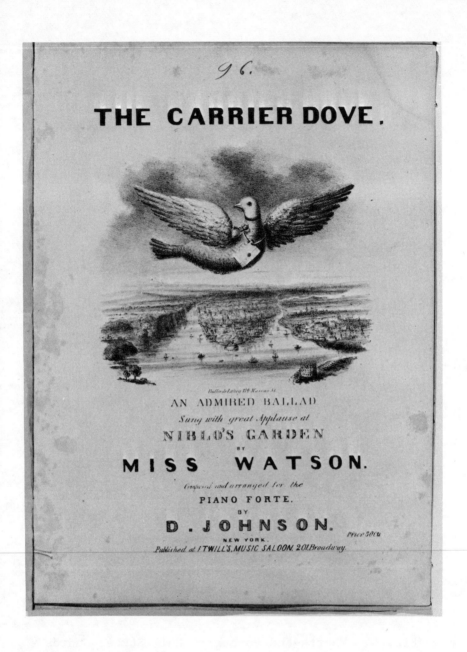

Fig. 6. "The Carrier Dove." New York: Atwill's
Music Saloon, 1836

surface--a picture that could not be reproduced.

Zachary Taylor's portrait on the cover of "The Grand Triumphal Quick Step" of 1847 testifies to his great popularity during and after the Mexican War (fig. 7). His victories at Matamoras and Buena Vista were also commemorated on the covers of sheet music. "The Capitol Quick Step," ca. 1843, with its impressive equestrian portrait of Henry Clay is another political song of the period.

William Henry Harrison's presidential campaign of 1840 was based upon his kinship with the common man. Known as the "Farmer of North Bend," Ohio, Harrison supposedly lived in a log cabin and drank hard cider. His reputation as an Indian fighter further enhanced his image. Martin Van Buren, the Democratic incumbent, in contrast, lived an extravagant and aristocratic life in the White House while the people suffered from hard times brought on by Van Buren and his predecessor Andrew Jackson. This was the Whigs' story, anyway, and they made the most of it with real log cabins, plenty of hard cider, and music. The songs included "Tippecanoe or Log Cabin Quick Step" (fig. 8), "The Log Cabin Song," "General Harrison's Grand March," "The Farmer of North Bend," and "The Hard Cider Quick Step." Whig editor Horace Greeley noted at one point during the campaign that "Our songs are doing more good than anything else."[6] The series of Harrison songs ended abruptly with Harrison's "Funeral March" in 1841.

European music dominated the American concert stage and polite musical society during the nineteenth century. Young musicians, as well as young artists, were expected to complete their studies in Europe. Many European musicians and dancers made long and profitable tours of American cities. Jenny Lind is the best known of these visiting performers. Many of her songs were published by American firms, and most of these had her portrait lithographed on the covers. Ossian E. Dodge, a Boston composer and performer, dedicated "Ossian's Serenade" to her shortly after her first Boston concert. The cover lithograph is captioned "P. T. Barnum, introducing Madelle. Jenny Lind to Ossian E. Dodge. The 'Boston vocalist' & purchaser of the $625 Ticket for the

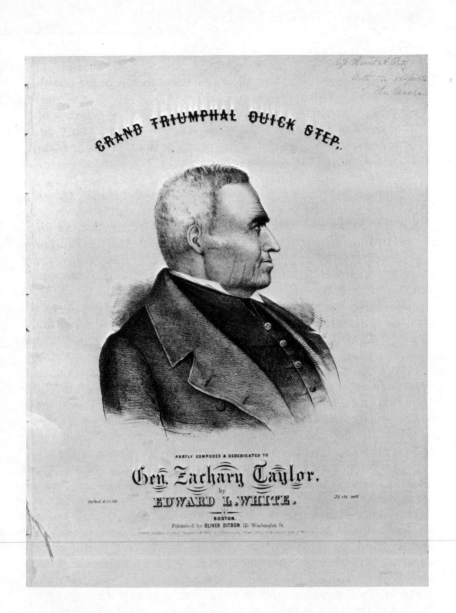

Fig. 7. "Grand Triumphal Quick Step." Boston:
Oliver Ditson, 1847

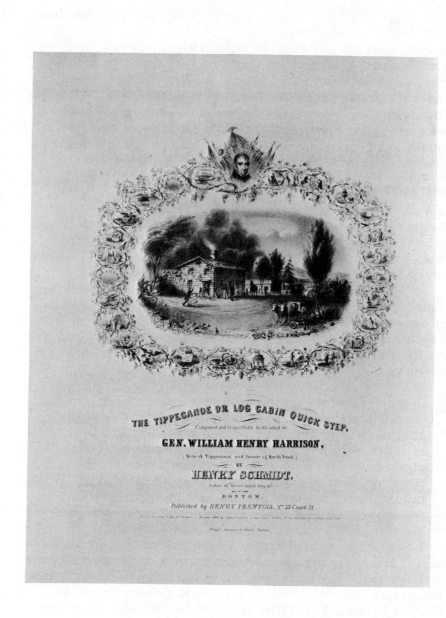

Fig. 8. "Tippecanoe or Log Cabin Quick Step."
Boston: Henry Prentiss, 1840

first Concert of the Sweedish [sic] Nightingale in Boston."
Barnum had held an auction to sell tickets to the first concert, and Dodge had paid $625 for the first ticket--three
times the price paid for the first ticket in New York. Dodge's
"own subsequent concerts were crowded with people who
were not so much interested in his entertainment value as in
seeing and hearing the man who was able to outbid everyone
else for a ticket to Jenny Lind's Boston Concert."[7]

Fanny Elssler toured the United States around 1840. The
Austrian ballerina was already extremely popular in Europe,
and she charmed Americans with such dances as "The
Cachucha" and "The Gitana." Although these tunes were
published separately, one all-purpose lithograph showing
Miss Elssler in five different costumes was used to illustrate
several different numbers.

Although the tradition of the singing family developed in
Alpine Europe, American singing families were popular and
prosperous during the 1840s and 1850s. The Hutchinson
Family of New Hampshire was especially well known (fig. 9).
A mill girl in Lowell, Massachusetts, heard them sing on the
Fourth of July, ca. 1840, and commented:

In the evening we had the Hutchinsons, from our own
Granite State, who discoursed sweet music so sweetly.
They have become great favorites with the public. It
is not on account of their fine voices only, but their
pleasant modest manners--the perfect sense of propriety which they exhibit in all their demeanor; and I
think they are not less popular here because they sing
the wrongs of the slave, and praises of cold water.[8]

Literary figures also appear on the covers of sheet music.
In 1842 Henry Prentiss published a portrait of Charles Dickens
with the song "The Stars their early Vigils keep . . . ." The
inscription reads "As Sung at the complimentary Dinner to
Charles Dickens Esq. Written by Dr. O. W. Holmes." The
portraits found on the covers of such songs, and on the
covers of music for the militia, are often the only existing
likenesses of many nineteenth-century figures. An ornate

Fig. 9. "Songs of the Hutchinson Family:
Excelsior." New York: Firth, Hall & Pond, 1843

colored border reflects a fad for designs based upon medieval
illuminated manuscripts.

Portraits of visiting performers were generally drawn with
utmost seriousness. The Austrian composer and pianist Alfred
Jaell, however, was caricatured in a complimentary fashion
on the cover of the "Caricature Schottische." Published
shortly after Jaell's magnificent Boston concert, the illustration for this music sheet was a "lithograph caricature of the
pianist . . . , drawn by E. Masson, which cleverly ex-
pressed the popular opinion by showing him unobtrusively
displaying his TEN-FINGERED hands."[9]

Humorous sheet music illustrations are generally uncommon. With the exception of the "Caricature Schottische,"
D. C. Johnston's sheet music covers, and a few touches in
Winslow Homer's lithographs, comic elements in music sheets
are broad and theatrical. The classic black-face minstrel
show was not developed until 1843, but "Ethiopian" melodies
such as "Jim Crow," ca. 1829, and "Jumbo Jum," 1840, were
popular before that time. Illustrated with stereotyped images
of happily singing blacks these numbers were usually sung
in Negro dialect. "Comic" songs, such as "The Cork Leg"
and "The Handsome Man," originated in the English musical
theater. Illustrations for these numbers were often borrowed
from English models that were probably based upon the stage
settings and costumes of the performances.

Songs with a moral were also popular. The songs of the
Hutchinson Family dealt with temperance and abolition. An
earlier song, "Think and Smoke Tobacco," reflects upon the
mortality of man.

> This Indian weed now wither'd quite,
> Though green at noon, cut down at night,
> Shows thy decay: All flesh is hay,
> Thus think and smoke Tobacco,
> Thus think and smoke Tobacco.

Both the song and the illustration are probably English in
origin. "The Washington Quick Step" cover shows a house
in ruins next to a house in good repair, symbolizing a man's

life with and without the companionship of Demon Rum. D. C.
Johnston's illustration for "The Total S'iety" is another of
many temperance lithographs.

Many sheet music lithographs are difficult to classify by
subject. "Charter Oak! Charter Oak Ancient and Fair!,"
written by Mrs. Sigourney, a popular lady poet, and composed
by Henry Russell, was one of many sentimental favorites.
Russell, an English composer who had studied music in France
and Italy, visited many American cities during the 1830s and
early 1840s to perform his own "descriptive songs." Among
his most popular compositions were "The Maniac," "Woodman!
Spare That Tree," and "The Ship on Fire."

Henry Russell was extremely popular, and greatly influenced genteel American taste. He made a fortune with his
stirring performances, and he had this to say about the relationship between composer and publisher:

> I have composed and published in my life over eight
> hundred songs, but it was by singing these songs
> and not by the sale of copyrights that I made money.
> There was no such thing as a royalty in those days
> and when a song was sold it was sold outright. My
> songs brought me an average price of ten shillings
> each . . . though they have made the fortune of
> several publishers. Had it not been that I sang my
> songs myself . . . the payment for their composition
> would have meant simple starvation.[10]

Another popular song of the 1830s was the Women's Libera-
tion anthem, entitled "I'll be No Submissive Wife."

> I'll be no submissive wife
> No not I no not I
> I'll not a slave for life
> No not I no not I
>
>   . . . . .
>
> Think you on a wedding day
> That I said as other say
> Love and honor and obey
>
>   . . . . .

No no no . . . not I

One edition appeared in New York in 1835, and the song was presumably still a best seller in 1838 when the sixth edition was published.

Three miscellaneous pieces complete this sample of lithographed sheet music covers. A set of dance tunes, "The Violet Quadrilles," is illustrated with an interior view of the ballroom of the Tremont House in Boston. This piece, printed between 1840 and 1845, was a perfect souvenir for those who attended the dance. "A Health to the Outward Bound," published about 1839, is one of many marine litho-graphs to be found on music covers. The last lithograph is on the cover of the dramatic piece "The Fireman's Call" (fig. 10). The song and the illustration are dedicated to the Fire Department of Boston, and reflect the honored and res-pected position of the fireman in American society in the nineteenth century.

Music sheets are still with us, but their role in American life is greatly diminished. The golden age of lithographed sheet music covers lasted from the late 1820s to the 1850s, when new techniques of printing and photoreproduction came into use. The artists and craftsmen who were employed by the lithographic shops now had numerous other opportunities. Art training became more readily available, and photography offered new horizons. Magazines required skilled and facile artists to do their wood engravings, and black and white lithography was rapidly becoming old-fashioned.

The field of lithographed sheet music covers is huge and largely unexplored. The thirty-odd prints mentioned here can give only a faint impression of the quality and variety of the music covers produced in the second quarter of the nineteenth century in America.

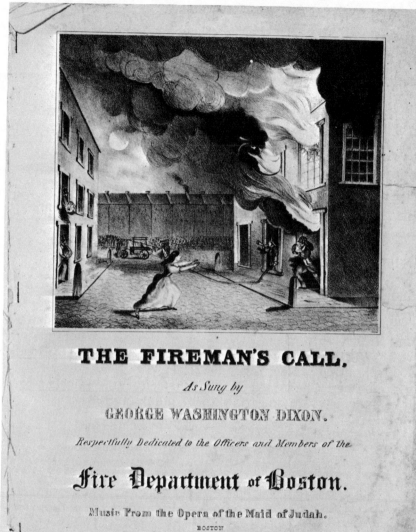

Fig. 10. "The Fireman's Call." Boston: Oliver Ditson, 1845

NOTES

1. Sixty Years' Memories of Art and Artists (Woburn, Mass., 1900), p. 10.

2. George H. Eckhardt, "Early Lithography in Philadelphia," Antiques, XXVIII (Dec. 1935), 251.

3. Harry T. Peters, America on Stone (Garden City, N.Y., 1931), p. 318.

4. Ibid., p. 317.

5. One Hundred and Fifty Years of Music Publishing in the United States: An Historical Sketch with Special Reference to the Pioneer Publisher, Oliver Ditson Company, Inc., 1783-1933 (Boston, 1934), p. 22.

6. Robert Gray Gunderson, The Log-Cabin Campaign (Lexington, Ky., 1957), p. 123.

7. Lester S. Levy, Grace Notes in American History: Popular Sheet Music from 1820 to 1900 (Norman, Okla., 1967), p. 11.

8. Carl Bode, ed., American Life in the 1840s (Garden City, N.Y., 1967), p. 38.

9. William Murrell, A History of American Graphic Humor (1933; reprint ed., New York, 1967), I, 193.

10. Gilbert Chase, America's Music from the Pilgrims to the Present, rev. 2d ed. (New York, 1966), p. 168.

SOURCES

Bode, Carl., ed. <u>American Life in the 1840s.</u> Garden City,
   N.Y.: Anchor Books, Doubleday & Company, Inc., 1967.
   _____. <u>The Anatomy of American Popular Culture, 1840-
   1861.</u> Berkeley and Los Angeles: University of
   California Press, 1959.
Champney, Benjamin. <u>Sixty Years' Memories of Art and
   Artists.</u> Woburn, Mass., 1900.
Chase, Gilbert. <u>America's Music from the Pilgrims to the
   Present</u>. Rev. 2d ed. New York: McGraw-Hill Book
   Company, 1966.
Cunliffe, Marcus. <u>Soldiers and Civilians: The Martial
   Spirit in America 1775-1865.</u> Boston: Little, Brown &
   Company, 1968.
Davis, Aaron. "Music Covers," <u>Antiques</u>, XII (Nov. 1927),
   394-96.
Dichter, Harry, and Shapiro, Elliott. <u>Early American Sheet
   Music: Its Lure and Its Lore, 1768-1889; Including a
   Directory of Early American Music Publishers.</u> New York:
   RR Bowker Company, 1941.
Eckhardt, George H. "Early Lithography in Philadelphia,"
   <u>Antiques</u>, XXVIII (Dec. 1935), 249-52.
Fisher, William Arms. <u>One Hundred and Fifty Years of Music
   Publishing in the United States: An Historical Sketch
   with Special References to the Pioneer Publisher,
   Oliver Ditson Company, Inc., 1783-1933.</u> Boston:
   Oliver Ditson Company, Inc., 1934.
Fuld, James J. <u>American Popular Music:. . . 1875-1950</u>.
   Philadelphia: Musical Americana, 1955.
   _____. <u>The Book of World-Famous Music: Classical,
   Popular, Folk.</u> New York: Crown Publishers, Inc., 1966.
Groce, George C., and Wallace, David H. <u>The New-York
   Historical Society's Dictionary of Artists in America,
   1564-1860</u>. New Haven and London: Yale University
   Press, 1957.
Gunderson, Robert Gray. <u>The Log-Cabin Campaign.</u> Lexington:
   University of Kentucky Press, 1957.

Hamilton, Sinclair. Early American Book Illustrators and Wood Engravers. Vol I. Main Catalogue. Princeton, N. J.: Princeton University Press, 1958.

Howard, John Tasker, and Bellows, George Kent. A Short History of Music in America. New York: Thomas Y. Crowell Company, 1967.

Johnson, Malcolm. David Claypool Johnston: American Graphic Humorist, 1798-1865. Catalogue for an exhibition jointly held by the American Antiquarian Society, Boston College, The Boston Public Library, and the Worcester Art Museum in March 1970.

King, A. Hyatt. English Pictorial Music Title-pages, 1820-1885: Their Style, Evolution and Importance. London: The Bibliographical Society, 1950.

Levy, Lester S. Grace Notes in American History: Popular Sheet Music from 1820 to 1900. Norman: University of Oklahoma Press, 1967.

Murrell, William. A History of American Graphic Humor. 2 vols. New York: Cooper Square Publishers, 1933.

Nye, Russell Blaine. 1776-1830: The Cultural Life of the New Nation. New York, Evanston, and London: Harper & Row, Harper Torchbooks, 1963.

Peters, Harry T. America on Stone. Garden City, N.Y.: Doubleday, Doran & Company, Inc., 1931.

_____. California on Stone. Garden City, N.Y.: Doubleday, Doran & Company, Inc., 1935.

_____. Currier & Ives: Printmakers to the American People. Garden City, N.Y.: Doubleday, Doran & Company, Inc., 1942.

Rublowsky, John. Music in America. New York: Crowell-Collier Press, 1967.

Sonneck, Oscar George Theodore. A Bibliography of Early Secular American Music. Revised and enlarged by William Treat Upton. The Library of Congress Music Division, Washington, 1945.

_____. A Survey of Music in America. Washington: Privately printed for the Author by the McQueen Press, 1913. Read before the "Schola Cantorum," New York City, April 11, 1913.

Spaeth, Sigmund. Read 'em and Weep. Rev. ed. New York:
    Arco Publishing Company, 1945.
    _____. Weep Some More, My Lady. Garden City,
    N.Y.: Doubleday, Page, and Company, 1927.
Tatham, David. "Some Apprentice Lithographs of Winslow
    Homer," Old-Time New England: Bulletin of the
    Society for the Preservation of New England
    Antiquities, LIX (April-June, 1969), 87-104.
    _____. "Winslow Homer and The Ratcatcher's Daughter."
    Reprinted from The Courier, no. 28 (Winter, 1967),
    Syracuse University.
Trollope, Mrs. Frances. Domestic Manners of the Americans.
    2 vols. 2d. ed. London: Printed for Whittaker, Treacher,
    and Company, 1832.
Van Deusen, Glyndon G. The Jacksonian Era: 1828-1848.
    New York: Harper & Row, Harper Torchbooks, 1959.
Wainwright, Nicholas B. Philadelphia in the Romantic Age
    of Lithography. Philadelphia: The Historical Society of
    Pennsylvania, 1958.
Winter, Marian Hannah. Art Scores for Music. Brooklyn
    Institute of Arts and Sciences. Brooklyn Museum, 1939.
Wolf, Edwin, 2nd. American Song Sheets, Slip Ballards and
    Political Broadsides 1850-1870: A Catalogue of the
    Collection of the Library Company of Philadelphia.
    Philadelphia: Philadelphia Library Company, 1963.

SHEET MUSIC LITHOGRAPHS MENTIONED IN "THE GRAND
TRIUMPHAL QUICK STEP OR SHEET MUSIC COVERS IN AMERICA."*

BANGOR MARCH (North front of Mercantile Row with a N.E.
   distant front of the Bangor House), ca. 1830,
   Pendleton's Lithography. Boston: Published for
   the Author by Chas. Bradlee.
THE BIRD AT SEA. (Four editions, five different illustra-
   tions.)
   First Edition. 1834, Lith. and artist: Thomas Campbell,
      Baltimore: John Cole & Son, Baltimore, pub. Illustra-
      tion: "Square rigged three masted ship."
   Second edition A. 1834, Lith. T. Campbell. John Cole
      & Son, Baltimore, pub. Illustration: "Single masted
      sailing craft, view of stern only, sailing before
      the wind. Probably a ketch."
   Second edition B. 1834, Lith. T. Campbell. John Cole
      & Son, Baltimore, pub. Illustration: "Italian Felucca
      one sail of special type. Mt. Vesuvius is dimly
      seen smoking in the background."
   Third edition. 1836, John Cole & Son, Baltimore, pub.
      Illustration: "Two masted schooner."
   Fourth edition. 1836, Lith: E. Weber & Co., John Cole
      & Son, Baltimore, pub. Illustration: "Two masted
      brig."
   Source: Harry Dichter and Elliott Shapiro, Sheet
      Music: Its Lure and Its Lore, 1768-1889. New
      York: RR Bowker Company, 1941. p. 55.
THE CAPITOL QUICK STEP. 1843-44, Lith. of Bouve &
   Sharp, [Boston].
CAPTN. E. G. AUSTIN'S QUICK STEP. 1837, F. H. Lane,
   del.; Moore's Lithogy. Boston: Parker & Ditson, 107
   Washington St. (Also entitled A YANKEE SHIP AND A
   YANKEE CREW).
CARICATURE SCHOTTISCHE. 1854, E. Masson, del.;
   Bufford's Lith. Boston: Oliver Ditson, 115 Washington St.
THE CARRIER DOVE. 1836, Bufford's Lithog., 114 Nassau St.
   [New York]: Atwill's Music Saloon, 201 Broadway.

*Quoted directly from the music sheets.

CHARTER OAK! CHARTER OAK ANCIENT AND FAIR! ca. 1840,
  W. K. H. (William K. Hewitt), del.; N. Currier's
  Lith., N.Y.: Hewitt & Jaques, 239 Broadway.
COAL BLACK ROSE: NEW VERSION. 1831-32, D. C. J. (David
  Claypool Johnston), del.; Published by D. C. Johnston,
  19 Water St., Boston. AAS.
THE CORK LEG. ca. 1835, C. A. Smith del.; Willig's Lith.,
  G. Willig, Jr., Baltimore.
ELSSLER QUADRILLES. 1840, Designed by S. C. Jollie,;
  Thayer's Lithography, Boston: Ferdinand C. Unger,
  No. 385 Broadway N.Y.
THE FARMER OF NORTH BEND (THE PATRIOTS HOME). 1840,
  Charles T. Geslain, N.Y. pub. Dichter & Shapiro, p. 60.
THE FIREMAN'S CALL. 1845, Boston: Oliver Ditson, 115
  Washington St.
FUNERAL MARCH: IN MEMORY OF WILLIAM H. HARRISON:
  LATE PRESIDENT OF THE UNITED STATES. 1841, Bufford,
  del.; B. W. Thayer's Lithography, Boston: Henry
  Prentiss, 33 Court St.
GEN. HARRISON'S GRAND MARCH. 1840, B. W. Thayer's
  Lith. Boston: John Ashton & Co. 197 Washington St.
GRAND TRIUMPHAL QUICK STEP. 1847, Bufford & Co's Lith.,
  Oliver Ditson 115 Washington St., Boston.
HALL'S QUICK STEP. 1840, R. Cooke, del.; Thayer's
  Lithogy, Boston: Oakes & Swan, 8 1/2 Tremont Row.
THE HANDSOME MAN. ca. 1837, E. Brown, Jr. del.; N.
  Currier's Lith. N.Y.: James L. Hewitt & Co. 239
  Broadway.
THE HARD CIDER QUICK STEP. 1840, Lith. E. Weber & Co.,
  S. Carusi, Baltimore, Dichter & Shapiro, p. 61.
A HEALTH TO THE OUTWARD BOUND. ca. 1839, Swett, del.;
  G. Willig, Jr., Baltimore.
HE DOETH ALL THINGS WELL. ca. 1841, Lane & Scott's
  Lith., Geo. P. Reed, 17 Tremont Row, Boston.
HEWITT'S QUICK STEP. 1840, N. Currier's Lith. N.Y.,
  Hewitt & Jaques, 239 Broadway.
I'LL BE NO SUBMISSIVE WIFE. 1835, Lithographer illegible,
  Firth & Hall, No. 1 Franklin Square (N.Y.).

JUMBO JUM. 1840, R. Cooke, del.; Thayer's Lith., Henry
   Prentiss, 33 Court St., Boston.
THE LOG CABIN SONG. 1840, J. H. B. (John H. Bufford),
   del.; B. W. Thayer's Lithy., Parker & Ditson, 135
   Washington St., Boston.
THE LOG HOUSE. 1826, D. C. Johnston, del.; Lith. of
   Pendleton, Boston.
THE MANIAC. 1840, F. H. Lane, del.; Thayer's Lithographic
   Press, Published by Parker & Ditson 135 Washington St.,
   Boston.
MINNIE CLYDE. 1857, (Winslow Homer, del.); J. H. Bufford's
   Lith., Oliver Ditson & Co. Washington St., Boston.
   Tatham. "Some Apprentice Lithographs...", pp. 96, 100.
NATIONAL GUARDS QUICK STEP. 1838, T. Moore's Lithogy,
   Henry Prentiss 33 Court St., Boston.
THE NEW YORK LIGHT GUARDS QUICK STEP. 1839, N.
   Currier's Lith., Hewitt & Jaques, 239 Broadway, New York.
NORTH END FOREVER: HULL STREET GUARDS QUICK STEP.
   ca. 1838, Thos. Moore's Lithogy. Boston: H. Prentiss,
   No. 2 Pemberton Hill.
THE OLD ARM CHAIR. 1840, Thayer & Co's Lithogy, Boston,
   Geo. P. Reed, 17 Tremont Row.
_____1840, F. H. Lane, del.; Thayer, successor to
   Moore. Oakes & Swan, 8 1/2 Tremont Row, Boston.
_____1840, 4th ed., B. Champney, del.; B. W. Thayer's
   Lithogy. Boston: Henry Prentiss, 33 Court St.
THE OLD SEXTON, 3d ed., 1841, B. Champney, del.; B. W.
   Thayer's Lithogy. Boston: Henry Prentiss, 33 Court St.
OSSIAN'S SERENADE. 1850. Oliver Ditson, 115 Washington
   St., Boston.
THE PIRATE'S SERENADE. 1838, R. Cooke, del.; T. Moore's
   Lithogy, Boston: Henry Prentiss.
RANGERS' TRIP TO WESTBOROUGH OR LION QUICK STEP. 1834,
   J. H. Bufford, del.; Pendleton's Lithogy. Boston,
   C. Bradlee,
RETURN QUICK STEP. 1844, Thayer & Co.'s Lith. Boston:
   Keith's Music Publishing House, 67 & 69 Court St.
ROGERS QUICK STEP. 1856, Des. by W. L. Champney,
   (Winslow Homer, del.), Lith. by J. H. Bufford.

H. B. Dodworth, 493 Broadway, N. Y. <u>Tatham. "Some</u>
Apprentice Lithographs..." p. 96.

SALEM MECHANICK LIGHT INFANTRY QUICK STEP. ca. 1836,
F. H. Lane, del.; Moore's Lithography. Boston, suc-
cessor to Pendleton. Published by Ives & Putnam, Salem,
Mass.

THE SCHOOLMASTER. 1839, D. C. Johnston del.;
T. Moore's Lith. Boston: Parker & Ditson 135 Washington
St., Boston.

SHAWMUT QUICK STEP, ca. 1840, R. Cooke, del.; B. W.
Thayer's Lithogy, Boston: Geo. P. Reed 17 Tremont Row,
Boston.

THE SHIP ON FIRE. ca. 1843, E. Brown, del. & lith.,
4 John St., Printed by Endicott, N. York: J. L. Hewitt
& Co., 239 Broadway.

SONG OF THE FISHER'S WIFE. 1840, F. H. Lane, del.;
Sharp & Michelin, Printers. Oakes & Swan, 8 1/2
Tremont Row, Boston.

SONGS OF THE HUTCHINSON FAMILY: EXCELSIOR. 1843.
Lith. of G. & W. Endicott, N. Y.: Firth & Hall No. 1
Franklin Sq. and Firth, Hall & Pond 239 Broad-
way.

THE STARS THEIR EARLY VIGILS KEEP. 1842, Thayer & Co.'s
Lithography, Boston: Henry Prentiss 33 Court St.

THERE IS THE WHITE HOUSE YONDER OR THE FREMONT
CAMPAIGN SONG, 1856, Lith. of Sarony & Co. N.Y.,
S. T. Gordon, 297 Broadway, N.Y.

THINK AND SMOKE TOBACCO. 1836, Designed by Joseph
Gear; Pendleton's Lithography, Published by John Ashton
& Company, 197 Washington St., Boston.

TIPPECANOE OR LOG CABIN QUICK STEP. 1840, Thayer,
successor to Moore, Henry Prentiss, 33 Court St.,
Boston.

THE TOTAL S'IETY. 1840, D. C. Johnston, del.; B. W.
Thayer's Lithogy, Boston: Henry Prentiss. Boston.
<u>AAS.</u>

VIOLET QUADRILLES, c. 1840, B. W. Thayer's Lithogy.
Boston: Henry Prentiss, 33 Court St.

THE WASHINGTONIAN QUICK STEP. 1842, Thayer & Co.'s
    Lithogy. Boston: Geo. P. Reed 17 Tremont Row.
WE WERE BOYS TOGETHER. 1841, B. Champney, del.;
    B. W. Thayer's Lith.; Boston: Firth & Hall, No. 1,
    Franklin Sq., N.Y.
THE WHEELBARROW POLKA. 1856, Photograph by Turner &
    Cutting [sic], (Winslow Homer, del.); J. H. Bufford's
    Lith., Oliver Ditson, 115 Washington St., Boston:
    Tatham. "Some Apprentice Lithographs...," pp. 86,96.
THE WINNISIMMET QUICK STEP. 1840. Bufford, del.;
    Thayer's Lithography, Boston: Henry Prentiss 33 Court St.
WOODMAN! SPARE THAT TREE! 1837, Lithoy of Endicott,
    N. Y.: Firth & Hall, No. 1, Franklin Sq.
ZIP COON. ca. 1835, Litho. of Endicott 359 Broadway, New
    York: Published by J. L. Hewitt & Co., 137 Broadway.
    Levy, p. 90.

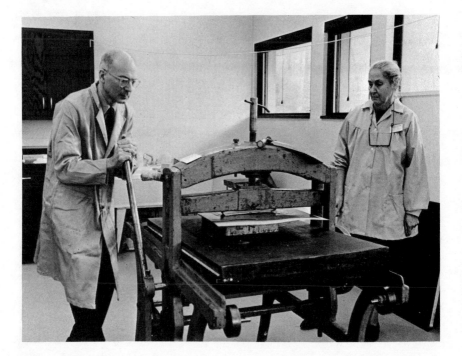

Lithographers Jerome Kaplan and Sallie F. Knerr pull a print. The stone with its drawing has been inked, and now resting on the bed of the press, is forced under the pressure bar. The Parks press, used here, was made in 1897 by Robert Mayer & Co., New York City.

Engravers Cantor and Weil roll the inked plate and
moist paper between cylinders and steel bed causing
the inked furrows to print black on the surface
while the unengraved portions of the plate, being
polished, print white. This etching press was made
by Karl Krause, ca. 1910, in Leipzig, Germany.

PRINTS AND THE AMERICAN ART-UNION

Jay Cantor

MOST students of American art are familiar with the history
of the founding and development of the American Art-Union.[1]
Organized in 1839, it operated under the name of the Apollo
Association for the Advancement of the Fine Arts in the United
States until it was renamed the American Art-Union in 1844.
The Association encouraged the growth of the fine arts in the
United States through its system of an annual lottery of works
of art which had been acquired during the year directly from
American artists. Purchase funds were provided by a five-
dollar subscription fee to the Association. This form of col-
lective patronage was operative in America at a time when the
mechanics for distribution of works of art had not yet been resolved by the development of major art dealers and an active
market place. The Art-Union extended its patronage throughout
the country, and even acquired works of American artists re-
siding abroad. The lottery, in turn, provided a vehicle for
the transfer of these works to the far reaches of a culturally
unsettled nation, until the lottery system was declared illegal
and the Union was forced to suspend its activities in 1852.

The choice of pictures for the lottery was limited to what
was made available to the Art-Union and what they considered
worthy of distribution. The Union frequently found itself
haggling with artists over subject matter and the prices of
their works, and often encountered greater difficulty in alter-
ing the convictions of artists than it did in influencing the
taste and attitudes of its subscribers.

In selecting a print for the annual distribution to all subscribers, the Union could choose the one work which seemed
the most appropriate to the purposes of the organization during

that year. In its earliest years it did so by depending entirely
on the loan of pictures from private collectors, and it did not
reproduce a painting which was part of the annual lottery until
1847.

The plan of the Art-Union, which states its charter purpose
as the "promotion of the Fine Arts in the United States," also
lists the means through which this "TRULY NATIONAL OBJECT"
of "uniting great public good with private gratification at small
individual expense" was to be accomplished. [2] The first of
their list of activities was to involve "the production of a
large and costly Original Engraving from an American painting
of which the plate and copyright belong to the Institution, and
are used solely for its benefit." [3] The implication is that the
print so issued was to be something more than a consolation
prize for the losers in the lottery. Secondly, the funds of
the Union were to be applied to the purchase of paintings and
sculptures which would be publicly distributed, and finally,
the Union intended to maintain a free picture gallery (fig. 1),
to be open throughout the year--an attractive feature in a
country which could not yet boast of a single successful
museum devoted to the fine arts. Thus the plan of the Art-
Union did not vary appreciably from the design of similar
institutions abroad. [4]

Nor was the creation of fine prints from works of art a
novel concept in America. Numerous attempts had been made
to foster a knowledge of the fine arts and, not incidentally,
the fame and fortune of an artist by the publication of prints
after his paintings. John Trumbull's Revolutionary War subjects (produced in England), Rembrandt Peale's Washington
portraits, and Asher Durand's famed engraving after John
Vanderlyn's "Ariadne" are convenient illustrations of the
tendency of these prints to deal with themes of national significance, historical events, portraits, or allegorical subjects.
The illustration of literary works was another major reason for
the production of printed images based on works of fine art,
but these tended to be small in scale and were usually included
as only occasional illustrations to literary journals or in one
of the sentimental gift books popular during the second quarter
of the nineteenth century. The literary character of these

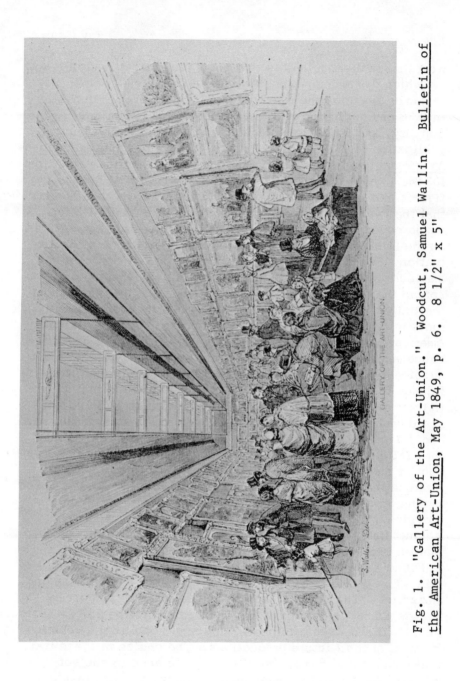

GALLERY OF THE ART-UNION

Fig. 1. "Gallery of the Art-Union." Woodcut, Samuel Wallin. Bulletin of the American Art-Union, May 1849, p. 6. 8 1/2" x 5"

works made them palatable to a populace not yet ready for an
art which demanded trained or experienced visual sensibility.

James Herring, the man who had founded the Apollo Gallery
in 1838 and dedicated it to the exhibition of "Paintings,
Statuary, and Engravings," had himself been involved in the
publication of The National Portrait Gallery of Distinguished
Americans (published with James Longacre in Philadelphia from
1834 to 1839), four volumes containing portraits of famous
figures and brief sketches of their lives. Herring had hoped
that the twenty-five-cent entrance fee to the Apollo Gallery
would cover operating expenses, but when the project tottered
on the brink of failure, it was reorganized as the Apollo Association. The Apollo was directed by a group of merchant
amateurs who, through nationalistic motives, sought to
spread the taste-elevating impulse of the fine arts throughout
the United States. Generally they were self-made men with
roots in rural America, and they felt personally indebted to
America for the opportunities she had given for their own advancement. They pursued the repayment of this debt with a
missionary zeal. Success of their Association brought confidence to the managers, who soon gained extraordinary faith
in their own powers of perception and articulation. They devised a hierarchy of subject matter which was both democratic
and didactic; democratic in the sense of fostering the values
they felt germane to a democratic society (which was the product of the American Revolution) and didactic because they
awarded the greatest value to history painting.

The prints distributed by the Apollo and the Art-Union
provide an index to the range of the managers' concerns.
Having distributed their first print, a mezzotint of "General
Marion in His Swamp Encampment Inviting a British Officer
to Dinner" by John Blake White (engraved by John Sartain,
printed by J. Dalton) to the 686 members in 1840 and a second
mezzotint, "The Artist's Dream," an allegorical subject by
George Comegys (engraved by John Sartain) to the 937 members
in 1841, the managers turned to line engraving as the vehicle
for most of their future productions. The choice of these two
works suggested something of their preference in subject
matter. The first print was, appropriately, a scene taken

from Revolutionary War history, while the second explored
the pantheon of genius in the history of art and suggested the
transfer of that fertile seed to America. Another allegory
depicted in a considerably earlier work by a patriarch of
American neoclassical painting, was offered to the members
of the Association in 1842: John Vanderlyn's "Marius Amidst
the Ruins of Carthage," painted by the artist in France in
1807. But by the early 1840s neoclassical allegory was being
displaced in the range of desirable subjects even as the
Greek Revival fashion was dying as an architectural style.
Having thus paid proper respect to the fashion of an earlier
moment with the reproduction of Vanderlyn's romantic expostu-
lation, the managers turned to the everyday life of modern,
albeit rural, America.

There exists throughout the Art-Union's history a dichotomy
between sophisticated and cosmopolitan values of high art and
the desire to promote a national art which must, of necessity,
be based on American life. Though genre subjects would seem
natural in this context, their position was usually preempted
by historical subjects which frequently had only the vaguest
relation to American iconography. With the publication of
William Sidney Mount's "Farmers Nooning" (engraved by Alfred
Jones, printed by Burton) the managers were allowing nationalistic motives to outweigh their love of grand themes (fig. 2).
Yet even this scene makes it clear that the Association favored
works that would have an instructive value or a moral implication. Advising a young artist a few years later, the Association stated a preference for works "taken from everyday scenes
of life, those that are not suggestive of, or create painful
emotions . . . anything, however that illustrates our country,
its history or its poetry."[5] Although we no longer believe
Mount to be the painter of homely scenes of domestic virtue,
it is not unlikely that "Farmers Nooning," which was borrowed
for engraving from Jonathan Sturges, must have had precisely
that appeal for the Apollo Association.

By borrowing from a private collector, the Association
could avoid paying the artist a reproduction fee. Mount never
received such a fee from the Association or later from his
French publishers, Goupil, Vibert & Co. The copyright

Fig. 2. "Farmers Nooning." Steel, engraving, Alfred Jones, after painting by William Sidney Mount, Art-Union premium in 1843. 16" x 12 3/4". New-York Historical Society

belonged to the Association, and Mount later complained:

> They did dispose of the old plate of the "Farmers
> Nooning"--and what miserable impressions Mr.
> Appleton has thrown out to the world,--a lie in
> comparison to the original and a disgrace to his
> taste--how a man can pick up dollars from a worn
> out plate--it is like a crow picking up a few
> pieces from an old dead carcase. [6]

A small version of the same print was used as the frontispiece to the Transactions for 1842 published by the Apollo
Association. Thus was begun what would eventually become
a fully illustrated journal of art--a journal which would, moreover, reach a sizable audience, for the Apollo Association
was gaining momentum and had, by 1843, 1,452 members on
its rolls. The following year it became the American Art-Union,
offering a chance at one of ninety-two paintings and two prints
to 2,080 members. [7] The lottery also included ten bound sets
of four plates of George Harvey's American Landscape Scenery.
It should be noted here that prints did not generally appear
in the Art-Union lotteries, and a specific injunction against
the inclusion of paintings based on prints had been issued. [8]
The only individual prints which were awarded by lot were
after two paintings by John Trumbull: "The Battle of Bunker's
Hill" and the "Death of General Montgomery," both distributed
in 1850. It did become the custom, however, to make the
prints of previous years available to members for an additional
five-dollar fee, which also brought a second chance in the
lottery. For this purpose the old plates were occasionally
reworked, a process which prolonged their life and the
currency of their images.
Sentimental scenes of home life were present among the
genre subjects that the Art-Union offered in the lottery, and
a print after Francis W. Edmonds's "Sparking" was engraved
for distribution in 1844 by Alfred Jones (fig. 3). The painting
was owned by a collector in Newburgh, New York, who presumably was aware of the preachings on the sanctity of rural
life published by his townsman, Andrew Jackson Downing.

Fig. 3. "Sparking." Steel engraving, Alfred Jones,
after painting by Francis W. Edmonds. Offered in
1845. 16 3/4" x 12 3/4". New-York Historical Society

The Art-Union recommended the picture as:

> The best of the kind yet produced in this country;
> and it is of that costly description that it could
> not have been produced but for the agency of the
> Art-Union. The subject of the picture is of homely,
> but of universal interest; one that will appeal to all
> hearts, and to all understandings, and will require
> no labelling to make it perfectly understood.[9]

Having approved of genre, the Union moved to American
history, a subject dear to its heart. The print of Asher B.
Durand's "Capture of Major Andre" (figures engraved by
Alfred Jones and landscape by Smillie and Hinshelwood,
printed by W. E. Smith), which is to our eyes an awkward
and frozen tableau, must have appeared to contemporaries as
a vivid recollection of an aspect of American life that was
suddenly turning from story into history (fig. 4). In addition,
the luster of Durand's reputation and the importance of his
recent election as the president of the National Academy of
Design (with which the Art-Union did not always have the
most cordial relations) must have added to the Union's pride
in presenting this work to the subscribers for 1845.

At the close of that year, the Union found it necessary to
explain to their now more than 3,000 members a delay that
had occurred in the distribution of the Durand print. The
managers noted the difficulty of procuring a proper picture to
be engraved. The Durand had to be borrowed from a private
collector, James Kirke Paulding. They also remarked on the
problem of estimating the time necessary to engrave a plate
in "the best style . . . of the size we require."[10] The
following year they added to their apology the fact that no
more than fifty prints a day could be taken from a plate.[11]
Consequently, the Durand was not to be available for distribution until the fall of 1846 and the plate for 1846, "Sir
Walter Raleigh Parting with His Wife," by Emanuel Leutze
(painted in Dusseldorf in 1842, engraved by Charles Burt
and printed by J. Dalton), would not be available until the

Fig. 4. "The Capture of Major Andre." Steel engraving, after painting by Asher B. Durand, Alfred Jones (figures), and Smillie and Hinshelwood (landscape). Offered 1845-46. 17 7/8" x 13 1/8". New-York Historical Society

spring of 1847. They also reported the collapse of negotiations for the engraving of another Leutze subject, "The Landing
of Columbus at Cadiz," after three years of protracted discussions. As a consolation, the managers offered two prints for
the following year: "Sybil," after a painting by Daniel
Huntington (engraved by John W. Casilear) (fig. 5), and "The
Jolly Flat Boat Men" by George Caleb Bingham (engraved in
mezzotint by Thomas Doney, and printed by Powell & Co.)
(fig. 6). No two paintings could better suggest the dichotomy
of thinking of the Art-Union managers and their mixed allegiance
to a notion of sophistication in the fine arts as opposed to an
essentially provincial nationalism.

Huntington was the artist-savant, specializing in classical
allegory, religious subjects, or somewhat arcane historical
themes which could hardly be more distant from the Art-Union's
own stated ideals. Yet Huntington continually sought and received the patronage of the Art-Union--even to the point of
having a one-man exhibition in the Art-Union Gallery. One
wonders how a work such as the "Sybil" was received in "the
most secluded villages of the far West--in Canada--in Texas--
in Mexico," regions claimed by the Art-Union as the perimeters
of its influence in this year.[12]

It is likely that George Caleb Bingham's "Jolly Flat Boat
Men" may have had a wider appeal to this public. While
the Union's support had helped Huntington to pursue his
career, it had also enabled Bingham to move from portraiture
into the field of genre painting.[13] His first contribution to
the Art-Union in 1845 included two such subjects--one being
the famous "Fur Traders Descending the Missouri." Three
pictures were submitted in 1846, of which two were distributed
by lottery and the third--"The Jolly Flat Boat Men"--was
withheld for engraving. In all, some twenty of Bingham's
canvases passed through the Art-Union's rooms, and it would
seem that here was an artist who satisfied the Union's
demands for national subject matter, although it never paid
him more than $350 for a painting.

Reviewing Bingham's contributions for 1849, the Art-Union
Bulletin explained:

Fig. 5. "A Sibyl." Etching, unidentified
engraver, after painting by Daniel Huntington,
1847. Frontispiece for the Transactions of
the American Art-Union for the Year 1846.
4 1/2" x 5 1/2"

Fig. 6. "The Jolly Flat Boat Men." Mezzotint
engraving, Thomas Doney, after painting by George
Caleb Bingham. Offered 1846-47. 24" x 19".
New-York Historical Society

These works are thoroughly American in their subjects, and could never have been painted by one
who was not perfectly familiar with the scenes
they represented. It was this striking nationality
of character, combined with considerable power in
form and expression, which first interested the
Art-Union in these productions, not withstanding
the existence of obvious faults. . . . His figures
have some _vitality_ about them. They look out of
their own eyes. They stand upon their legs. They
are shrewd or merry or grave or quizzical. They
are not merely empty ghosts of figures--mere
pictures of jackets and trousers, with masks
attached to them.[14]

Yet in the same year these enthusiastic comments were made,
the Art-Union proudly trumpeted the results of its beneficent
patronage. It was announced that three costly pictures had
been purchased: Henry Peter Gray's "The Wages of War," for
$1,500; "The Attainder of Stafford," commissioned by the Art-
Union from Leutze for $1,000; and a $1,200 picture by
Huntington, "Marys at the Sepulchre." All of these subjects
were remote from American life, and although distribution
prints were not made after them, small reproductions appeared
in the _Bulletin_ for 1849. The previous year, the Union had
expanded their semimonthly catalogue into a _Bulletin_ which
was at this moment being transformed into a full-fledged
journal of the fine arts. The membership had expanded rapidly:
from 9,666 in 1847 to 16,475 in 1848. The increase was due,
in part, to the presence in the collection of the entire series
of the "Voyage of Life" by Thomas Cole--all four pictures
being offered as a single lot in the annual distribution.

   With such a considerable audience, the Union could do
much to sway opinion and direct both public taste and
artistic energies. The _Bulletin_ became the prime vehicle for
this campaign:

The Committee believe that this small tract will become, at no very distant day, one of the most powerful

means within their control for the promotion of
the Fine Arts in the United States. Twenty-three
thousand copies of the first number, and fifteen
thousand of the second, have been printed and
distributed.[15]

The Bulletin was sent free to members and sold for six cents
a copy at the Gallery--now in newly expanded quarters designed by the architect of the Smithsonian Institution, James
Renwick, Jr. The fact that the Bulletin was not a "money
speculation" allowed, according to the editors, for a greater
"independence" of discussion.
   In order to capitalize on the distribution of the "Voyage of
Life" during the preceding season, the committee decided to
commission an engraving after one of the paintings, "Youth"
(fig. 7). Difficulty in securing "proper subjects for engraving,"
the committee felt, was:

   becoming a serious obstacle to the satisfactory progress of the Institution in this department of Art;
   but it is one which your Committee hope, ere long,
   to see removed, in the more frequent production,
   from the easels of our eminent artists, of American
   scenes, of a higher order of talent, and possessing
   historic dignity and truth.[16]

In discussing the Cole, they noted:

   The proper completion of this engraving has been en-
   trusted to Mr. Smillie, one of the most distinguished
   engravers of landscape; and it is sincerely believed
   that this work, which is now in progress, when
   finished in the manner designed, will redound to the
   credit of this Institution, and to the repuation of
   American Art.[17]

Buried not too deeply beneath the surface of their rhetoric
were the tastes and attitudes of a merchant class. Having

Fig. 7. "The Voyage of Life-Youth." Steel engraving, James Smillie, after painting by Thomas Cole. Offered in 1849. 22 7/8" x 15 1/4". New-York Historical Society

placed the "credit of the Institution" ahead of the "reputation of American Art," they concluded by boasting: "An engraving by <u>Smillie,</u> in the highest style of his peculiar department, of the largest size, of one of the best works of the lamented <u>Cole,</u> the Committee are induced to think, will meet the expectations of the most fastidious subscriber."[18]

In 1850, the <u>Bulletin</u> was considerably enlarged in both size and intention. Not only was this elaborate enterprise to include illustrations of works on exhibition in the gallery; the committee also desired to publish:

> from time to time, original etchings, and would be pleased to receive drawings for this object, or completed works on steel, for which, if adopted, a proper price will be paid. They intend also, if practicable, to embrace lithography, and wood engraving, in their plan. For all these purposes, they would prefer subjects illustrating national character, or history, or scenery. They would also cheerfully include in the <u>Bulletin</u> prints from woodcuts, furnished to them of good original designs for Art-manufacturers, similar to those found in the London Art Journal.[19]

The Union had, by this time, a membership of 18,960, and it was clear that a single print was not enough to satisfy the multitudes. The committee was not oblivious to the tremendous scale its operations had assumed, nor were the members ignorant of the visual hunger of the public. They reported in 1849 that in addition to the 1,300 paintings which had been offered in the ten years of the Union's existence, more than 50,000 engravings had been distributed—12,000 in mezzotint and the rest in line. In addition, nearly 20,000 sets of engravings in outline had been published. The outlines (actually lithographs) were offered as bonuses in 1848 and 1849. The prints, in sets of six plates each, were the only original compositions in print media which the Union had commissioned for general distribution. They illustrated the popular American stories of Washington Irving, "Rip Van Winkle" (fig. 8) and "The Legend of Sleepy Hollow." The Art-Union considered these works by Felix O. Darley as a "missionary of art, throughout the length and breadth of the land," and felt they had "awakened thousands to a knowledge of the magic power which lies in simple lines when traced by the hand of Genius."[20]

The limitations of the Art-Union's print productions were becoming the subject of some criticism. One observer, writing in the Boston Daily Advertiser, found a dull familiarity in the Union's prints:

> The public have, long ago, seen quite too much of 'The Jolly Flat-boat Men,' (of which, indeed, one inspection is quite sufficient). . . . On every other center table will be Darley's illustrations, in every other parlor will hang the picture of Queen Mary ["The Signing of the Death Warrant of Lady Jane Gray," by Daniel Huntington, the distribution print for 1848, engraved by Charles Burt and printed by J. Dalton]. There is, therefore, really no inducement for a subscriber to induce his friends to subscribe with him, for they will all together become weary of the pictures which meet them every day as they pass from house to house in friendly intercourse.[21]

The Union replied that "twenty-thousand copies of a single work become rare enough when distributed over so vast an extent of territory as ours."[22] But it was clear that the production of a single large engraving, even if supplemented by a companion volume such as Darley's, was no longer sufficient recompense for membership. In addition, as the membership grew, the Art-Union was encountering increasing difficulty in producing the quantity of prints they required. It was noted in connection with the engraving of the Cole plate that it took at least two years for the plate to be engraved, and another nine or ten months to pull the prints.[23] The engraver received two to three thousand dollars for his labor, and another two thousand had to be spent for paper. Printing

Fig. 8. "Rip van Winkle." Lithograph, Felix O. Darley.
Published by the American Art-Union, 1848. 11 1/8" x
8 5/8". Library of the Metropolitan Museum of Art

costs brought the total expense to well over nine thousand
dollars (about 10 percent of the year's receipts). The following year, although the membership had dropped slightly from
the 1849 high of 18,960, the Art-Union was able to produce
for nearly the same price 16,500 copies of each of five smaller
plates which they offered, in addition to a large engraving.
The Bulletin format was, as we have seen, expanded at the
same time to include a wider variety of visual materials, and
the Union moved a step closer toward the production of the
type of popular illustrated journal which would do much to
undermine its own position as the purveyor of art to the
masses.

The smaller plates for 1850--Cole's "Dream of Arcadia,"
Durand's "Dover Plains," Emmanuel Leutze's "The Image
Breaker," Edmonds's "The New Scholar," and Richard
Woodville's "Card Players"--were planned "to give as elaborate and truthful an exhibition as engravings of the size proposed (7 1/2" by 10") can give of the genius of five of the
most distinguished American painters." Woodville, an artist
whose activities in Dusseldorf, Germany, were thoroughly
recorded through the pages of the Bulletin, also provided the
painting "Mexican News," which was the subject of the large
engraving of 1851 (engraved by Alfred Jones, printed by J.
Dalton), while one of the five smaller plates of that year illustrated his "Old '76 and Young '48 " (fig. 9). Both subjects
were calculated to appeal to a broad cultural nationalism,
with clever references in the latter to America's Revolutionary
history. The Bulletin carefully remarked on the bust of
Washington which Woodville included, but it failed to notice
the print after the "Signing of the Declaration of Independence"
by Trumbull which adorned the overmantle in this scene. In
Woodville's works, genre and history were pleasingly combined and their approbation by the Union again illustrates
the predilection for didactic themes.

The other smaller plates for 1851 included Jasper Cropsey's
"American Harvesting," Mount's "Bargaining for a Horse "
(fig. 10), John Kensett's "Mount Washington from the Valley
of the Conway" and William T. Ranney's "Marion Crossing
the Pedee " (fig. 11), another Revolutionary War subject.

Fig. 9. "Old '76 and Young '48." Steel engraving,
J. I. Pease, after painting by Richard Catton
Woodville. Offered 1851-53. 9 5/8" x 7 1/2".
New-York Historical Society

Fig. 10. "Bargaining for a Horse." Steel engraving,
Charles Burt, after painting by William Sidney Mount.
Offered 1851-53. 10" x 7 3/4". New-York Historical
Society

Fig. 11. "Marion Crossing the Pedee." Steel engraving, Charles Burt, after painting by William Ranney. Offered 1851-52. 11 7/8" x 8". New-York Historical Society

The Art-Union witnessed a second crossing the same year
which, ironically, turned out to be a double crossing. Later
that season, Emanuel Leutze crossed the Atlantic, returning
from Dusseldorf, where he had worked and studied for ten
years. Leutze brought with him his latest production,
"Washington Crossing the Delaware " (fig. 12) (ultimately
acquired by William H. Webb who also owned "Marion
Crossing the Pedee"). The Art-Union Bulletin had contained
periodic dispatches from Dusseldorf on the progress of
"Washington" and eagerly anticipated its arrival. The Union,
as we have seen, had been a constant patron and promoter of
Leutze's work. The managers were therefore somewhat shocked
to learn that Leutze had sold the painting for $6,000 to the
French print publishers Goupil, Vibert & Co., who planned
to publish "the most beautiful and largest line engraving ever
produced."[25] Goupil had been operating a New York branch
since 1846. Because its stock had consisted primarily of the
modern French school, it had not been seen as a threat by
the Art-Union but rather as an indication of the advance in
healthy activity in the fine arts at every level. But Goupil
had passed the boundaries of propriety when, in 1848, the
company founded a competing organ, the International Art
Union, a private business speculation which served primarily
to help the firm divest itself of undesirable stock of inferior
French art, an art, moreover, which the Art-Union had sometimes found meretricious and wanting in the proper moral tone.

The presence of competing commercial firms specifically
devoted to the exhibition and sale of works of art and prints
of all schools, was but one indication of the expanding art
market and the growing cosmopolitanism of collectors, now
eager to begin making decisions for themselves. Had it not
been legally terminated, the Art-Union, I suspect, would have
found it difficult to meet the competition and to maintain the
same level of operations it had enjoyed. Its print activities
were to be superseded. The fashion for line engraving was
fading in light of the increasing sophistication of chromo-
lithographic technology on the one hand and the evolution of
professional reproductive techniques combining photography
and wood engraving on the other. In 1849, the Bulletin had

Fig. 12. "Washington Crossing the Delaware." Steel engraving, Paul Girardet, after painting by Emanuel Leutze. Offered in 1853. 38 1/2" x 22 3/8". The New York Public Library

noted that a chromolithograph produced by P. J. Duval of
Philadelphia, was a specimen:

> which for finish and richness of color, rivals the
> best European work. In this specimen are brillant
> garlands of flowers, architectural ornaments,
> mythological designs of figures, in which the flesh
> tints and draperies are all properly colored, and
> decorations in gilding and en grisaille, which are
> truly beautiful. In a few years the most accurate
> copies in color of pictures, will be printed, and
> the great work of popularising Art, which is one
> of the distinguishing characteristics of the age,
> carried nearly to perfection.[26]

Bingham and a few others persisted in their devotion to steel
engraving as a vehicle for fashionable reproduction--and
perhaps appropriately so for the graphic nature of his genre
subjects. Mount's paintings, however, were quite successfully translated into chromolithographs in Paris by Goupil,
Vibert & Co. during the 1850s. Genre, with its illustrative
moral content, was giving way to a harder, more realistic
style of reportage, increasingly the domain of illustrated
weekly magazines and journals such as Frank Leslie's
Illustrated Weekly Newspaper (1855) or Harpers Weekly (1857).
The homely, picturesque, and generally rural images which
the Art-Union seemed to prefer were to become the meat of
popular and inexpensive lithographs--works which the Art-
Union had realized "will attract more attention and find more
purchasers than the finest engravings or the most exquisite
paintings."[27] In 1849, they turned down a painting of "East
Rock near New Haven" by George Henry Durrie, whose paintings were to provide the basis of some of the most popular
and enduring prints issued by Currier & Ives, because the
Union found the picture "not being of a degree of merit to
warrant its distribution."[28]
        Chromolithography was particularly well suited to the
subtle effects demanded for the reproduction of what was becoming the primary class of American paintings--landscape.

The Art-Union had shunned landscape generally, and although references to the work of landscape artists and occasional reproductions of their work had appeared in the Bulletin, the Union had found that "there are certain other branches which demand higher powers of mind and hand, and upon which the fame of this country (if she shall ever attain fame in this region of mental effort,) alone can rest."[29] One cannot imagine the Art-Union paying, as Williams and Stevens were to do a few years later, $2,000 merely for the chromolithographic rights to Frederick Church's "Niagara."

For the Art-Union, prints were to be the instructive vehicle for the improvement of taste and for the advancement of the fine arts. Subject matter was primary, and only secondarily was a print to be considered a work of art, although engraving was preferred to other techniques because it seemed somehow a more elevated medium. The Art-Union would have been somewhat surprised by, although not necessarily out of sympathy with, the jocular notion of William Sidney Mount when he remarked: "One of the great enjoyments of life is looking at paintings and engravings--they kill time so profitably."[30]

NOTES

1. Mary Bartlett Cowdrey, <u>American Academy of Fine Arts and American Art-Union</u>, with introduction and a history of the American Academy by Theodore Sizer (New York, 1953). Contains essays dealing with the history of the Art-Union; "The American Art-Union," Charles E. Baker, pp. 95-240 and "Publications of the American Art-Union," Mary Bartlett Cowdrey, pp. 241-93. Also useful is the "Addendum: Sale of Art-Union Holdings, 1852," Malcom Stearns, pp. 295-311, and Volume II which contains the "Exhibition Record" of the two institutions. See also E. Maurice Bloch, "The American Art-Union's Downfall," <u>New-York Historical Society Quarterly</u>, XXXVII (Oct. 1953), 331-59.

2. "Plan of the American Art-Union," reprinted in Baker, pp. 114-15.

3. <u>Ibid.</u> Article III of "By-Laws of the Committee of Management of the American Art-Union" states the duties of the committee upon engravings: "Sec. 5. The Committee upon Engravings shall have power to inquire and report from time to time, as to what Pictures may be suitable to be engraved for the Association; to make arrangements with the owners of such pictures as may be selected for that purpose; to make contracts with engravers; under the direction of the Committee of Management; to superintend the engraving of plates for the Association; and the printing from such plates" (<u>ibid.</u>, p. 128).

4. <u>Ibid.</u>, p. 100. The earliest influence on the organization of the Apollo Association was the report issued by the Edinburgh Association for the Promotion of Fine Arts in Scotland. See also the discussion of "The American Art-Union," <u>Knickerbocker Magazine</u>, XXXII (Nov. 1848), 442-47.

5. A. Warner to Frederick E. Cohen, New York, Aug. 12, 1848, as quoted in E. Maurice Bloch, <u>George Caleb Bingham: The Evolution of an Artist</u> (Berkeley and Los Angeles, 1967), I, 81.

6. William Sidney Mount to Jonathan Sturges, Stony Brook, March 14, 1854, Mount Collection, New-York Historical Society. Mount was writing to Sturges to warn him of the Art-Union's intention of selling the plate of "Bargaining for a Horse" which had been a distribution print for 1851. Mount urged Sturges, who represented the New-York Gallery of Fine Arts, the owner of the

painting, to intervene in the negotiations. He enjoined Sturges,
"I hope you will not suffer the small plate 'Bargaining for a
horse' to be sold for the purpose of being magnified--and thereby
lose the spirit of the painting . . . If another engraving is ever
taken of the Bargaining--it should be from the original painting.
Also the artist paid for the copy-right."

7. In addition to "Sparking" by Francis W. Edmonds,
which is discussed below, the Art-Union published a plate of
the "Escape of Captain Wharton" illustrating a scene from
James Fenimore Cooper's Spy (T. F. Hoppin, engraved by F.F.E.
Prudhomme, printed by C. Thomas).

8. Report of the Apollo Association for the Year 1839,
quoted in Baker, p. 148.

9. "Proceedings of the Annual Meeting," Transactions of
the American Art-Union, 1844, p. 9.

10. Ibid., 1845, p. 9.

11. Ibid., 1846, p. 9.

12. Ibid., 1847, p. 25.

13. "What Has the American Art-Union Accomplished?" in
Bulletin of the American Art-Union, II (Oct. 1849), 12:
"Bingham acknowledges his indebtedness to us as the first
patron of his higher efforts, and his main-stay in all attempts
beyond the line of portraiture." See also John Francis
McDermott, "George Caleb Bingham and the American Art-
Union," New-York Historical Society Quarterly, XLII (Jan.
1958), 60-69.

14. Bulletin, Aug. 1849.

15. Ibid., June 1849, p. 6.

16. Transactions, 1848, p. 42.

17. Ibid., pp. 43-44.

18. Ibid.

19. Bulletin, April 1850, p. 1.

20. Ibid., Oct. 1849, p. 17. Six watercolor drawings,
considered to be the originals for the "Rip Van Winkle" plates
are in the collection of Sleepy Hollow Restorations.

21. Boston Daily Advertiser (1848), undated clipping bound
in scrapbook of American Art-Union Newspaper Clippings, New-
York Historical Society.

22. <u>Bulletin,</u> Oct. 1849, p. 17.

23. <u>Ibid.</u>, May 1850, p. 17. The cost estimated in the article was $8,000, but the print had already cost $9,256.24 according to the Treasurer's Report to December 21, 1849, published in the <u>Report of the Annual Meeting,</u> 1849, p. 37.

24. <u>Bulletin</u>, May 1850, p. 17.

25. As quoted in John Howat, "Washington Crossing the Delaware," <u>The Metropolitan Museum of Art Bulletin</u>, March, 1968, p. 291.

26. <u>Transactions</u>, 1847, p. 26.

27. "The Fine Arts in America," extract from <u>Southern Quarterly Review</u>, July 1849, reprinted in <u>Bulletin</u>, Sept. 1849, p. 25.

28. George Henry Durrie to American Art-Union, Nov. 13, 1849, New-York Historical Society.

29. <u>Transactions</u>, 1847, p. 26.

30. William Sidney Mount to Goupil, Vibert & Co., Stony Brook, Dec. 13, 1848, Mount Collection, New-York Historical Society.

EARLY AMERICAN PRINT RESEARCH RESOURCES
IN THE UNITED STATES

Wendy J. Shadwell

This listing has been compiled to provide scholars and
students with a useful catalogue of the most significant
research resources for prints in and of America to 1850.
Following the name of the institution or collection and its
location is a short description of the nature of the collection, its limitations and its strengths. Publications are
mentioned only when a major catalogue on a collection exists,
or when a periodical includes pertinent material about the
print collection of an institution.

AMERICAN ANTIQUARIAN SOCIETY, Salisbury Street and Park Ave.,
Worcester, Massachusetts 01609
    Holdings of the Society include a miscellaneous collec-
tion of American engravings (many of them book illustrations)
through 1850. Notable are an unrivalled collection of Revere
material; important collections of works by Turner, Hurd,
Callender, Doolittle, Norman, Maverick, Tanner, Tiebout,
Peter Pelham, and David Claypoole Johnston; an excellent
collection of political cartoons; a map collection strong in
eighteenth- and early nineteenth-century New England items;
and collections of bookplates, paper money, trade cards,
watch papers, and sheet music covers.

See: "Early New England Printmakers" (in collaboration
       with the Worcester Art Museum), in Art in New
       England. /Cambridge, Mass.: Harvard University
       Press, 1939./

       Clarence S. Brigham. Paul Revere's Engravings. (rev.
       ed., 1969.) Worcester, Mass.: American Antiquarian
       Society, 1954.

AMERICAN PHILOSOPHICAL SOCIETY, 105 South Fifth Street, Philadelphia, Pennsylvania 19106
    The print collection is a miscellany of American and related European engravings and lithographs through 1850. Emphasis of the portrait collection is on likenesses of Benjamin Franklin and other members of the Society and the American Indian. Most notable among the city views is an excellent collection of Philadelphia prints including several by William and Thomas Birch. The collection of natural history prints features a complete set of the elephant-folio edition of Audubon's Birds of America. There is a special card file of bookplates. The map collection numbers some 2,000 items, principally American, and it features rare seventeenth- and eighteenth-century maps of Pennsylvania and, more specifically, of Philadelphia.

THE BANCROFT LIBRARY, University of California, Berkeley, California 94720
    The collection formed by Robert B. Honeyman, Jr., is a major source of nineteenth-century American and related European prints at the Library. The graphic media best represented are lithography and steel engraving. Among subjects featured are western cities, especially San Francisco, and events connected with the 1849 Gold Rush. The Library also has major holdings of maps, charts, and certificates.

See: University of California. The Bancroft Library Index to Printed Maps. Boston: G. K. Hall and Co., 1964.

THE BOSTON ATHENAEUM, 10½ Beacon Street, Boston, Massachusetts 02108
    The general collection of American prints and illustrated books and periodicals through 1850 includes some volumes from George Washington's personal library. The print collection features mainly portraits and town views, especially of Boston.

BOSTON PUBLIC LIBRARY, Copley Square, Boston, Massachusetts 02117
    Boston Archive contains some prints of Boston arranged architecturally and geographically. American Prints, arranged chronologically, includes portraits, cartoons, and

military scenes. The collection of American Views has
prints of the United States other than Boston and includes
the rare lithographs of the Baltimore and Ohio Railroad in
1830 by Swett and Endicott. There is a collection of about
290 illustrated sheet music covers dating from 1840. The
Rare Book Department holds Revere's "Boston Massacre" and a
good collection of military prints.

THE ANNE S. K. BROWN MILITARY COLLECTION, 357 Benefit Street,
Providence, Rhode Island 02903
     The American portion of this collection is now owned
by Brown University (to which the whole is eventually to be
given). It consists of a large number of prints and
illustrations in books through 1850, all having military or
naval connotations - battle scenes, drills, military and
naval life, portraits, and particularly uniforms. There is
a catalogue and subject index.

THE JOHN CARTER BROWN LIBRARY, Brown University, Providence,
Rhode Island 02912
     A superb collection of early American prints, maps,
books, periodicals, and related materials from before the
seventeenth century to 1801, it features many exceedingly
rare items. The entire collection is expertly catalogued.

See: Lawrence C. Wroth and Marion W. Adams. American
      Woodcuts and Engravings, 1670-1800. Providence, R.I.:
      The Associates of the John Carter Brown Library, 1946.

      The French and Indian War, An Album. Providence, R.I.:
      The Associates of the John Carter Brown Library,
      /1960/.

      Annual Reports, issued since 1910, record acquisi-
      tions, etc.

CALIFORNIA HISTORICAL SOCIETY, 2090 Jackson Street, San
Francisco, California 94109
     The Society has a collection of graphic art, primarily
lithographs from 1850 on, which relates to California. A
number of these prints were formerly in the Harry T. Peters
Collection, which is currently on loan to the Society from
the De Young Memorial Museum in San Francisco. There is

also an important special collection of California letter
sheets which illustrate life in the area immediately after
the Gold Rush.

See: Harry T. Peters. California on Stone. Garden City,
      N.Y.: Doubleday, Doran & Co., 1935.

      Joseph A. Baird, Jr. California's Pictorial Letter
      Sheets. San Francisco, Calif.: David Magee, 1967.

MARIAN S. CARSON COLLECTION, 706 South Washington Square,
Philadelphia, Pennsylvania 19106
      This varied, private collection of American prints and
periodicals up to 1850 contains a large body of works by
John Rubens Smith.

AMON CARTER MUSEUM OF WESTERN ART, 3501 Camp Bowie Blvd.,
Forth Worth, Texas 76101
      The prints in this collection are concerned with the
western United States and the American frontier. Nineteenth-
century scenes, particularly city views, constitute the
major holding, and new material is being actively acquired.

CHICAGO HISTORICAL SOCIETY, North Avenue and Clark Street,
Chicago, Illinois 60614
      The collection of eighteenth-century prints includes
some portraits, battle scenes, cartoons, and allegorical
pieces. The nineteenth-century material, strong in the
area of American city prints, relates not only to American
history but especially to the history of Chicago. The
prints are arranged according to subject matter. Maps are
housed in the Library.

WILLIAM L. CLEMENTS LIBRARY, University of Michigan, Ann
Arbor, Michigan 48104
      The general collection of early American prints, maps,
and related materials includes numerous reprints and
facsimiles of significant originals not represented in the
collection.

COLONIAL WILLIAMSBURG, Williamsburg, Virginia 23158

An excellent collection of American and European prints pertaining to America of the colonial period (to 1795), the material is strong in political prints and English social satires. A collection of English and American maps (1635-1795) features rare items. Selected pieces are hung in appropriate period buildings open to the public, and a study room is available to scholars.

THE CONNECTICUT HISTORICAL SOCIETY, 1 Elizabeth Street, Hartford, Connecticut 06105

This collection of American prints, maps, bookplates, trade cards, paper money, and related material of Connecticut origin or content includes notable collections of works by the Doolittles and Abner Reed, Kellogg lithographs, and Hartford Graphic Company bank notes.

DARTMOUTH COLLEGE LIBRARY, Dartmouth College, Hanover, New Hampshire 03755

The Class of 1926 Memorial Collection of Illustrated Books published in New England from 1769-1869, the first century of the College's existence, includes books illustrated with wood engravings, steel engravings, and lithographs. The Collection has been in formation since 1960, and now numbers about 1,300 volumes. A checklist is scheduled for completion by year's end.

See: Howard C. Rice, Jr. Sampler from the Class of 1926 Memorial Collection of Illustrated Books. Dartmouth, N.H.: Dartmouth College Library, 1970.

THE DETROIT INSTITUTE OF ARTS, 5200 Woodward Avenue, Detroit, Michigan 48202

This is a general collection of about one hundred American and related European prints, the earliest of which is dated ca. 1756. There are a few eighteenth-century portraits and bookplates. Between 1800 and 1850 the collection includes views, portraits, naval scenes, Audubon's Birds of America, and an apparently unique set of John Hill's Picturesque Views of American Scenery, Philadelphia, 1820, a complete series of 44 plates with pure etching proofs and uncolored and finished proofs.

ESSEX INSTITUTE, Salem, Massachusetts 01970
A small collection of early American prints and related
material, it contains some rare items. In formation since
1848, the collection emphasizes works related to Essex
County. Selected items are exhibited in contemporary buildings and in the museum galleries.

HENRY FORD MUSEUM, Dearborn, Michigan 48121
This general museum of American history has a varied
collection of American prints from the eighteenth century
through 1850. The collection, which has been in formation
since the 1920s, is strongest in nineteenth-century material
and includes many Currier and Ives lithographs and a comprehensive collection of eighteenth- and nineteenth-century
bookplates.

THE FREE LIBRARY OF PHILADELPHIA, Logan Square, Philadelphia,
Pennsylvania 19103
The general collection of American prints from 1800
through 1850 places emphasis on Pennsylvania and, specifically,
on Philadelphia-oriented items. Good collections of works
by William and Thomas Birch, J. C. Wild, and Augustus Kollner
are included, as well as an important collection of Philadelphia views (some of which are housed in the Social Science
Department and some in the Rare Book Room, along with numerous eighteenth- and nineteenth-century illustrated books and
periodicals).

HERITAGE FOUNDATION, Deerfield, Massachusetts 01342
A varied collection of eighteenth-century prints and
maps--many English, some European, and a few American--
that are exhibited in appropriately furnished colonial
houses and a tavern.

THE HISTORICAL SOCIETY OF PENNSYLVANIA, 1300 Locust Street,
Philadelphia, Pennsylvania 19107
The general collection of American Prints and related
material through 1850, with emphasis on Pennsylvania items,
contains a superb collection of Philadelphia town views.
The entire collection is catalogued; the Society Small Print

Collection (which includes photographs as well as prints) is arranged by subject. All of the print collection is administered by the Manuscripts Division of the Historical Society, although a part of it is housed in the adjoining Library Company building.

HOUGHTON LIBRARY, Harvard University, Cambridge, Massachusetts 02138

This excellent collection of American prints and related material of the seventeenth and eighteenth centuries, including some of the rarest early examples, emphasizes items relating to the University.

HENRY E. HUNTINGTON LIBRARY AND ART GALLERY, San Marino, California 91108

This well-rounded collection ranges from engravings of America in early European books of voyages and travels to native productions through 1850. American lithographs are broadly represented by the earliest examples in the medium, portraits, social scenes, and a good collection of Currier and Ives cartoons. There is a large collection of American bookplates, and a small but important group of American trade cards. The holdings of American maps are very good. All American prints are in the charge of the Curator of Rare Books; only European prints are administered by the Curator of Prints.

KENDALL COLLECTION, South Caroliniana Library, University of South Carolina, Columbia, South Carolina 29208

The outstanding collection of maps formed by Henry P. Kendall includes early European maps of the world, the Western Hemisphere, North America, and the English colonies; and European and American maps of the United States, the Carolinas, and adjoining regions through 1850.

See: Louis C. Karpinski. Early Maps of Carolina and Adjoining Regions. Privately published, 1937.

THE KENDALL WHALING MUSEUM, Sharon, Massachusetts 02067

This unique collection of American and European prints in all media through 1850 features scenes of whaling vessels, stranded whales, sea life, sealing and walrus hunting, world

ports, toys and games, natural history, cartoons, and caricatures.

See: Marion V. and Dorothy Brewington. Kendall Whaling
      Museum Prints, Part I, The Kendall Whaling Museum, 1969.
      Catalogues 597 of the whaling prints, each of which is
      illustrated. Part II, covering natural history, car-
      toons, and caricatures, is in preparation.

THE LIBRARY COMPANY OF PHILADELPHIA, 1314 Locust Street,
Philadelphia, Pennsylvania 19107
     This is a sizable general collection of American prints,
including periodical illustrations, through 1850. It
contains notable collections of portraits, of cartoons, of
lithographic prints advertising Philadelphia businesses,
and of views of Philadelphia in all media, the last group
being especially rich in works by William and Thomas Birch.

THE LIBRARY OF CONGRESS, Washington, D.C. 20540

Prints and Photographs Division
     The Library of Congress has an excellent collection of
American and pertinent European prints up to 1850 covering
a wide variety of subjects: people, places, events, things.
The collection includes prints deposited for copyright in
the various District Courts of the United States and formally
transferred to the Library under the Copyright Act of 1870.
The extensive collection of lithographed music covers in the
Division is arranged by subject, complementing the collection in the Music Division held by composer. There are
several hundred British political cartoons relating to the
American Revolution, cartoons by William Charles of the War
of 1812, and many American political and social cartoons in
the Division. Pictures are available through a visual card
catalogue and through subject and artist card files. The
Division also has indexes to prints used as illustrations
in books published in the United States up to 1850. An
extensive collection of maps of the period is in the custody
of the Geography and Map Division; many related items are
in the Manuscript Division; and the Rare Book Room contains
many books of significance for their plates.

LOUISIANA STATE MUSEUM, 751 Chartres, New Orleans,
Louisiana 70116
  Although the bulk of the Museum's print collection dates
after 1850, there are certain notable earlier holdings.
These include a group of mainly eighteenth-century gazetteer
book plates relative to French Colonial Louisiana; works by
Carlos Nebel dealing with Mexico and the Mexican-American
War, which were published 1839-51; and a large number of
prints by the local artist, Jules Lion, ca. 1840.

THE MARINERS MUSEUM, Newport News, Virginia 23606
  The collection includes American and related European
prints in all graphic media from the seventeenth century
through 1850. Among the maritime topics featured are harbors
and port scenes, navy yards, naval battles, naval and
merchant vessels, fishing, lighthouses, marine disasters,
and portraits. The Museum owns six original Currier lithographic stones. There is an efficient card catalogue with
cross-index system.

See: The Mariners Museum. Boston: G. K. Hall & Co., 1964.

MASSACHUSETTS HISTORICAL SOCIETY, 1154 Boylston Street,
Boston, Massachusetts 02215
  In formation since 1791, this excellent collection of
American prints and related material features many rare
(and several unique) items, with emphasis on the Massachusetts
area.

See: Yearly publication of the Massachusetts Historical
      Society Picture Book.

      Listing of new acquisitions in the annual volume of
      Proceedings.

THE METROPOLITAN MUSEUM OF ART, 1000 Fifth Avenue, New York
City 10028
  The extensive general collection of American and related
European prints up to 1850 includes the Edward W. C. Arnold
Collection are on loan to the Museum of the City of New
York. There are duplicate impressions of many items.

MIDDENDORF COLLECTION, 80 Broad Street, New York City 10004
    The most complete collection of American and related
English prints up to 1820 in private hands, it has been in
formation since 1955. Included are several unique, and many
rare, items; also maps, bookplates, and periodicals.

See: <u>American Printmaking: The First 150 Years, 1670-1820</u>.
    New York: The Museum of Graphic Art, 1969.

MUSEUM OF THE CITY OF NEW YORK, Fifth Avenue at 103 Street,
New York City 10029
    Holdings of the Museum include an extensive collection
of lithographs--a large number of views of New York City
from 1835 on, and the Harry T. Peters Collection of Currier
and Ives. The collection also contains some seventeenth-
and eighteenth-century prints and maps. Emphasis of the
collection is on material relating to the history of New
York City.

See: Harry T. Peters. <u>Currier and Ives: Printmakers to the
    American People</u>. 2 vols. New York: Doubleday, Doran
    & Co., 1929-31.

MUSEUM OF EARLY SOUTHERN DECORATIVE ARTS, Salem Station,
Winston-Salem, North Carolina 27108
    This small collection of American and English prints
through ca. 1820 is exhibited in the museum's fifteen
period rooms. Included are town views of southern settlements and portraits of eminent southerners.

MUSEUM OF FINE ARTS, 479 Huntington Avenue, Boston,
Massachusetts 02115
    The broad general collection of American prints is
strong in nineteenth-century material. Included is the
Karolik Collection of Prints from 1720 to 1820 (notable
portraits, views, and bookplates), which was given in
1939.

NEW JERSEY HISTORICAL SOCIETY, 230 Broadway, Newark, New
Jersey 07104
    American prints in all media have been acquired by the
Society since its founding in 1845. A major strength of

the collection is a group of 1,700 town views and scenes of New Jersey through 1850. A multivolume iconographical catalogue, geographically arranged, which has been prepared by the Society and which may be consulted there, also includes references to New Jersey scenes owned by other institutions and private collections. (Book illustrations are covered in this source.) The Society also holds about 1,000 portraits of New Jersey personages; 700 trade cards of New Jersey businesses; 328 maps of New Jersey; and about 100 miscellaneous prints of general historic interest, all published before 1850.

THE NEW-YORK HISTORICAL SOCIETY, 170 Central Park West, New York City 10024

The excellent collection of American prints, views, sheet music covers, bookplates, trade cards, political caricatures, portraits, maps, and related materials up to 1850 features a strong general collection of the Revolutionary period. Emphasis of the nineteenth-century material is increasingly on New York City, New York State, and the surrounding states. The collections include about two-thirds of the Irving S. Olds Naval Collection, and the Bella C. Landauer Collection of Advertising Art.

See: Irving S. Olds. Bits & Pieces of American History. New York, privately published, 1951.

Treasures of Americana from the Library of the New-York Historical Society. New York, New-York Historical Society, 1969.

Acquisitions are recorded in the illustrated Annual Reports

NEW YORK PUBLIC LIBRARY, Fifth Avenue at 42 Street, New York City 10018

Print Room

This superb collection of American and pertinent English prints and related materials through 1850 includes the I. N. Phelps Stokes Collection, the Stauffer Collection, the Emmet Collection of prints (mounted prints and documents in bound volumes are housed in the Manuscript Division), the Amos F. Eno Collection of New York City views, the McAlpin Collection of

George Washington portraits and Washingtoniana, and a large
collection of Benjamin Franklin portraits.

See: Frank Weitenkampf, "The Eno Collection of New York City
      Views," Bulletin of the New York Public Library. 1925.

      I. N. Phelps Stokes and Daniel C. Haskell. American
      Historical Prints: Early Views of American Cities, etc.
      1497-1891. New York: New York Public Library, 1932.
      (Out of print; a revised edition is contemplated.)

Map Room
    Holdings include a large collection of maps and emphasize
    the colony, city, and state of New York. Many facsimiles of
    Revolutionary battle maps; strong holdings of original
    nineteenth-century maps, atlases, and charts; and seventeenth-
    century and later European atlases dealing with North America
    are included.

Rare Book Room
    American publications prior to 1825 are housed in the
    Rare Book Room. Therefore, early original maps, periodicals,
    books, and related materials are found here.

PEABODY MUSEUM, Salem, Massachusetts 01970
    In formation since 1799, the collection comprises about
    4,000 American prints through 1850. There are a few eigh-
    teenth-century items; the bulk of the material is from the
    nineteenth century and is divided by subject matter into
    three main groups: maritime, ethnological, and natural
    history.

THE PEALE MUSEUM, 225 North Holliday Street, Baltimore,
Maryland 21202
    This collection of about 2,000 prints in various media
    features views, scenes, and rare maps of Baltimore through
    1850, mostly by local print makers. The Hambleton Collec-
    tion is one of the major holdings. There is also a good
    representation of sheet music, paper currency, and related
    material. The collection is accurately catalogued and
    cross-indexed.

See: John Hill. An Analytical Catalogue of Print Views
      of Baltimore Covering the Period from the Beginning

of the Nineteenth Century to 1860. (Unpublished term
paper for course at Winterthur Museum——University of
Delaware, 1965. Typescript.)

PHILADELPHIA MARITIME MUSEUM, 427 Chestnut Street, Philadelphia, Pennsylvania 19106
    The Museum has a small, high-quality collection of
maritime prints pertaining primarily to Philadelphia and
environs and the Delaware Bay and River.

PHILADELPHIA MUSEUM OF ART, Benjamin Franklin Parkway at
Twenty-sixth Street, Philadelphia, Pennsylvania 19101
    The general collection of American prints before 1850
is small, mostly Philadelphia city views of little distinction, but there is an important group of one hundred and fifty
Benjamin Franklin portraits.

PRINCETON UNIVERSITY LIBRARY, Princeton, New Jersey 08540
    A varied collection of American and related European
prints up to 1850 will be found in the Department of Rare
Books and Special Collections, which includes Rare Books,
Manuscripts, Graphic Arts, Theatre, Maps, and Numismatics
divisions. The Library's greatest strength is in prints
which appear as book illustrations. The Sinclair Hamilton
Collection is notable. Separate prints are located chiefly
in the Graphic Arts division. Other collections containing
material in various graphic media are Princetoniana and New
Jerseyiana, American travel books and illustrated albums,
Western Americana, angling, paper money, and bookplates.

See: Sinclair Hamilton. Early American Book Illustrators
       and Wood Engravers, 1670-1870. A Catalogue of American
       Books ... in the Princeton University Library.
       Princeton University Library, 1958; reprinted 1968 by
       Princeton University Press. Vol. II, Supplement.
       Princeton University Press, 1968.

SMITHSONIAN INSTITUTION, Washington, D.C. 20560

National Collection of Fine Arts, G Street at Eighth, N.W.
    In formation only since 1967, this varied collection
of about 200 American prints through 1850 contains but few

eighteenth-century items. Prints calculated to produce a
general survey of American printmaking are being acquired.

National Museum of History and Technology, Constitution
Avenue at Fourteenth, N.W.

Division of Cultural History
    This division holds the Harry T. Peters Collection of
American lithographs, other than Currier and Ives.

See: Harry T. Peters. America on Stone: The Other Print-
      makers to the American People. New York: Doubleday,
      Doran & Co., Inc., 1931.

Division of Graphic Arts
    The purpose of the print collection in this division is
to record the development of the technology of printmaking
and to illustrate the various graphic media. The collection
includes a few early American prints, some early lithographs,
and a strong selection of wood engravings.

National Portrait Gallery, F Street at Eighth, N.W.
    This is a study collection of over 40,000 engravings,
etchings, lithographs, and photographs of American personages.
The earliest print dates from 1793; however, the majority of
the Gallery's pre-1850 prints was published after 1830. Many
of the prints were originally published in books or periodicals. A checklist and cross indexes are being compiled.

THE SOCIETY FOR THE PRESERVATION OF NEW ENGLAND ANTIQUITIES,
141 Cambridge Street, Boston, Massachusetts 02114
    The Society has a varied American print collection of
engravings and lithographs, mostly of an architectural
nature; bookplates; maps; and trade cards and billheads
through 1850. Their holdings are limited to items of New
England interest.

THE STATE HISTORICAL SOCIETY OF WISCONSIN, 816 State Street,
Madison, Wisconsin 53706
    The remarkable collection of American and related
European maps through 1850 at this American History Library
has been in formation since 1854. The majority concern
North America and the United States; about one-fourth concern the state of Wisconsin alone. The holdings of nineteenth-century atlases are outstanding. Each item in the

collection is individually catalogued and is readily
accessible. The Society also owns a few American prints
issued before 1850.

VIRGINIA HISTORICAL SOCIETY, Boulevard and Kensington Avenue,
Richmond, Virginia 23221
     The Society has in its Special Collections Division
prints of persons associated with Virginia, of places in
Virginia, and of events that took place in Virginia from the
earliest period through 1850. It also has excellent collections of Virginia bookplates, paper currency, sheet music,
trade cards, and related material. The Society has an outstanding collection of early Virginia maps.

THE HENRY FRANCIS DU PONT WINTERTHUR MUSEUM, Winterthur,
Delaware 19735
     This is a broad collection of American and related
English prints, which are exhibited in appropriate contemporary surroundings. The collection, which is still in
formation, features mezzotints, political prints, and illustrated books and includes many rare items.
     The Libraries contain a large collection of American
illustrated books (especially color-plate books), prints
published after 1850 (especially city views), and books on
architecture.

See: "Philadelphia Reviewed -- The Printmakers' Record
      1750-1850." Multilithed sheets, 1960.

      Prints Pertaining to America. /Portland, Maine7:
      The Walpole Society, 1963. (Extensive bibliography.)

WORCESTER ART MUSEUM, 55 Salisbury Street, Worcester, Massachusetts 01608
     The general collection of American prints up to 1850
includes the Goodspeed Collection of about 250 folios and
4,000 smaller prints, acquired in 1910. Featured is an
extraordinarily complete collection of the work of John
Cheney.

See: "Early New England Printmakers" (in collaboration
      with the American Antiquarian Society), in Art in
      New England. /Cambridge, Mass.: Harvard University
      Press, 1939/.

YALE UNIVERSITY, New Haven, Connecticut 06520

Yale University Art Gallery, 1111 Chapel Street
    The Garvan Collection of approximately 2,000 American
prints, including a superb group of Currier and Ives, and
the Anson Phelps Stokes Collection make up the bulk of the
Art Gallery's holdings, which run through 1850. There is an
excellent collection of prints by Amos Doolittle, as well as
a representative collection of mezzotint portraits.

Yale University Library
    Some early American prints that have long been in the
University's collection are housed in the Library. Emphasis
is on items pertaining to the University and to New Haven.
Printed and manuscript American maps are included in the Map
Collection of the Library.

CONFERENCE EXHIBITION OF PRINTS IN AND OF AMERICA TO 1850

From the Collection of The Henry Francis du Pont Winterthur
Museum

Allegory and Emblem

"America," stipple engraving, sepia, Joseph Strutt, after a
painting by Robert Edge Pine, London, 1781. 20" x 25" (61.499)

"Triumph of Liberty," etching and engraving, Peter C. Verger,
after a drawing by John Francis Renault, New York, (dated)
November 1796. 11 7/8" x 18 7/16" (58.48)

"Emblem of the United States of America," etching and engraving, tinted with water color, Samuel Harris, Boston, (dated)
September 7, 1804. 13¼" x 9½" (58.1)

"America guided by Wisdom," etching and line engraving,
Benjamin Tanner, after a drawing by John J. Barralet, Philadelphia, ca. 1815. 17¼" x 23½" (58.23.1)

Bookplate

/Bookplate of Nathaniel Tracy/, line engraving, Nathaniel
Hurd, Boston, ca. 1770-1771. 3½" x 2½" (Mss 69x163)

Broadsides

"Washington's Farewell Address . . .," line engraving, Gideon
Fairman, Philadelphia, 1810-1827. 39" x 25 9/16" (64.1601)

/Abolition of Slavery/, woodcut and printed text, possibly
Boston, ca. 1818-1820. 18½" x 11 1/8" (Mss 69x28)

City Views

/View of Charleston, South Carolina/, etching and engraving,
William Henry Toms, after a drawing by B. Roberts, London,
(dated) June 9, 1739. 18" x 54" (57.532)

"A View of Savanah . . .," etching and engraving, Pierre
Fourdrinier, after a design by Peter Gordon, London, 1734-
1750. 15 3/4" x 21 3/4" (61.1699)

"Quebec, The Capital of New France . . .," line engraving,
tinted with water color, Thomas Johnston for Stephen Whiting,
Boston, (dated) October 1, 1759. /State II/ 6 3/4" x 8 7/8"
(60.13)

"Broadway, New-York," aquatint, tinted with water color, drawn
and etched by Thomas Hornor, aquatinted by John Hill, New York,
(dated) 1836. 21 3/4" x 30 1/8" (67.152)

Commerce and Trade

/Paper Currency in four, five, six and ten shilling notes/,
line engraving, printed by James Adams, Wilmington, Delaware,
(dated) 1776. 8¼" x 13 3/4" (Mss 65x624.41)

/Trade Card, Kneeland & Adams/, line engraving, printed by
Elisha Babcock, Hartford, Connecticut, ca. 1793. 8 7/8" x
7" (Mss 67x93)

/Watch Paper/, line engraving used by Nathaniel Dominy IV,
East Hampton, L. I., New York, ca. 1798. 1 7/8" diameter.
(64.1805.1)

/Watch Paper/, line engraving, Abraham Simmons, used by John
Sayer and Thomas Richards, New York, ca. 1813. 2 1/16"
diameter. (64.1809)

Illustrations

"Narrative of the troubles with the Indians in New England
. . .," book, woodcut, type, printed by John Foster, /attached
is a facsimile of Foster's woodcut map: _"A Map of/ New.
England," called the White Hills version/, Boston, 1677.
Map: 13½" x 16½"; Book: 7 3/4" x 5½"

"The Natural History of Carolina, Florida, and the Bahama
Islands . . .," book, printed text, engraving, tinted with
water color, original drawings by Mark Catesby, London, 1731-
1734. 19" x 13½"

"Essay on the Invention of Engraving and Printing in
Chiaroscuro," book, printed text, woodcut, tinted with water
color, London, 1754. 10" x 7 3/4"

"Discourses concerning government," by Algernon Sydney, book,
printed text, line engraving, London, 1763. 11 5/16" x 8 5/8"

"Philadelphia Directory for 1796 . ._.," /attached is "Stephens/
Plan/ of the City of/ Philadelphia."/ Printed for Thomas
Stephens by W. Woodward. 6 3/16" x 3 3/8"

"Baltimore Directory for 1804 . . .," book, line engraving,
type, /Attached is "Improved/ Plan/ of the City of/ Baltimore."/
Printed by Warner and Hanna. 6 3/4" x 4"

"American Ornithology . . .," book, engravings, tinted with
water color, A. Lawson and G. Murray, from drawings by Alexander
Wilson, Philadelphia, 1808. 13 3/8" x 10 3/8"

"American Medical Botony . . .," book, aquatint, tinted with
water colors, W. B. Annin, Boston, 1817. 9 9/16" x 5 7/8"

"Picturesque Views of American Scenery," book, printed text,
aquatint, tinted with water color, John Hill, after drawings by
Joshua Shaw, Philadelphia, 1819-1820. 14 1/8" x 20 7/8"

"American Entomology . . . by Thomas Say," engravings, tinted
with water color, printed text, Cornelius Tiebout, after drawings by Titian Ramsey Peale, Philadelphia, 1824. 9" x 5½"

"The Cabinet of Natural History and American Rural Sports . . .,"
book, lithography, tinted with water color, line engraving,
type, lithographs by Childs and Inman, after drawings by Thomas
Doughty, Philadelphia, 1830. 11" x 8 7/8"

"Broadway Sights," /Title page from sheet music/, lithograph,
J. H. Bufford, New York, ca. 1835. 12 3/8" x 9 5/16" (Mss 69x6)

"My Sister Dear, Remember Me," /Assorted sheet music/, book,
lithograph and printed text, printed by Thayer & Co., Lithographers, Boston, (dated) 1842. 13½" x 10 3/8" (Mss 69x218.1)

Landmarks

"View of the Pennsylvania Hospital," line engraving, James
Claypoole, Jr., Philadelphia, 1761. 11 3/4" x 15¼" (59.1551)

"A View of the House of Employment, Almshouse, Pennsylvania
Hospital, & part of the City of Philadelphia," J. Hulett after
a drawing by Nicholas Garrison, Philadelphia, ca. 1767. 13½"
x 27 3/4" (57.501)

"Federal Hall," line engraving, tinted with water color, Amos
Doolittle after a drawing by Peter Lacour, New Haven, Connecticut, (dated) 1790. 18 1/8" x 14 3/8" (57.816)

"Girard College . . .," engraving, reengraved by James W.
Steel after an engraving by A. W. Graham, Philadelphia, 1847.
14¼" x 30" (60.358.3)

Maps

"Map of New Jersey," line engraving, tinted with water color,
Jo. Clerk after a design by John Seller, London, ca. 1664.
17¼" x 21 3/4" (64.740)

"Plan of Baltimore," line engraving, tinted with water color,
Francis Shallus, Philadelphia, (dated) 1801. 19 3/4" x 28 3/4"
(67.160)

Military & Naval

"The Bloody Massacre," Paul Revere, line engraving, tinted
with color, Boston, 1770. 10 3/4" x 9¼" (55.500)

"The Bloody Massacre . . .," line engraving, tinted with
water color, Jonathan Mulliken, Newburyport, Massachusetts,
1770-1782. 10 3/8" x 9" (55.501)

"The Battle of Lexington . . .," etching and engraving, tinted
with water color, Amos Doolittle, after a painting by Ralph
Earl, New Haven, Connecticut, 1775. 13 3/4" x 19" (65.23)

"The Engagement at . . . Concord," etching and engraving,
tinted with water color, Amos Doolittle, after a painting by
Ralph Earl, New Haven, Connecticut, 1775. 13½" x 18½"
(65.24)

"An Exact View of the Late Battle at Charlestown . . .," line
engraving, Bernard Romans, London, (dated) June 4, 1776.
12 5/16" x 17" (59.1550)

"Brilliant Naval Victory," etching, engraving and aquatint,
colored with water color, Samuel Seymour, Philadelphia, (dated)
1812. 14" x 18" (57.809)

"Sprigs of Laurel," aquatint, tinted with water color, William
Strickland, Philadelphia, 1814-1815. 19 7/8" x 14½" (57.811)

Politics and Satire

" . . . Industry and Idleness . . .," line engraving, William
Hogarth, London, ca. 1750. /One of 12 plates/. 7 3/4" x
10 7/8" (56.42.11)

"The Idle Prentice prophaning the Sabbath . . .," William
Hogarth, London, ca. 1750. 7 3/4" x 10 7/8" (56.42.8)

"The Industrious Prentice, a Favorite . . .," line engraving,
William Hogarth, London, ca. 1750. 7 3/4" x 10 7/8"
(56.42.10)

"The Industrious Prentice, Out of his Time . . .," line
engraving, William Hogarth, London, ca. 1750. 7 3/4" x 10 7/8"
(56.42.9)

"The Repeal/ or the Funeral of Miss Ame-Stamp," line engraving,
England or America, ca. 1766. 9 5/8" x 13 7/8" (65.8.1)

"Political Electricity," line engraving, /print bears the
following satirical signatures: "Bute & Wilkes inven.^{t}" and
"Mercurius & Apelles fec.^{t}/ 28 5/8" x 16 3/8" (60.58)

"Bunkers Hill," /Caricature/, line engraving, tinted with
water color, London, (dated) March 1, 1776. 10" x 17 1/16"
(54.51.3)

"Mal Lui Veut Mal Lui Tourne Dit le Bon Homme Richard," etching and engraving, France, ca. 1777-1778. 9¼" x 11" (67.238)

"Tea-Tax-Tempest," line engraving, probably Carl Guttenbert,
Nuremberg, Germany, 1778. 16" x 19 1/8" (66.30)

/Rebus letter America to Her Mistaken Mother/, etching,
tinted with water color, London, (dated) May 11, 1778. 14"
x 10" (54.51.5)

/Washington and Jefferson/, etching and engraving, New York,
(dated) June, 1807. 10½" x 13½" (55.597)

"John Bull and the Baltimoreans," etching and engraving, William
Charles, Philadelphia, 1814. 9 7/8" x 13 15/16" (68.93)

"The Hartford Convention," etching and engraving, William
Charles, Philadelphia, 1815. 9 5/8" x 14" (69.45)

"The Four Indian Kings," mezzotint and engraving, after drawings from life, Bernard Lens, Jr., London, ca. 1710. 13 9/16"
x 10" (69.218)

"Ho Nee Yeath Tan No Ron," mezzotint and engraving, John Simon,
after a painting by I. Verelst, London, ca. 1710. 16 3/16"
x 10 1/16" (70.4)

"Sa Ga Yeath Qua Pieth Tow," mezzotint and engraving, John
Simon, after a painting by T. Verelst, London, ca. 1710. 16 3/16"
x 10 1/16" (70.5)

"Sir William Pepperrell," mezzotint and engraving, Peter Pelham,
 Boston, 1747. 17½" x 11 5/8" (67.232)

"Sir William Johnson," line engraving transfer printed on
glass, colored with oils, Charles Spooner, after a drawing by
T. Adams, London, (dated) February 2, 1756. 14 1/16" x 10 1/8"
(55.15.3)

"George III, William Pitt, and General Wolfe," line engraving,
tinted with water color, Nathaniel Hurd, Boston, (dated) 1762.
4½" x 5¼" (58.2374)

"Worthy of Liberty, Mr. Pitt . . .," Charles Willson Peale,
mezzotint and engraving after his painting, London, ca. 1768.
22 7/8" x 14 3/4" (59.1488)

"Samuel Adams," mezzotint and engraving, Samuel Okey, after a
drawing by J. Mitchell, Newport, Rhode Island, (dated) April,
1775. 12¼" x 9 3/4" (56.11.4)

"Commodore Hopkins," mezzotint, Johann Martin Will, Augsburg,
Germany, after 1776. 16" x 11" (trimmed) (68.282)

"George Washington," line engraving, John Norman, after a drawing by Benjamin Blyth, Boston, (dated) March 26, 1782. 11½"
x 9¼" (58.2412)

"Thomas Jefferson," aquatint, tinted with water color,
Michel Sokolnicki, after a drawing by Thaddeus Kosciuszko,
Europe, 1798-1799. 14½" x 10¼" (65.79)

"A New Display of the United States," line engraving, Amos
Doolittle, New Haven, Connecticut, (dated) August 14, 1803.
/Print contains portrait of John Adams/. 16 5/8" x 20 7/8"
(61.1783)

/Portrait of Charles Carroll/, line engraving, Charles Balthazar
Julien Fevret de Saint-Memin, Baltimore, Maryland, 1804. 2½"
x 2½" (67.95)

"Alexander Hamilton," stipple engraving, William Rollinson,
after a painting by Archibald Robertson, New York, (dated)
September 1, 1804. 17½" x 13 3/4" (58.2058)

"Stephen Girard," lithograph, Albert Newsam, after a painting
by Bass Otis, Philadelphia, 1832. 10" x 10" (60.357.5)

Nature and Natural Phenomena

"May," line engraving, Thomas Bowles, London, 1735-1755.
14 1/8" x 10 1/8" (66.1048.5)

"Niagara Falls, Part of the American Fall . . .," aquatint,
tinted with water color, John Hill, after a painting by William
James Bennett, New York, 1820-1830. 23½" x 18 7/16" (58.2059)

PARTICIPANTS

Adams, Mrs. James F.
  Goodspeed's Book Shop
Ahlborn, Richard E.
  Smithsonian Institution
Ashmead, John
  Haverford College
Babcock, Mrs. Sumner H.
  Consultant, Lecturer
Barnes, Jairus B.
  The Western Reserve Historical
  Society Museum
Bartlett, Mrs. Edmund
  Winterthur Fellow, 1971
Bastedo, Philip R.
  University of Delaware
Belden, Mrs. Gail C.
  Winterthur Museum
Belknap, Miss Helen R.
  Winterthur Museum
Brownell, Charles
  Oakland University
Bumgardner, Mrs. George H.
  American Antiquarian Society
Butler, Patrick Henry III
  Johns Hopkins University
Cannon, Clawson
  Brigham Young University
Cantor, Jay
  Cornell University
Carson, Cary
  Harvard University
Carson, Mrs. Cary
  Radcliffe Institute
Clapp, Miss Anne E.
  Winterthur Museum
Cooper, Miss Wendy A.
  Winterthur Fellow, 1971
Cowdrey, Miss Mary Bartlett
  Author, Collector
Cox, John Craib, Jr.
  Winterthur Fellow, 1970

Craven, Wayne
  University of Delaware
Crompton, Robert D.
  Researcher and Collector
Cross, Mrs. George H., Jr.
  Winterthur Museum
Davis, John D.
  Colonial Williamsburg
Davis, Miss Julia F.
  Eleutherian Mills Historical
  Library
Davison, Mrs. Nancy R.
  Boston Public Library
Dawson, John
  University of Delaware
Dee, Mrs. Joseph
  Cooper-Hewitt Museum of Design
Dependahl, Miss Deborah L.
  Winterthur Fellow, 1971
De Silva, Ronald A.
  Winterthur Fellow, 1970
Dolmetsch, Mrs. Joan
  Colonial Williamsburg
Donaghy, Miss Elisabeth
  Winterthur Fellow, 1970
Doud, Richard K.
  Winterthur Museum
Duprey, Wilson G.
  New-York Historical Society
Eastburn, Mrs. David A.
  Winterthur Museum
Elder, William V.
  Baltimore Museum of Art
Evans, Mrs. Nancy Goyne
  Winterthur Museum
Failey, Dean F.
  Winterthur Fellow, 1971
Fairbanks, Jonathan
  Winterthur Museum
Farnham, Mrs. Clayton H.
  The Briggs Gallery

Fennimore, Donald L.
   Winterthur Fellow, 1971
Fern, Alan Maxwell
   Library of Congress
Fikioris, Mrs. Dimitrios
   Winterthur Museum
Fleming, E. McClung
   Winterthur Museum
Flint, Miss Janet
   Smithsonian Institution
Forman, Benno M.
   Winterthur Museum
Fowble, Miss E. McSherry
   Winterthur Museum
Frangiamore, Mrs. Roy P.
   Cooper-Hewitt Museum of Design
Freeman, John
   University of Victoria
Frick, George
   University of Delaware
Gardiner, Rockwell
   Antiquarian
Garrett, Wendell D.
   Antiques Magazine
Garvin, James L.
   Strawberry Banke, Inc.
Garvin, Mrs. James L.
   Strawberry Banke, Inc.
Gates, Warren J.
   Dickinson College
Giffen, Mrs. Jane C.
   Old Sturbridge Village
Gilborn, Craig
   Delaware State Arts Council
Goodyear, Frank H., Jr.
   Rhode Island Historical Society
Greenlaw, Barry A.
   Colonial Williamsburg
Greer, Miss Dorothy W.
   Winterthur Museum

Grotz, Mrs. George
   Winterthur Museum
Grubbs, Miss Karol A.
   Winterthur Museum
Hall, Elton W.
   U.S. Naval Historical Display Center
Hamilton, Mrs. Suzanne C.
   Winterthur Museum
Hamlin, Miss Elizabeth
   Winterthur Museum
Harlow, Thompson R.
   Connecticut Historical Society
Harris, Miss Elizabeth
   Smithsonian Institution
Hayward, Miss Mary Ellen
   Winterthur Fellow, 1971
Heacock, Walter J.
   Eleutherian Mills-Hagley Foundation
Hendricks, Gordon
   Lecturer
Herdeg, John
   Winterthur Museum
Hicks, Frederick S.
   Collector
Hicks, Willis R.
   Winterthur Museum
Hill, John H.
   Winterthur Museum
Hitchings, Sinclair H.
   Boston Public Library
Hoberg, Perry F.
   West Chester State College
Holman, Richard B.
   Holman's Print Shop, Inc.
Homer, William I.
   University of Delaware
Hotchkiss, Horace L., Jr.
   Winterthur Museum
Hugo, E. Harold
   Meriden Gravure Company

Hummel, Charles F.
  Winterthur Museum
Hunt, Miss K. Conover
  Winterthur Fellow, 1971
Hutton, Mrs. Charles W.
  Winterthur Museum
Hyder, Darrell
  Barre Publishing Company
Irving, Mrs. A. Duer
  Winterthur Fellowship Donor
James, Mrs. Albert W.
  Winterthur Museum
Johnson, Miss Susan
  Winterthur Museum
Jones, Mrs. Wilmot R.
  Winterthur Museum
Kaplan, Jerome
  Philadelphia College of Art
Karshan, Donald H.
  New York Cultural Center
Klein, Arnold
  The Detroit Institute of
  Arts
Knerr, Mrs. Hugh S.
  School of Gibbes Art Gallery
La Fond, Edward F., Jr.
  Pennsylvania Historical and
  Museum Commission
Landon, Mrs. George K.
  Winterthur Museum
Lanmon, Dwight P.
  Winterthur Museum
Lanmon, Mrs. Dwight P.
  Cornell University
Lawrence, Mrs. A. Hicks, Jr.
  Winterthur Museum
Looney, Robert F.
  Free Library of Philadelphia
Macuga, Mrs. Stephen J.
  Winterthur Museum
Martin, Mervin
  Winterthur Museum

Marzio, Peter C.
  Smithsonian Institution
Maxwell, Mrs. Catherine H.
  Winterthur Museum
McElroy, Miss Cathryn J.
  Winterthur Fellow, 1970
McGee, Mrs. Lemuel C.
  Winterthur Museum
McKendry, John J.
  The Metropolitan Museum of Art
McKenney, Mrs. Daniel J.
  Winterthur Museum
Melody, John W.
  Winterthur Museum
Milley, John C.
  Independence National Historical
  Park
Mitchell, James R.
  New Jersey State Museum
Montgomery, Charles F.
  Winterthur Museum
Mooz, R. Peter
  Winterthur Museum
Morse, John D.
  Winterthur Museum
Mundt, Miss Alice
  Worcester Art Museum
Munroe, John A.
  University of Delaware
Munsing, Miss Stefanie
  Winterthur Fellow, 1971
Naeve, Milo M.
  Colonial Williamsburg
Noyes, Mrs. John H.
  Winterthur Museum
O'Brien, Miss Maureen A.
  Eleutherian Mills-Hagley
  Foundation
Page, Mrs. John F.
  Concord, New Hampshire
Pillsbury, William M.
  New York State History Museum

Prown, Jules D.
    Yale University
Puffer, Nathaniel
    University of Delaware
Quimby, Ian M. G.
    Winterthur Museum
Raley, Robert L.
    Old Brandywine Village
Ransom, Mrs. John T.
    Winterthur Museum
Ray, Miss Mary Lyn
    Winterthur Fellow, 1970
Reps, John W.
    Cornell University
Rhymer, Mrs. Paul
    Chicago Historical Society
Richards, Miss Nancy E.
    Winterthur Museum
Richardson, Dr. Edgar P.
    Philadelphia Academy of the
    Fine Arts
Ridington, Dr. Thomas
    La Salle College
Rippe, Peter
    Harris County Heritage and
    Conservation Society
Rittenhouse, Mrs. Jane
    Winterthur Museum
Roth, Miss Elizabeth
    New York Public Library
Roth, Miss Rodris
    Smithsonian Institution
Rothroch, O. Joseph
    Princeton University Library
Rubenstein, Lewis C.
    Hudson River Valley Commission
Rumford, Miss Beatrix
    Colonial Williamsburg
Sayre, Miss Eleanor
    Museum of Fine Arts, Boston
Schmidt, Frank J.
    Pennsylvania Historical and
    Museum Commission

Shadwell, Miss Wendy
    Middendorf, Colgate &
    Company
Sharp, Miss Ellen
    Detroit Institute of Arts
Sharp, Lewis I.
    University of Delaware
Shepherd, Raymond V.
    Philadelphia Museum of Art
Snyder, John J., Jr.
    Winterthur Fellow, 1970
Sommer, Frank H. III
    Winterthur Museum
Sorber, James C.
    Antiquarian
Spruance, Mrs. James H., Jr.
    Winterthur Museum
Sullivan, Mrs. Matthew C.
    Winterthur Museum
Sweeney, John A. H.
    Winterthur Museum
Tatham, David
    Syracuse University
Tatum, Dr. George B.
    University of Delaware
Teagarden, Mrs. John E.
    Winterthur Museum
Townsend, Mrs. Walter P.
    Winterthur Museum
Turley, Mrs. Louisa F.
    Winterthur Museum
Van Devanter, Willis
    Collector
van Ravenswaay, Charles
    Winterthur Museum
Warren, David B.
    Museum of Fine Arts of
    Houston
Webster, Richard J.
    West Chester State
    College
Weekley, Miss Carolyn
    Winterthur Fellow, 1971

Weil, Martin E.
    Price & Dickey, Architects
Whitehill, Walter Muir
    Boston Athenaeum
Wolcott, Miss Eliza
    Historical Society of
    Delaware
Wolf, Edwin II
    The Library Company of
    Philadelphia
Wolfe, Mrs. Homer B.
    Winterthur Museum
Wood, Charles B. III
    Antiquarian Bookseller
Wortman, Jeffrey
    Dartmouth College
Zigrosser, Carl
    Philadelphia Museum of Art